' … an invaluable resource for anyone studying Film A level. The book is split into three accessible and logical sections; Film forms, Film theories, and Context and forms, and is well supported throughout by relevant and interesting examples. Written with the student in mind, the revision activities and exemplars ought to help pupils achieve at a high level in their A level exams. The "Experimental film" and "Lighting" chapters are great examples of how to break down complex topics into digestible and fathomable content, allowing access across all ability ranges. This text is equally useful for 1st-year undergraduate students who are bridging into a film-related course.'

Leigh Adams, *British Film Institute:*
Director of Education and Skills

'Essential in more than just name! With written examples relating to exam set texts and chapters on technical aspects of film, theories and contexts, Mark Dixon's *Essential Revision for A Level Film Studies* is the perfect companion for any student embarking on an A level Film Studies course, or any teacher who wants to secure their subject knowledge.'

Claire Pollard, *Editor of EMC Media Magazine*

T0247845

Essential Revision for A Level Film Studies

This comprehensive revision guide contains everything students need to know to succeed on their A Level Film Studies course.

Essential Revision for A Level Film Studies features engaging and accessible chapters to help learners develop a deeper understanding of the key elements of film form, including cinematography, mise en scène, performance, lighting, editing and sound. The book offers detailed explanations of the specialist study areas required for the A Level course, including auteur theory, spectatorship, genre, key critical debates, narrative and ideology, as well as overviews of key film movements like French New Wave cinema, German Expressionism and Soviet Montage. Also included are practical exercises designed to help students apply essential concepts to film set texts, sample exam responses for both Eduqas and OCR exam boards, and challenge activities designed to help students secure premium grades.

With its practical approach and comprehensive scope, *Essential Revision for A Level Film Studies* is the ideal resource for students and teachers.

The book also features a companion website at EssentialFilmRevision.com, which includes a wide range of supporting resources including revision flashcards and worksheets, a bank of film set text applications for exam questions for all film specifications and classroom-ready worksheets that teachers can use alongside the book to help students master A Level Film exam content.

Mark Dixon works as a principal examiner for Eduqas and is the head of Media and Film at Durham Sixth Form Centre. He is also the author of *Essential Theory for Media A Level* (also published by Routledge) as well as having written for the *Guardian*, *Media Magazine*, *TES* magazine and *Wired*.

Essential Revision for
A Level Film Studies

Mark Dixon

Routledge
Taylor & Francis Group

LONDON AND NEW YORK

First published 2022
by Routledge
2 Park Square, Milton Park, Abingdon, Oxon OX14 4RN

and by Routledge
605 Third Avenue, New York, NY 10158

Routledge is an imprint of the Taylor & Francis Group, an informa business

British Library Cataloguing-in-Publication Data
A catalogue record for this book is available from the British Library

Library of Congress Cataloging-in-Publication Data
Names: Dixon, Mark (Teacher), author.
Title: Essential revision for A level film studies / Mark Dixon.
Description: London; New York: Routledge, 2021. |
Includes bibliographical references and index. |
Identifiers: LCCN 2021004393 | ISBN 9780367634506 (hardback) |
ISBN 9780367634490 (paperback) | ISBN 9781003119241 (ebook)
Subjects: LCSH: Motion pictures–History. |
Motion pictures–Production and direction.
Classification: LCC PN1994 .D5385 2021 | DDC 791.4309–dc23
LC record available at https://lccn.loc.gov/2021004393

ISBN: 9780367634506 (hbk)
ISBN: 9780367634490 (pbk)
ISBN: 9781003119241 (ebk)

Typeset in Bembo
by Newgen Publishing UK

Access the companion website: EssentialFilmRevision.com

To Mam and Dad

Contents

Part I
Film forms

1   Cinematography

Table 1.1 What do you need to revise cinematography for?

Study of cinematography is core to all aspects of Film Studies. To provide effective analysis you should be able to discuss the use and impact of camera movement, shot distance, depth of field as well as the impact of composition and framing decisions (covered in Chapter 2).

Essential background: paradigmatic and syntagmatic meaning-making

Filmmakers have two central jobs when planning a film. First, they must decide upon the overriding story – to identify the characters, major plot points, subplots and so on. To complete this task, filmmakers must order scenes so that their audiences can make sense of the narratives presented. Script writers must invent dialogue, craft characters and work out where crucial plot moments must happen to maximise the emotional impact of their story.

The second, and equally vital, task for filmmakers is to think about the styling and aesthetics of the individual shots that their cinematic story will be composed from. Camera positioning must be worked out to capture actor movement, while locations and sets must be styled to reflect a specific aesthetic look. Those two central planning roles produce meaning in the following two ways:

- **Syntagmatic meaning-making** describes the effects produced by film stories as a result of the way narrative material is sequenced; through, for example, the choices made by script writers and editors in shaping the narrative flow of a product.
- **Paradigmatic meaning-making**, the second function, is less concerned with the way a story builds or changes direction, but in the way that single shots relay meaning.

The study of cinematography is largely concerned with the second form of meaning-making described above.

Cinematographic decisions, in this sense, are made from a fixed menu of shot types, wherein the technical application of a specific shot type constructs a specific connotative effect. If, for example, a shot is filmed using a low-angle tilt to depict a character, the intended effects can be decoded relatively quickly. We do not need to know the narrative events that have taken place before or after the shot to understand that the character has been deliberately framed to look powerful. Conversely, the use of a high-angle tilt would tell an audience that a character lacks authority.

Importantly, the routine use of these fixed shot types means that audiences are well acquainted with their effects and significance. The connotative meanings of tilt, canted shots or tracking camera movements, for instance, are so readily applied that audiences intuitively or subconsciously understand their significance and effect. The range of camera-oriented shot types available to filmmakers are subdivided as follows:

- The use of angle and tilt
- Depth of field
- Camera movement
- Shot distance

Figure 1.1 Pulp Fiction (top): Tarantino's trademark boot shot deploys low-angle cinematography to create character power. *La La Land* (middle): Damien Chazelle's 2017 film uses a high-angle tilt to suggest Mia's vulnerability. *Boyhood* (bottom): Linklater's choice of a canted angle infers the unstable viewpoint of his central character.

Angle and tilt

Angle refers to the vertical or horizontal positioning of the camera during filming. Tilt describes the extent to which shots look downwards or upwards to the subjects being filmed (see Figure 1.1). The canted or Dutch angle shot is a horizontal variant of the tilt, initially used by director auteurs like Carol Green in her film noir classic *The Third Man* to encode the mental collapse of the film's central characters. Dutch angles skew compositions to make scenes appear slanted or off-centre (see Figure 1.1).

Table 1.2 Angle and tilt revision essentials

• *Low-angle tilts* point up to the subject being filmed, so they appear powerful or dominant.
• *High-angle tilts* look down upon the subject being filmed, making them appear powerless or weak.
• *Dutch angles* suggest character instability or can connote anxiety, tension or terror. The strong diagonal compositions created by Dutch angles can also generate a dynamic or energetic tension within a shot.
• *Dutch angles* can be used to depict dream states or hallucinations.

Depth of field

Depth of field: *deep focus shooting*

Deep focus photography is constructed when fore, mid and background elements are kept in focus. The use of deep focus compositions enables directors to use screen depth as a creative tool and to arrange shots so that they convey both background and foreground interest (see Figures 1.2 and 1.3).

Table 1.3 Deep focus revision essentials

• *Deep focus* compositions prompt viewers to think about the symbolic significance of the settings in which actors are placed.
• *Deep focus* can be used to emphasise the space or the distance between objects/actors.
• *Deep focus* photography can also produce strong diagonally configured compositions that inject energy into a scene.
• *Deep focus* photography injects realism as a result of its mimicry of human vision.

Depth of field: *shallow focus shooting*

Conversely, shallow depth of field – the ability to control the focus of a shot so only the background or foreground is held in focus – provides filmmakers with the ability to guide and direct spectators to key aspects of the cinematic frame (see Figures 1.2 and 1.3).

Table 1.4 Shallow focus revision essentials

- Holding only foreground characters in focus directs spectator attention on the actions or dialogue of that character.
- A sense of alienation, claustrophobia or separation can also be constructed when characters are depicted using shallow depth of field compositions.
- *Rack focusing* – the shifting of focal depth during a shot – can be used to alternate audience attention from foreground to background elements, literally shifting the focal point of the frame mid focus.
- *Rack focusing* slows down the editing tempo of sequences, omitting the need for cuts or shot changes, and, as a result, can intensify the dramatic qualities of a scene during moments of character interaction.

Figure 1.2 Citizen Kane (top): Gregg Toland's use of deep focus
emphasises fore and background elements within the scene.
Under the Skin (bottom): Glazer's use of shallow focus in the
shot above isolates Johansson's alien character from the world
around her.

DEPTH OF FIELD

shallow focus guides spectators to specific focal points in the fore, back or mid ground of a shot

shallow focus

shallow depth of field

deep focus

large depth of field

can convey both foreground and background interest

SHOT DISTANCE

very long shot

long shot

medium long shot

mid shot

medium close-up

close-up

big close-up

extreme close-up

makes subject look vulnerable

often used for dialogue

great for showing emotion

Figure 1.3 Depth of field and shot distance effects © Tom Zaino.

Camera movement

Some of the most significant evolutions in the development of film language have been prompted by the various technological and mechanical advances that have freed the camera from its fixed filming position. The separate inventions of the crane, dolly, track, handheld camera and Steadicam have contributed to the 'how' of filmmaking by giving cinematographers the capacity to rotate, lift or track across a scene. Understanding the effects of the following technologies will help you produce extended discussion of camera produced meanings in exam responses.

Camera movement: *cranes and tracks*

Mounting cameras on cranes produces vertical movement, enabling filmmakers to lift the camera upwards or downwards. The track shot similarly liberates directors from the confines of static filming, allowing cameras to move horizontally across the frame on wheel-mounted tracks or to dolly-in or out of a scene (see Figure 1.4).

CAMERA MOVEMENT

Figure 1.4 Camera movement effects © Tom Zaino.

Table 1.5 Crane and track revision essentials

- *Crane-up*: shots that lift upwards produce emotional uplift or can be used to underline the spiritual subtext of a filmic moment.
- *Crane-up*: fast moving crane-ups can disorientate the spectator or produce a sense of vertigo.
- *Crane-down*: conversely, dropping the spectator into a scene with the slam of a crane down produces a grounding effect or can be used to suggest a downbeat emotional moment in a scene.
- *Crane shots*, more generally, are used to empower or disempower audiences during sequences in much the same way that high-angle tilts position the audience above characters or that low-angle tilts reduce audiences to a ground-level view.
- *Motivated track:* track shots are said to be motivated when they follow a subject as they move across the frame. Motivated tracks are usually used to reinforce character alignment or to help audiences identify significant characters in a scene.
- *Scene track* describes a movement where the camera tracks towards or away from a static character. Scene tracks are often used to suggest the enormity or scale of a location or to emphasise the immobility of a character in a scene.
- *Track-right:* shots that move from left to right are usually said to move in the correct direction (mimicking the way that we read a book). Track-rights might suggest adventure, purpose or optimism.
- *Track-left:* shots that track from right to left move in a way that feels hostile or alien to viewers. Track-lefts can suggest a return to the past, nostalgia, a potential meeting with danger or can connote impending tragedy.
- *Dolly-outs* take place when the camera tracks outwards from the frame towards the spectator. Dolly-outs pull audiences into unknown threats or distance them from framed characters.
- *Dolly-ins* move spectators into the frame, magnifying the drama or intensity of a film moment.

Camera movement: *handheld shooting*

The invention of light weight cameras like the Arriflex in the 1950s led to something of a filmmaking revolution. French New Wave directors like Jean-Luc Godard took their Arriflex cameras onto the real streets of France, using lightweight cameras in ways that resembled human observation. Handheld camerawork has become a staple ingredient in filmmaking ever since and is routinely used to suggest a subjective viewpoint or to infer an amateur feel.

Table 1.6 Handheld revision essentials

- Handheld camera work suggests the perspective of a character
- Handheld shots allow filmmakers to engage a subjective film view or to explore a scene with a sense of human frailty.

Camera movement: *Steadicam shooting*

Handheld camerawork has given way to the current Hollywood vogue for Steadicam shooting. The Steadicam is best described as a device that combines the smoothness of the track shot with the freedom of the handheld camera. Steadicams, essentially, are body vests that house spring mounted cameras – as a result, camera shake is ironed out of shots and cinematographers are given the ability to track characters in a free-floating dreamy style.

Table 1.7 Steadicam revision essentials

- The Steadicam smooths out camera movement and allows for a free-flowing filmic style.
- The floating evenness of the Steadicam is often showcased by long-takes and hidden edits.
- The Steadicam is often used to enhance chase sequences.
- Slow Steadicam movements can be used to produce a dreamlike feel.
- The Steadicam shot can also construct a subjective form of filmmaking, suggesting, perhaps, the viewpoint of a hidden character.

Shot distance

The use of shot distance (see Figure 1.3) also produces a discrete range of paradigmatic connotations. Essentially, the more we see of the settings in which characters are depicted, the less important those characters appear.

Table 1.8 Shot distance revision essentials

- *Long-shots:* shots that frame characters within the expanse of a location emphasise setting as more significant than the characters depicted in those locations. Benh Zeiltin's *Beasts of the Southern Wild*, for example, uses long shot dominated sequences to emphasise character vulnerability and to foreground the poverty of the film's Louisiana inhabitants (see Figure 1.5).
- *Close-up and extreme close-up* shots emphasise character emotion. Where the long shot diminishes character physicality, close-ups inject drama and emotional intensity by overwhelming the cinema screen with an actor's profile.
- *Mid-shot:* the mid-shot is generally used to communicate dialogue or to provide spectator relief during scenes that are dominated by close-up shot choices.

Figure 1.5 *Beasts of the Southern Wild* (top): Zeiltin's use of wide-angle long-shots allows the film's Louisiana setting to overwhelm its central characters. *Apocalypse Now* (bottom): Coppola's iconic depiction of Colonel Kurtz was filmed using close-ups to construct a claustrophobic emotional intensity.

Table 1.9 Analyse it: explore the effects of cinematography in key set text sequences

Use the following questions to help you analyse the impact of cinematography in key sequences of your set text films.	
Cinematography feature	**Key questions**
Depth of field	• Does the sequence use shallow depth of field at key moments? Does the use of limited focal depth train audience attention on specific subject action? Does shallow depth of field construct a claustrophobic or isolating effect? • Do key moments utilise deep focus? What background, foreground and midground elements does the use of deep focus make visible? • In what ways do background and foreground elements compete with one another or reinforce the thrust of screen action? • Does the film's author use depth of field in a stylised or idiosyncratic way?
Dutch angles & tilts	• Are Dutch angles or tilts used and with what connotative effects? • What do the use of Dutch angles suggest about a character's inner world? • What does tilt tell us about the power or lack of power of the character depicted? • Why does the director want to strip away or enhance the power of a character when tilt is used? • Does the film's author use tilt or Dutch angles in a stylised or idiosyncratic way?
Camera movement	• Does the camera crane up or down? What emotional impact does that movement produce?

(continued)

Table 1.9 Cont.

	• Does the camera track left or right in the sequence? What impact does tracking have on audience perceptions of screen action? • What objects/subjects does camera movement track? What do motivated tracks or scene tracks suggest about the significance of the shot's subjects? • Does the camera dolly-in or dolly-out of the scene? What emotional effect does that movement produce? In what ways does camera movement bring us closer to characters, or, indeed, separate us from the subjects of shots? • Are camera movements quick or slow? What connotative effects does the speed of camera movement inject? • Does the shot use a handheld aesthetic? With what effect? Does it suggest a point of view? Why has a point-of-view shot been chosen to depict that film moment? • Does camera movement produce a subjective or objective aesthetic?
Shot distance	• How is shot distance used to heighten or reduce the emotional intensity of the scene? • What does shot distance suggest about a character's relationship with the world in which they are placed? • What distance is used to frame the last shot in the scene? Why has the filmmaker chosen to end the sequence in this way?

Exemplar: *Under the Skin* (Eduqas). Glazer provides us with a deliberately juxtaposed shooting style in *Under the Skin*. Handheld long-shots construct the subjective viewpoint of Scarlett Johansson's predatory search at the start of the movie. Importantly, the absence of anything other than long-shots in these montages help to delineate Johansson's isolation from mainstream society. The handheld aesthetic also constructs cinematic realism, presenting the audience with an unnerving sense of the familiar from an alien perspective.

Table 1.9 Cont.

We might also suggest that these sequences encode the real world using a masculine viewpoint with the female alien depicted as a predatory lone wolf of sorts. Yet, Glazer deliberately contrasts these long-shot montages with moments where Johansson gazes into the rear-view mirror of her van: the alien's self-scrutiny framed within a closed-frame close-up during these moments of painful self-regard. These shots help to suggest the female alien's anxiety in perfecting her human disguise, and, moreover, in being forced to carry out the kidnapping of her male victims. The juxtaposition of shot distance across these early sequences also produces a jarring cinematic experience for the audience – throwing viewers from long-shot to close-ups in a way that helps to underline the conflicted mindset of the alien protagonist.

Links to exemplar film clips and exemplars for other OCR/Eduqas film texts can be found at www.essentialfilmrevision.com

Extending exam responses

Paradigmatic resistance

Yes, filmmakers encode meaning through the careful control of shot distance, movement, lens type and depth of field, but to regard the meaning of a film as solely determined by these paradigmatic influences is hugely problematic. Indeed, exam questions that ask students to assess camera usage often reward responses that provide detailed evaluations of how the meanings produced by a film's cinematography fit within the wider context of the films discussed. Indeed, some questions specifically guide students to challenge the notion that cinematography alone produces meaning.

Depending on the area of study and the films studied, high-level exam responses could assess the impact of cinematography by exploring the following:

• **The ways that cinematographic choices reinforce or challenge other macroelements.** Exam responses of this sort evaluate the way that shot choice reinforces wider narrative themes or helps to construct character meanings. Responses might zone in on key sequences where character outlooks are defined, or even redefined, by the choice of shots used by the film's director.

- **The way that filmmakers combine cinematography with other microelements**. Exam responses could evaluate the way that cinematographic decisions work alongside sound, mise en scène or editing decisions to enhance meaning.

- **The selective use of cinematography by auteurs to create a heavily stylised film aesthetic**. The unwritten rule book of film syntax isn't universally applied by all directors in the same way. Questions might ask you to identify the specific shooting styles of key filmmakers and to offer explanations as to why those makers construct their films using these stylised applications of cinematography.

- **The extent to which camera style is experimental or is driven by wider technological/historical factors**. The language of cinema is subject to continuous change. New filmmaking technologies present filmmakers with new tools and techniques to create meaning. Films, too, absorb the shooting styles and fashions that prevail at any given historical point or can replicate genre-driven rules regarding cinematographic choices. Evaluations that assess the impact of these contextual forces can help students gain premium marks.

- **The representational/ideological effects of shot choice on audiences**. Films construct ideological effects, positioning audiences to think about key social groups using problematic or celebratory representations. Evaluations might seek to understand a film's ideological role by exploring the use of camerawork in scenes where key groups are portrayed. The camera might, for example, diminish the presence or importance of key groups via a shooting style that uses tilts and long-shots to reduce the screen-based presence of those groups.

- **The varied ways that audiences interpret cinemato-graphic choices**. The notion that camera work creates universally understood paradigmatic meanings is seriously challenged if we accept the idea that individual audience members read films differently. Audience reactions are inevitably governed by the context of spectatorship. Inevitably, some audiences will read beyond the paradigmatic readings of what they see.

Table 1.10 Challenge it: evaluate the effects of cinematography for exam questions

Use the following questions to help you **evaluate** the impact of cinematography in key sequences of your set text films:	
Macrocodes	• How does cinematography reinforce or reflect wider narrative themes? • How does cinematography reflect character-based representations? Does it challenge or reinforce what we already know about the characters depicted?
Other microcodes	• Does cinematography alone control audience reactions? • How is cinematography enhanced by the sound, editing, lighting or mise en scène of key sequences? • How are the meanings produced by cinematographic decisions stretched or distorted by other microcodes?
Technology effects	• When was the film made? What technological advances were available to filmmakers during this period? • What equipment was used to film the sequence? • What freedoms or restrictions did available equipment produce?
Auteur-based effects	• Does the sequence's author approach cinematographic aspects of the film using a specific style or approach? • What were the author's intentions in using shots in this stylised way?

(continued)

Table 1.10 Cont.

Exemplar: *Vertigo* **(Eduqas and OCR).** Robert Burks' cinematography in *Vertigo* propels the film beyond the conventions of 1950s Hollywood storytelling. Burks adds a rich variety of shot types to the classic mid-shot, dialogue-heavy sequences of Hollywood film in the post-war period. The Dutch angles used during the trial sequence, for instance, connote the instability of Scottie's internal reality, while Scottie's vertigo episodes were ingeniously constructed by Burks through the then innovative use of the zoom in/dolly out shot. The injection of wide-angle aerial shots by Burks also helped to construct the disorientating effects of the lead character's fear of heights.
Yet beyond these fringe moments of invention, the studio-driven impulse for fixed camera, studio-centred cinematography dates the film's overall aesthetic. Perhaps, more significant to the overall impact of Hitchcock's masterpiece was Bernard Herrmann's stylised score. The spiralling layers of harp and piano are undercut by the stabbing bass notes of Hermann's roaring score. Importantly, that roar reinforces the much-lauded smashed zoom shots used to represent Scottie's vertigo. The psychological terror of these moments exaggerated through the minor key instrumentation of the film. By itself the camera work of Burks is important, but when combined with Herrmann's modernist soundtrack the effect is magnified tenfold.

Table 1.11 Cinematography: ten-minute revision

Paradigmatic meaning-making
• Cinematographic decisions provide filmmakers with the 'how' of storytelling. • Cinematographic choices are often paradigmatic – certain types of shot construct or connote specific meanings. • The language of cinematography is closely aligned to developments in camera technology. • Cinematographers create meaning through the use of depth-of-field, camera movement and shot distance.
Paradigmatic resistance
• Cinematography inevitably works alongside other microelements (editing, sound, lighting, mise en scène) to produce meaning. • Cinematography works in conjunction with other macroelements (principally narrative and character) to produce meaning. • Filmmakers stylise or hallmark their films via the use of cinematographic choices.

2 Mise en scène and performance

Table 2.1 What do you need to revise mise en scène for?

Study of mise en scène is core to all aspects of Film Studies. Students ought to be able to identify the symbolic or connotative effects of a film's setting, props, costume, make-up and lighting (see Chapter 5), as well as the impact of composition, actor performance or colour coding. Students should also be able to identify how mise en scène works in conjunction with other microcodes.

Essential background

Mise en scène when translated means 'placing on stage' and refers to the way that visual elements – props, sets and costuming – are styled. The control of mise en scène in film is usually devolved to the director of photography, who coordinates set and costume designers, location support personnel as well as a whole host of electricians, joiners and artists to realise the look and feel of a film.

The control and styling of mise en scène should not be underestimated, with considerable levels of production budgets given over to mise en scène elements to ensure that the visual look of a film is coordinated with the artistic vision required. The control of mise en scène produces an enormous range of effects for film audiences, principally enabling filmmakers to fulfill the 'show don't tell function' of film storytelling and to guide audiences towards a range of inferred reactions. Other core functions of mise en scène are as follows:

- **Mise en scène constructs a film's environment:** directors use carefully orchestrated mise en scène to construct the world of their film. That portrayal might author an escapist otherworldly experience or replicate a version of the real world that builds audience relatability. The construction of a film's overarching setting also outlines a set of tonal qualities – an emotional ambience that sits behind the action depicted.

- **Mise en scène decisions reinforce or challenge genre-based expectations:** mise en scène plays a crucial role in building genre recognition. Westerns, for example, are referenced via the use of desert landscapes, cowboy hats and horses. Thrillers are recognisable for their use of urban locations, suits and spy-based gizmos. Contemporary directors, of course, deploy cinematic subtleties by using hybridised mise en scène-based traits from across a number of genres.

- **Mise en scène suggests character traits and archetypes:** the use of stylised costuming decisions help to delineate character archetypes. The overuse of black in costumes might, for example, infer a character's villainous qualities, while Proppian Princesses are recognisable via the use of blond hair treatments and costuming decisions that deliver conventional beauty ideals. Mise en scène might also symbolise the internal world of a character: the neatness of a character's hairstyle, for example, might infer the extent to which they are in control of narrative events. Symbolic props, too, might be used to suggest important character backstory or to help outline a character's beliefs or attitudes.

- **Mise en scène outlines a character's relationship with their surroundings:** characters interact with the worlds that are constructed for them – the extent to which those worlds work harmoniously or disharmoniously with characters is often inferred via controlled mise en scène decisions.

- **Mise en scène choices position the audience to react with specific emotional responses:** audiences do not read films – they feel them, and the use of mise en scène is central to the construction of audience emotion. Horror-based fear, for example, is constructed using claustrophobic settings, while the uplifting euphoria of a romcom is often delineated through the use of primary colour palettes and high-key lighting.

Setting types and impact

A film's setting refers to the locations selected or constructed in which film action takes place. Film sets, typically, are either location or studio based, with directors increasingly using ever-more sophisticated green-screen-based technologies to produce setting effects that would have been impossible to craft until relatively recently.

Setting is significant in that opening shots in scenes often introduce a film world and its location to spectators before delineating character action. Steve Neale further suggests that the setting of films is partly determined by genre-driven requirements, and, generally speaking, that they fall into one of the following three categories:

- **Verisimilitudinous worlds:** the word verisimilitude is applied when settings appear real or natural. Films that are verisimilitudinous use locations that the viewer has direct experience of. Romances, crime thrillers, coming of age dramas and war films, for example, build stories using the same settings and logic that we experience in everyday life. As a result, these film worlds produce audience relatability, producing narratives that immerse spectators in story settings that are highly believable.
- **Non-verisimilitudinous worlds:** settings that are escapist or other worldly are used in non-verisimilitudinous worlds. Science fiction and fantasy films, for example, provide good examples of genres that use locations that are fantastical or imaginary. The satisfaction of consuming these kinds of narratives lies in their capacity to transport us to places that lie beyond our everyday reality.
- **Partial verisimilitude:** the third category of films use settings that combine reality and unreality. Horror films, for

example, inject otherworldly supernatural elements into our known world, and, in so doing, help to construct the genre's fear-oriented narrative pleasures.

The symbolic function of film locations

The styling of sets is often used for emotive or symbolic purposes. Settings can be constructed to convey pathetic fallacy or to suggest the emotional landscape of a character – stormy backdrops, for example, are conventionally used by filmmakers to suggest emotional upheaval or character sadness. Similarly, the colour palettes used in settings help to enforce an emotional or symbolic response: heavy use of reds might suggest anger, browns and greys might connote a somber landscape, while blues and greens might suggest sadness or depression. Settings also work as hidden characters in films – environments, for example, might present insurmountable barriers to protagonists or enclose actors in worlds that are chaotic or overwhelming, while remote or desert settings can help author character isolation.

Some common setting types that are popular within contemporary mainstream and independent cinema include the following:

- **Urban jungles:** busy city worlds that imprison their central characters are constructed. Urban jungles are often crime ridden, forcing protagonists to join gangs or to commit inhumane acts so that they might survive. The symbolic subtext of urban-jungle films centre on the dehumanising effects of urban life. The decayed dystopian landscapes of *City of God* provide an excellent example of an urban-jungle setting.
- **Inhospitable lands:** characters when placed in desolate landscapes are forced to draw upon their own inner strength to survive. Inhospitable landscapes often induce themes of escape and loneliness, producing worlds that characters are compelled to flee. The empty scrub of the Coen Brothers *No Country for Old Men* provides a version of an inhospitable landscape setting.

- **Social realist settings:** British cinema output regularly uses gritty urban settings to explore the effects of poverty. Social realist settings usually use run down council estates or inner-city locales. Much like the urban jungles of *City of God*, the social realist settings used in contemporary British film work as hidden antagonists in that they trap characters in bleak crime-driven worlds where human morality is pushed to its limits.

- **Magical realist settings:** magical realism fuses the real with the imaginary, often using fantasy-based elements to outline character desires and motivations. *Pan's Labyrinth*, for example, combines the cruel reality of Franco's fascist Spain with the fairytale landscape that Ofelia constructs for herself as an escape from that world.

Table 2.2 Revise it: settings revision analysis

How real is the film world portrayed?	• Does the setting help to convey the genre of a film? How? • Does the setting help to construct genre hybridity? • Does the setting create audience familiarity? • Does the setting present the audience with an unfamiliar world? • Does the setting construct an escapist viewing experience?
The symbolic values of settings	• Is the look of the setting symbolic? • What colour palettes are used to depict the location? • What colour connotations do set palettes infer? • Is the setting open or closed? Busy or empty? Lifeless or energised? What do those qualities suggest about the world the central character of the film lives in? • Is weather used for symbolic purposes? Does weather help to outline the emotional landscape of the film's central character? • Do sets change at crucial moments in the film? What meanings do those changes convey to audiences?

Table 2.2 Cont.

Settings as barriers	• Does the setting entrap the central characters of the film? • What physical barriers does the set construct for central characters? • Does the setting isolate the characters of the film? • Do settings enable character freedoms?

Exemplar: *We Need to Talk about Kevin* (**Eduqas & OCR**).

Lynne Ramsay's training as a photographer is evident within the sophisticated and precise detailing offered within the sets of *We Need to Talk About Kevin*. A carefully orchestrated palette of muted browns suggests the mundane landscape of Kevin's childhood, a landscape that is punctuated with carefully controlled shades of crimson that Ramsay uses to foreground the horror of Kevin's mass killing spree. It is no accident that those crimson shades increasingly dominate set designs as the film progresses, gradually suffusing Eva's world with the increasingly cruel actions of Kevin.

Ramsay, too, uses setting details to symbolically suggest Eva's internal world. A faded clown picture in the doctor's surgery connotes her broken interior, an unbroken wall of soup (see Figure 2.1) in the supermarket suggests both her entrapment and the emotional sterility of her life in the aftermath of Kevin's killing spree, while jaded posters of cliched holiday destinations – Tampa, Jamaica and the Rockies – tease Eva when she goes for a job interview – a cruel and ironic reminder of her lost freedom as a travel writer, and, more importantly, a potent symbol of her inability to escape the hard reality of her pariah status.

Links to exemplar film clips and exemplars for other OCR/Eduqas film texts can be found at www.essentialfilmrevision.com

Figure 2.1 We Need to Talk About Kevin (top): Ramsay's supermarket setting suggests the monotony of Eva's life in the wake of her son's mass killing spree. Also notice the use of oversized costuming to diminish the character's physical presence. *Pulp Fiction* (bottom): Butch's watch is used to symbolise the character's relationship with his father.

Props

Props are objects or items that are given visual prominence by filmmakers. The purpose of props in films, like settings, is hugely diverse, but can include the following:

- **Character symbolism:** props can be used to identify characters or relay symbolic information about a character without the need of dialogue. Katniss' bow and arrow in the *Hunger Games*, for example, symbolises her independence while also reminding us of her hunter role and self-reliance.

- **Hermeneutic props:** filmmakers often draw attention to scene-based objects in order to suggest mystery. Gaff's paper unicorns in *Blade Runner*, for example, infer his knowledge of Deckard's unicorn dream, but are never fully explained to the audience. The mysterious obelisk in *2001: A Space Odyssey* similarly drives the film's narrative forward but is never fully explained (see Figure 2.3 middle).

- **Chekhov's gun functions:** the playwright Anton Chekhov famously wrote, 'If in the first act you have hung a pistol on the wall, then in the following one it should be fired. Otherwise don't put it there'. Props used in this way provide a promise of future action to the viewer. Rey's discovery of Luke Skywalker's lightsaber, for example, in *The Force Awakens* connects longstanding Star Wars fans to Abram's reboot of the franchise, but the discovery also promises audiences that Rey will have to use the weapon in a climactic fight scene later in the film.

- **MacGuffins:** a specific prop-based device that writers use to drive stories forward, yet aren't enormously important to the story itself. MacGuffins are objects (or even characters) that protagonists must find or return to complete their film quests – they represent narrative goals that may or may not be realised before the movie ends. The mysterious briefcase, for example, must be returned to Marcellus in *Pulp Fiction*, the restroom water fountain must be dislodged in *One Flew Over the Cuckoo's Nest*, while in *Casablanca* a never-explained collection of letters of transit must be attained so that Ilsa and Victor might escape.

- **Genre reinforcement:** props, much like setting, perform a vital role in delineating genre. Guns and fast cars help us to identify thrillers, while lasers and robots add technological ambience to science fiction. The use of genre-driven props might also suggest or enable explicit genre-driven viewing promises. The presence, for example, of rifles and revolvers in westerns underscores the potential of such films to offer moments of action and violence.

- **Genre-driven narrative functions:** some props are used to enable a set of genre-specific narrative functions in films. In supernatural horror films, for example, what are loosely called 'portal props' are used to connect the spirit world with that of the real. The arrival, for example, of the mysterious children's book in the *Babadook* gives the supernatural demon entry into the real world of the film's child protagonist.

Table 2.3 Revise it: props analysis

Character-based functions	• What props are associated with the lead characters of the film? • What symbolic function do those objects serve? What do they tell us about the characters' relationships or their outlooks? • Do props help to delineate character archetypes or the roles of characters within films?
Narrative functions	• Do props work like Chekhov's gun? Are they given prominence in scenes to foreground future narrative action? • Are props used enigmatically? Do they make us question characters or infer unknown backstories? • Are props used as MacGuffins? Do they propel character action or provide the film with an underlying motive?
Genre-based functions	• What props help to convey the genre or subgenre of the film? • What kinds of viewing gratifications do props promise the audience? • How do props contribute to scene tone? How do they underscore the emotional pleasures of the genre? • What genre-specific narrative functions do props serve?

Costume and make-up

Costume and make-up decisions help to communicate important information about characters via a rich variety of visual cues. Indeed, costuming decisions tend to be made very early on in films and are the subject of intense research. Students should be alert to those cues when providing analysis and also to the meanings relayed when the application of costume and make-up is transformed during a film. Students should be mindful of the following details:

- **Costuming decisions communicate character archetypes and stereotypes:** character costuming choices help filmmakers to communicate character archetypes (see Table 2.4 for more details).
- **Costumes communicate social identity:** costuming decisions suggest how rich or poor a character is or can quickly reveal the social status of a character. Formal suits, for example, might suggest a character's desire to conform or a middle-class social position, whereas a washed-out or unkempt appearance might suggest an outsider status or that the character has little economic power. Consider too, the accessories worn by a character: jewellery might signify wealth while a wedding ring communicates marital status. Even small details like shoe choice can connect characters to a particular youth-oriented subgroup or can be used to suggest a character's sexual availability: high-heels, for example, can be used to construct objectification while Doc Martin boots might infer a character's identification with punk subculture.
- **Costumes communicate emotional outlooks:** the colour of costuming is a particularly significant indicator of a character's emotional disposition. Warm colours can suggest a more optimistic outlook while colder shades can suggest depression, sadness or apathy. Look out too for moments when the dominant colours of costumes change significantly – these deviations can be used to suggest a shift in the emotional outlook of characters. Filmmakers also think carefully about the way that costume colours combine with other set

details: costuming, for example, that clashes with location palettes can help to suggest a character's incompatibility with their environment, while sympathetic or blended colour use can connote a character's lack of individuality.

- **Costuming decisions shape actor physicality:** costuming inserts and padding, for example, can enhance an actor's physical presence. Conversely, physicality can be reduced by using oversized clothing to convey the suggestion that a character is smaller or thinner than they really are.
- **Costuming decisions help to build the world of the film:** period-specific costuming can reinforce historical settings, while culturally specific costumes might infer a specific geographic location for a film. Filmmakers might also use genre-driven conventions when thinking about character dress to help situate their film within a recognisable film environment.

Table 2.4 Common character archetypes and stereotypes

Character archetype	Narrative function	Costume/make-up
Proppian hero	The central character who undertakes the central quest of the film	Often presented as an 'ideal' presence for the target audience. Costuming inserts might enhance the physical presence of the character. Lighter costume coding could be used to suggest that the character is virtuous.
Proppian villain	Fights or pursues the hero of the story	Identified via darker costumes, make-up and hair. Costume choices are often juxtaposed with those of the lead hero. Formal attire might be chosen to contrast with the informal dress codes of heroes, for example. Villains, stereotypically, are also identified via blemishes, scars or other markers that contrast with acceptable beauty ideals.

Table 2.4 Cont.

Proppian princesses	The princess represents the goal or reward of the hero's quest.	Costuming might emphasise traditional female beauty ideals or produce objectified female characters. Costume colours might reinforce the innocence of the character through pastel shades or lighter colours.
Femme fatale	A female character who uses seduction to mislead or trap male characters.	Often depicted using black in costuming and dark hair colouring. Red lipstick is often used to signify the character's sexual availability.
Anti-heroes	Likeable but flawed characters who pursue equally flawed quests. Anti-heroes often realise the error of their ways just as their tragic fates are sealed.	Tragic backstories might be inferred through scars or other visible blemishes. The immorality of anti-heroes is also inferred via the use of dark colour palettes in costuming. Traditionally, anti-heroes are also given a strong physical presence (which might be constructed using inserts or padding), while their outsider status might be connoted via the use of washed-out wardrobes.

Table 2.5 Costume and make-up essential revision questions

Character archetype	• How do costume styles, hair, make-up or colour coding connote character archetypes?
Character identity	• What do costume and make-up decisions suggest about a character's class, social position, status or occupation? • In what ways do costuming decisions communicate the outlook or beliefs of a character? • What do costume decisions suggest about the character's relationship with the wider world as well as their relationship with other characters?

(continued)

Table 2.5 Cont.

Character physicality	• Does costuming and make-up enhance a character's physical presence? How and why? • Does costuming restrict or reduce character physicality? • How does make-up affect perceptions of age or health? • How do costuming decisions change over the course of a film? How do these changes link to the wider themes of the narrative?
Genre-driven functions of costume and worldbuilding	• What aspects of costuming decisions help to convey the genre of the film? • How does costuming and make-up help to build the historical or geographical setting of the film?

Composition

Composition refers to the arrangement of props, actors and set-based objects within a particular shot. Much like shot distance and shot movement, several techniques are widely deployed by filmmakers to convey a number of overarching connotations and paradigmatic effects.

Table 2.6 Composition revision essentials

• *Closed frame compositions* are produced when the edge of a shot is framed or bordered by object(s) (see Figures 2.2 (top) and 2.4 (top)). This composition technique can suggest that characters are trapped or restrained. • *Open frame compositions* are created when the frame edges of a shot are left open (see Figure 2.2 (bottom)). Open frames can suggest freedom or liberty, or, if coupled with a long-shot, can suggest isolation or vulnerability.

Table 2.6 Cont.

- *Asymmetrical compositions* are produced when scene objects/ subjects are positioned on either the left or right of the screen (see Figure 2.3 (top)). Asymmetrical photography can be used to juxtapose screen elements (as in shot/reverse shot sequences where characters are placed on either side of the frame) or to suggest that the elements given dominance in the frame are narratively powerful. Asymmetry might also be used to suggest narrative disharmony.
- *Symmetrical compositions* arrange scene elements into balanced compositions (see Figure 2.3 (middle)) – often used to direct viewer attention to central objects or to suggest a state of underlying harmony.
- *Right and left character positioning:* character placement in shots can be significant – especially within shot/reverse shot dialogue sequences, with, traditionally speaking, the left-hand side of the screen used for those characters that filmmakers want audiences to empathise with – protagonist, leading characters and anti-heroes, for example, see Figure 2.3 (bottom). Conversely, the right-hand side of the screen is given over to antagonists or secondary characters. Breaking the left-hand rule and positioning lead characters/protagonists on the right-hand side of a frame might connote a lack of character authority during the scene.
- *Leading lines:* often shots are arranged so that scene elements produce strong diagonals (see Figure 2.4 (middle)) – those diagonals inject energy and drama into shots. Leading lines also lead viewer attention to key focal points in a shot.
- *Off-screen space:* actors often gaze out of shot to the left or right of a frame, suggesting the existence of something or someone beyond the frame (see Figure 2.4 (bottom)). This inference of off-screen space is usually followed by a shot that the audience naturally assumes to be the object that the character is looking at. Inferring and revealing off-screen space is a key tool that filmmakers use to surprise or to shock audiences – a cinematic peek-a-boo that subconsciously arouses and appeases viewer interest. Off-screen gazes also enable character alignment by connecting a protagonist's viewpoint with that of the audience.
- *Eyeline control:* traditionally character eyelines are positioned using an imaginary line that runs horizontally across the frame – a third of the way down from the top of the shot. This allows the gaze of characters to be level with that of the audience. Placing eyelines above or below that imaginary line can construct the same effect as a low or high-angle shot, with low eyelines suggesting the powerlessness of a character while high eyelines are used to construct authority (see Figure 2.5).

Figure 2.2 Raging Bull (top): LaMotta's homelife is often depicted using closed frame compositions to add both claustrophobia and menace. *Captain Fantastic* (bottom): The film ends with a series of open frame shots that symbolise the family's newfound freedom.

Figure 2.3 Ex Machina (top): The asymmetry above allows director, Alex Garland, to suggest the dominance of Ava over Caleb's other AI inventions. *2001, A Space Odyssey* (middle): Kubrick uses symmetrical compositions to enforce what is called a one-point perspective. These viewpoints concentrate viewer attention on a clearly defined central focal point. *The Hunger Games* (bottom): illustrates the use of traditional left and right character placement to delineate protagonist and antagonist roles.

Figure 2.4 *Carol* (top): Todd Haynes uses asymmetrical compositions and closed frames throughout *Carol* to construct narrative disharmony. *Inception* (middle): Nolan exemplifies the use of line to direct spectators towards a key focal point in the frame. *This is England* (bottom): actors are often directed to look beyond the frame, thus constructing an imaginary off-screen space for audiences.

Figure 2.5 Selma: A high eyeline composition (top) is used to invest Martin Luther King with power during this sequence, but in his meeting with Lyndon Johnson (bottom) the same character is disempowered via a lower eyeline than that of the US President.

Table 2.7 Composition: essential revision questions

Closed/ open frame compositions	• Is the frame bordered by objects or is it left open? • What effect does the use of open/closed frame compositions have? What do they suggest about character outlook or the potential outcome of narrative events?
Symmetrical/ asymmetrical compositions	• What narrative connotations does the use of symmetry/asymmetry suggest? Is the world of the film in harmony or is narrative disruption inferred? • What focal points does the use of symmetry produce? • Does asymmetry invite audiences to compare the elements depicted?
Left/right positioning	• Which characters are positioned on the left during dialogue-driven moments? What does that tell us about their status or power in the film? • Which characters are placed on the right of the screen during dialogue? Why are they positioned in less important areas of the screen? • Do characters shift left/right positioning during the film? How does this link with the narrative events depicted? How does screen positioning change the audience's relationship with a character?
Eyelines	• What does eyeline positioning suggest about a character's power or status? Do eyelines shift over the course of the film? Why or why not?
Leading lines	• Are leading lines used to construct key focal points? What are those focal points and why are they significant? • Are diagonals used to inject visual energy into a shot? Are they used at key moments in the narrative to underline wider themes?
Off-screen space	• Do characters look at objects beyond the frame of the screen? • Which characters are given off-screen gazes? Do those shots privilege the viewpoint of those characters?

Table 2.7 Cont.

> **Exemplar:** *Raging Bull* **(OCR)**. Michael Chapman's mastery of composition in Raging Bull invests the film with a subtle and rich range of meanings. The claustrophobic closed framing of the steak scene, for example, suggests LaMotta's turbulent domestic world, with the deliberate composition of the couple on the right hand side of the frame during the shot-reverse-shot sequences of this scene producing a series of rapid-fire asymmetrical compositions that underline the abusive, chaotic and unbalanced nature of LaMotta's relationship with Vickie. The use, too, of off-screen compositions during this and other scenes aligns the audience with LaMotta's viewpoint, constructing an emotive and highly subjective portrait of Jake. The use of composition here provides Scorsese with the means to narrate the human, and ultimately tragic, story of La Motto's boxing obsession, and, more importantly, to relate the adverse effects of the story on those characters closest to the protagonist.

Acting style

Mise en scène questions also give students license to discuss the meanings produced as a result of the approaches taken by actors in set text films. Traditionally film analysis focuses on the following elements of performance:

- **Voice quality:** the tone, volume or fluency of actor dialogue delivery conveys a rich range of meanings during performance.
- **Body language:** the microgestures of actors – the duration of eye contact with other characters, their use of submissive or dominant body language or even the range of movements deployed while delivering a scene can radically shift the underlying intent of scene dialogue.
- **Pose:** the positioning of characters can also reveal significant subliminal details. The way that actors might reposition themselves in reaction to other characters, for example, can convey meaning without the presence of dialogue.

Table 2.8 Know it: acting school styles

A number of acting methodologies or schools of thought are used in contemporary filmmaking. Each school emphasises the use of specific techniques that subtly shape the style and effect of actor performance.

Classical Acting
An umbrella term for a range of acting styles that foreground a film's script as the most central prompt in directing performance. Classically trained actors deliver dialogue and action as described in scene prompts and written dialogue, using their skills and knowledge to add carefully controlled expression and emotion to those lines. Classically trained actors are highly skilled in delivering controlled performances that instantly evoke the emotion required for a particular scene moment. Performances that use a classical acting approach leave little room for improvisation. The classical approach is sometimes critiqued as producing shallow or an overly rehearsed delivery of character emotions.

Use in analysis: we could argue that classically trained actors play a minimal auteurial role in film texts in that their performances are largely directed by script content and director-based instruction.

The Chekhov Acting Technique
Actors who approach films using this technique explore underlying character motivation and emotions in more detail than classical acting. In the Chekhov technique, actors try to connect themselves with the feelings and reactions of characters so that they might authentically express those outlooks to audiences through gesture, body language or movement. Actors who deliver characters via this technique will invite more detailed analysis of body language, facial expression and gesture codes.

Use in analysis: actors who approach performance in this way play an important role in constructing the meaning of scenes. Their interpretation of scripts – and improvised performances that arise from those interpretations – add a layer of meaning to films other than those constructed by screenwriters and directors. Johnny Depp is perhaps one of the most significant actors to draw upon this technique in the contemporary film landscape.

Table 2.8 Cont.

Method Acting

Popularised from the 1950s onwards, method actors work on the assumption that authentic performances can only be achieved if a performer actively assumes the role of a character being played. Some method actors will draw upon personal experiences and traumas to help them deliver believable characters, while others go to extraordinary extremes to construct believable performances. In *Raging Bull*, for example, Robert De Niro spent six years researching Jake LaMotta before filming, interviewing the boxer's colleagues and acquaintances, collecting and reading as many score cards, news stories and fight reports as he could to gain a detailed psychological insight into the life of the film's subject. De Niro also famously put on 60 pounds of weight so that he could accurately capture the physicality of LaMotta's later life excesses.

Use in analysis: actors who use method acting use their own insight to improvise script dialogue. Their research and input prior to filming can suggest a significant auteurial role in films.

Meisner Acting Technique

A technique devised that builds performance by intensely focusing on and reacting to the cues of fellow actors. Meisner critiqued classical acting as overly performative or fake, and argued, conversely, that the real role of an actor was to capture the authentic emotions that might be naturally experienced if staged events were to take place in the real world. The Meisner technique, as a result, emphasises the relationships of characters, and prods actors to build performance as a unit.

Use in analysis: Meisner performances can generate profound scenes of character interplay and are readily used in independent cinema or drama-driven products where character interaction is foregrounded within narratives. Sam Rockwell's performance in *Moon*, for example, is shaped by the Meisner technique.

Table 2.9 Revise it: performance essential revision questions

Voice quality	• How do actors use voice volume to construct meaning? • What is significant about the actors' delivery of dialogue in terms of tone or fluency?
Body language	• What emotions are communicated by actor body language during key sequences? • What does an actor's eye contact or lack of eye contact with other characters suggest about their relationship?
Pose	• Are poses defensive or engaged? • Are poses assertive or timid? Formal or slouched? Masculine or feminine? Active or reactive?
Acting style	Research the key actors in your set texts and try to find out the acting style that they use when approaching films. • **Classical style:** does the actor foreground action over an emotive performance? Does the acting style affect the emotional impact of the film? • **Chekhov/Method acting**: does the actor's approach emphasise the inner world of the character? Does the acting style help to construct a more subjective or personal portrait? Where are the subjective effects of the performance style given notable prominence in the film? • **Meisner style:** how does this style affect the portrayal of character relationships? Are character reactions and relationships given a heightened sense of realism?

Table 2.10 Mise en scène: ten-minute revision

Setting
• Settings can be styled to play a symbolic role and to help audiences connect with a character's emotional reactions. • Settings play an important role in communicating the genre of a film. • Settings can be styled to constrain characters or to present characters with barriers.
Props
• Chekhov guns are used to foreground narrative events or to suggest potential action that might appear later in a film. • Hermeneutic props construct enigma. • MacGuffins drive plots forward and can be used to construct character motivation. • Props, like settings, can play a symbolic role in films.
Costume and make-up
• Help audiences to decode character archetypes and stereotypes. • Play an important function in communicating character identity. • Are used to enhance or diminish the physical presence of a character.
Composition
• Composition can provide important cues about character outlooks and their relationships with other characters/the world around them. • Composition can help to construct focal points in shots. • Composition can infer off-screen space and align characters with audiences. • Composition plays an important role in producing character authority or, conversely, their lack of authority.
Acting
• Voice, body language and character positioning are used to convey meaning in scenes. • Actors subscribe to several different schools of thought. Each school of thought produces different sorts of performance styles.

3 Editing

Table 3.1 What do you need to revise editing for?

Study of editing is core to all aspects of Film Studies. Students should be able to identify the use and effects of both continuity and expressive editing techniques.

Essential background

Editing is a process that orders production footage to best relate a film story. Editors decide what material ought to be included and where. Equally importantly, they decide what shooting footage doesn't make the final cut of a movie, or, indeed, where shots ought to be cut to achieve maximum emotional impact. The overriding functions of editing are as follows:

- **To shape film space:** perhaps one of the central appeals of film as an art form lies in its ability to tell stories using multiple settings. Conversely, photography or art-based narratives are restricted to single location messages, while the physical limitations of theatres significantly restrict the number of settings that a single play can comfortably recon-struct. Film, on the other hand, can establish action across several locations, and, importantly, editing plays a vital role in connecting or relating those settings so that audiences can make sense of the locations used to establish action. Establishing shots, for example, are used to introduce location choices at the start of scenes, while off-screen gazes coupled with eyeline matches orientate character action within the imagined space of a film.

- **To shape time:** editing concentrates film action, removing dead time from story lines to produce narrative excitement. Editing also enables storytelling to span durations of months, years or even longer, while elliptical edits can consolidate key moments in those periods into concentrated sequences of film action. Editing, too, can stretch time, with slow-motion treatments, for example, used to add dramatic intensity to key moments.

- **To privilege viewpoints and to create audience identification:** the order in which characters are presented, or, indeed, the way that character reveals are structured can align audiences to the viewpoint of specific characters. Dialogue sequences, for example, that give more weight to the reactions of one character over another can lend weight to that character's viewpoint.

- **Enigma and revelation:** at a very basic level, we might argue that editing constructs audience engagement through the presentation of shots that arouse audience interest followed by moments that offer explanation. Some shots, in other words, are used to pose questions or enigmas, while others provide resolutions to those questions. This twin pulse of enigma/resolution works like a binary switch or series of question/answer moments throughout a film. At a microlevel, this binary switch might provide immediate resolutions to enigmas posed: a two-character dialogue sequence, for example, might include moments where character A probes character B for information. Enigmas are posed through character A's questioning with shot/reverse-shot editing delivering answers to those questions via character B's dialogue. This disequilibrium/equilibrium metronome also works across film narratives: a lingering close-up of a significant prop, for example, might alert audiences that an object is important, a significance that is finally fully explained much later in the film. Editing, in this sense, can be described as a series of setups and payoffs, with narrative information supplied and withheld across a film's runtime. Importantly, the decisions taken by editors control the flow and sequencing of those setups and payoffs.

Table 3.2 Revise it: essential editing analysis

Editing analysis: top tips
• Identify key moments that exemplify the filmmaker's general approach to editing.
• Identify moments where a film's editing style varies.
• Analyse moments where key characters make their entrance.

Film-space analysis questions	• How is editing used to tell us about the world in which the film takes place? Are establishing or long-shots given prominence in edits? • Do edits foreground film environments and settings or does editing focus audience attention on character action? • How much time is spent depicting the world of the characters in the film?
Time-shaping questions	• Do film events take place at the same time as the spectator (a screen edit)? • Do film events take place over longer time periods than the timeframe of the spectator (an elliptical edit)? • Are events related in a chronological order (a linear edit)? • Is slow motion (stretched editing) used to add emphasis to a particular scene or moment?
Character alignment	• Which characters are given the most screen time during scenes? • Are character viewpoints privileged via reaction shots? • Which character(s) do we see first and last in scenes? How might these entrances and exits help to privilege character viewpoint?

Table 3.2 Cont.

	• How is editing used to convey viewpoint? Are off-screen glances restricted to just one or two characters in the story? • How does editing stop us from empathising with key characters? Is character empathy prevented via an absence of reaction shots?
Enigma and revelation	• Where does the film use enigma? Where are enigmas resolved? • Does the film overly rely on enigma set ups for narrative impact? • Are enigmas resolved by dialogue, action or imagery?

Approaches to editing

Broadly speaking two overarching editing approaches are used by filmmakers:

- **Continuity editing** is largely associated with Classical Hollywood output and mainstream film. Continuity editing orders shots to suggest a seamless flow of action. Footage is also sequenced to suggest a logical or chronological progression of events and action.
- **Expressive editing** breaks the rules of continuity editing – providing audiences with film moments that don't readily connect or that offer discontinuous timeframes. Expressive editing techniques are commonly found in experimental film narratives and independent output, but, increasingly, are widely used in contemporary mainstream output too.

Continuity editing

Continuity editing provides linear storytelling – sequencing material so that scene action moves progressively forward in time, presenting, too, the illusion that action takes place within the same timeframe as the viewer. Of course, scenes are really filmed in discontinuous blocks, with shots assembled in post-production using tried and tested editing routines to affect the illusion of a seamless flow. Those techniques include the following:

- **Match-on-action editing:** this technique is produced by joining two film clips that end and start with the same action but are filmed from different angles. Match-on-action cuts enable filmmakers to suggest continuity without the need for long-takes.
- **Eyeline matches:** this technique is used to suggest a connection between characters and/or objects. Eyeline matches essentially show a character looking at something followed by a shot of the object or character they are looking at. Eyeline matches also help to privilege the viewpoints of the characters depicted within matched edits.
- **Shot/reverse-shot dialogue:** these are sequences that usually depict dialogue exchanges between two or more characters. Shot/reverse shot edits cut between the characters involved in those exchanges.
- **Scene set-ups:** conventionally, scenes are introduced using shots that establish scene location, followed by a wide shot to outline the characters who are present within the scene.
- **Scene progression routines:** once scene locations are established, edits conventionally close in on actors, using mid-shots and close-ups to progress the action of the scene. Moving from establishing shots and mid-shots to close-ups helps to inject intensity as the scene progresses.

Table 3.3 Practical revision: continuity-editing planning exercise

Plan a continuity sequence for a thriller that depicts a character entering a classroom in your school or college. The sequence should use no more than ten shots. Try and include the following elements in your sequence:

- Establish the overarching location of the sequence with an introductory shot.
- Use match-on-action editing to suggest continuity.
- Use eyeline matches to reference the character's viewpoint or to identify significant objects in the character's world.

Continuity variations

It could be suggested that the use of continuity editing outlines a standardised approach to filmmaking that leaves little room for creative expression. Editors and directors, however, assemble continuity sequences in a highly idiosyncratic manner, adapting standardised approaches to enact their own authorial style or to give prominence to a range of film-specific narrative themes. To help identify those individual editing characteristics and their effects in your set text films think about the following:

1. **The overriding approach that filmmakers use in adapting and disrupting continuity-editing expectations**. Films establish their own editing routines, providing audiences with adapted versions of continuity-editing templates. Key shots within sequences, for example, might be held or repeated for dramatic effects or other meaning-making reasons. *No Country for Old Men*, for instance, prefaces most scenes with establishing shots that are held for unusually long time periods – thus enabling the film's audience to gain a sense of the inhospitable emptiness of the film's Texan setting (see Figure 3.1). Conversely, Tarantino routinely abandons the convention of using establishing shots to introduce new scenes, instead replacing them with disconcerting mid-shots, or fourth wall breaks where characters stare beyond the cinema screen into the eyes of the audience, or cutting directly to close-ups of symbolic props in a manner that disconnects the audiences from a scene's location entirely. (see Figure 3.2).

2. **Moments that demonstrate internal variation:** filmmakers use familiar patterns of shots in films to narrate action or dialogue-based sequences – dialogue sequences, for example, might follow a defined sequence of shot types. Those internal patterns establish a familiar rhythm, helping spectators to engage and understand essential plot points and characterisation. Filmmakers, too, construct moments of editing variation, authoring subtle changes in those patterns when the film story demands a different approach. If we

return, for example, to the editing style of *No Country for Old Men*, the scene that introduces Llewelyn starts, unusually, with a rifle-crosshair point of view (POV) instead of the long-take establishing shots found elsewhere in the film. This aberration in scene set up is no accident and is used to nurture audience alignment with Llewelyn from the outset of the character's first appearance.

Table 3.4 Revise it: continuity-editing analysis questions

Continuity-editing impact assessment	• How extensive is the use of continuity editing in your set text films? • How does continuity editing help to construct realism? • Does the use of continuity editing produce passive spectatorship? • Does the film focus more on dialogue-driven sequences or action-based continuity? What effect does this have on the film?
Assessing continuity-editing variation	• At what points in the film does the filmmaker depart from a continuity-based approach? • Is a stylised version of continuity editing used? Does the filmmaker give emphasis to or omit generic shot types in continuity sequences? • Does the filmmaker vary their approach to continuity editing across the film narrative (internal variation)? At which points in the film do these variations occur and why?
Diagnosing auteurial editing effects	• How does the editing style of your set text film compare with other films made by the director?

Figure 3.1 No Country for Old Men: the coin toss scene exemplifies the Coen Brothers' stylised editing approach.

Figure 3.2 Pulp Fiction: Tarantino often starts scenes with close-ups of objects or characters to purposefully disorientate his audience.

Editing tempo

Filmmakers use editing tempo to affect expressive control in continuity-driven sequences, either increasing the number of cuts to generate a more energised edit or reducing cuts to slow the pace of a film. Analysis could also consider the following effects of editing-tempo control:

1. **Overarching editing tempos:** films that predominantly deploy long-takes give audiences time to process scene action or allow for slow-moving performances. A slow-tempo approach, arguably, is best suited to character-driven dramas where dialogue-heavy scenes necessitate longer clips or where audiences need time to process character action. Jonathan Glazer's long take/minimal cut approach, for example, in *Under the Skin* slows the film's tempo to a predatory stall, allowing audiences to fully focus on the character's dawning self-scrutiny. Conversely, frequent cutting produces a faster edit tempo, and produces more energised sequences. Danny Boyle's high-tempo approach in *Trainspotting*, for example, is ignited by the film's opening chase scene and helps to reflect the drug-induced desperation of the film's protagonists.
3. **Tempo variations:** editing tempos vary across the narrative arc of films. Scenes, conventionally, tend to pick up speed as they progress to inject narrative energy, while the editing tempo towards the end of films also tends to increase to concentrate narrative climaxes. Tempos might noticeably decrease during significant plot points too – where, for example, character revelations or important narrative information needs to be communicated to a film's audience.

Table 3.5 Revise it: editing-tempo analysis

Sample several scenes across the film and count the number of shot changes per minute to assess the overarching editing tempo of set text films.

- How does editing tempo contribute to the emotional tone of the film?
- Is slow editing used to construct a reflective narrative style?
- Is a slow editing tempo used to promote active audience engagement? Does it give audiences space to question or interrogate character action?
- Is a fast editing tempo used to suggest character activity or to inject energy into a scene?
- Does the editing tempo deliberately slow or increase at key moments in a film? Why and with what effect?

Star/primary characters entrances

Stars and principal characters in films need to exude audience relatability, yet familiarity alone is not enough to lift an actor or lead character to the status of a star. Stars and lead characters are often given elevated entrances in films via the use of a number of editing/compositional strategies that purposefully attempt to dial up a lead character's initial presence. Films too might tease audiences by withholding a star's entrance for as long as possible in order to affect character or star-driven mystique. Key strategies used to author lead-character entrances include the following:

- **Distance-based delays:** long-shot sequences might be used where a star's distant presence stalls audience recognition. Extreme close-ups too can be used to obscure or disguise a star's profile before any final reveal.
- **Object/character-based delays:** often filmmakers reference a star/lead character's presence in advance of a reveal via the use of what are known as synecdoche props. These are objects that are associated with a well-known character – objects that suggest the presence of that character in advance of their appearance in an edit. Captain America's

stars and stripes shield, Thor's Hammer or the Bat Signal, for example, are objects that can be referenced to suggest the imminent appearance of those characters in a film. Filmmaker's, too, might foreground reaction shots of secondary characters before star personas are fully revealed to audiences. The emotional response of those secondary characters when confronted by the star's presence – awe, fear or elation – might guide audiences towards a similar reaction when a film's lead character is finally unveiled.

- **Slowed editing tempos:** this strategy is widely used to delay star entrances. Edits, for example, might hold preceding shots for longer than is necessary or effect scene-based cutaways before a lead character is fully introduced,

Table 3.6 Revise it: lead-character entrances

Identify scenes where primary and secondary characters appear for the first time. Use the following questions to help you diagnose the specific effects of those scenes:

- Is editing used to delay actor reveals?
- How do secondary characters react to the entrance of the star/lead character?
- Does the film hint at the presence of the star/lead character using key props before actors are fully revealed?
- Does the entrance of the star reinforce or challenge the off-screen persona of the actor playing the character?

Exemplar: *Inception* **(Eduqas and OCR).** Leonardo DiCaprio's entrance in *Inception* exemplifies the use of star power in contemporary American mainstream cinema. Stars convey ready-made appeals to specific audience segments, their inclusion in blockbuster films is also used as a visible marker of big-budget spends, and, moreover, can reinforce the genre-driven direction of a film if it deploys stars who are readily associated with a certain kind of output. DiCaprio's presence in *Inception* certainly helps to seal the film's credentials as an intelligent spy/thriller hybrid given his association with a range of similar movies prior to *Inception's* release (*Shutter Island*, *Blood Diamond* and *Gangs of New York*).

(continued)

Table 3.6 Cont.

DiCaprio's screen entrance in *Inception* also typifies the editing tactics used by contemporary big-budget productions in delaying or obscuring star entrances to magnify the mystique of big-name actors. *Inception*, for example, teases its audience, obscuring DiCaprio's profile with close-ups and backlit long-shots, while reaction shots from secondary characters further delay a final DiCaprio reveal. The held cutaway of Cobb's iconic spinning-top is also used to infer and delay DiCaprio's entrance – the spinning-top operating as a synecdoche prop to signal DiCaprio's nearness. Clearly, the combined purpose of this carefully crafted sequence during the film's opening is to delay star-based audience satisfactions, and, moreover, to amplify the aura that DiCaprio's big-spend presence lends the film.

Links to exemplar film clips and exemplars for other OCR/Eduqas film texts can be found at www.essentialfilmrevision.com

Cross-cutting

The creative logic of continuity editing is stretched further using cross-cutting – or using editing to alternate attention between different stories or locations. Cross-cutting, for example, can narrate the stories of several characters by bouncing from the timelines of one character to another. Key forms and uses of cross-cutting include the following:

- **Parallel cross-cutting** progresses action in two or more separate locations without the promise that the action will meet.
- **Collision cross-cutting** infers that the timelines of cross-cutting strands will meet, usually used to suggest that protagonists and antagonists' timelines will collide in a climactic battle.
- **Reflective cross-cutting** is similar to parallel action, but where the events in separate timelines mirror one another. Reflective cross-cutting magnifies moments of jeopardy or is used to heighten action by bouncing from one timeline to the next.

Expressive editing styles

Expressive editing is a term that encompasses a variety of techniques that challenge the invisibility of continuity editing. Expressive edits are usually constructed using sequences that contain juxtaposed or non-sequential shots. Arguably, when audiences are presented with edits that deploy familiar story-telling patterns they are more likely to submit to the flow or steer of the narrative presented – disrupting continuity editing asks audiences to take a more active role in decoding the meaning of a film, and, more importantly, to work out the potential connections that such imagery throws into question. Expressive editing techniques include the following:

- Jump-cutting
- Juxtaposition
- Angle violations
- Montage edits
- Long-take disruptions
- Screen-time control

Jump-cutting

We might further suggest that as audiences have become more experienced consumers that filmmakers have been able to employ ever more complicated editing patterns and techniques. Godard's jump-cut montages for example, were once seen as anarchic or overly disorientating, yet jump-cutting is now readily absorbed across film output.

Jump-cutting is best described as the use of continuous shots which are spliced together after part of the shot is removed. The result produces sequences of film that skip forward in time. Jump-cuts can be used to remove dead footage, but are also deployed to produce a choppy, fast-moving editing aesthetic. Jump-cutting also produces a more abrasive viewing experience than sequences that transition shots via dissolves or fades.

Jump-cutting – as a self-conscious editing style – was first used by the French New Wave director Godard in his 1960 film *À Bout de Souffle*, giving Godard's first major feature an amateur aesthetic that was initially greeted with a great deal of criticism. Since Godard, jump-cutting has assumed a more conventional aura as a result of its widespread application.

Juxtaposition

Some continuity editing can readily produce jarring effects or focus audience interest through the deliberate juxtaposition of sound or imagery in sequences. Common juxtaposition approaches include the following:

- **Scale and composition-based juxtapositions:** the invisibility of continuity editing breaks down if audiences are presented with edited sequences that switch between contrasting shot distances or jarring frame-based compositions. Scale-based contrasts – moving from extreme close-ups to long-shots, for example – might be used to demonstrate a narrative disruption or character conflict. Edits might also switch the focal points of consecutive shots, demanding, for example, that audiences refocus their viewing from the bottom left of the screen to the top right.
- **Colour/lighting juxtapositions:** these are constructed when successive shots use contrasting colour palettes or lighting styles. Switching abruptly from high to low-key lighting or suddenly cutting from warm to cold colour palettes disrupts film continuity and can infer symbolic meanings.
- **Sound-based juxtapositions:** editors control aural or sound-based elements as well as visual information, and where continuity editing conventionally effects gentle transitions from one soundscape to the next through cross fades or subtle volume changes, expressive edits might force a more abrupt transition to an audience's listening experience. Contrasting soundscapes can be used to realign audience perceptions or to infer extreme or contradictory messaging.

Table 3.7 Revise it: jump-cutting and juxtaposition analysis

Jump-cutting effects	• Is jump-cutting reserved for key moments in the film? Why has it been applied to those moments? • What material is excluded as a result of jump-cutting? Is material excluded to speed up the narrative? • Is jump-cutting used to disorientate the spectator? • How does jump-cutting affect the editing tempo?
Juxtaposition effects	**Scale and composition juxtapositions** • Do any editing sequences move quickly from close-ups or extreme close-ups to long-shots? With what effect? **Colour/lighting juxtapositions** • Are there any moments where the film switches abruptly from one colour palette to another? • Do editing sequences alternate between low- and high-key lighting? Where and with what effect? **Sound-based juxtapositions** • Do soundscapes transition suddenly? • Do scores change from major to minor keys or employ disjointed instrumentation? • Are there any moments in the film where ambient volume levels change as a result of juxtaposition in editing? **Effects of juxtaposition** • Are juxtapositions used to suggest character or narrative conflicts? • Are they used to suggest change? • Are they used to suggest adversarial character outlooks or clashing social positions perhaps?

(*continued*)

Table 3.7 Cont.

Exemplar: *Carol* **(Eduqas).** The central characters of *Carol* yearn to escape the closed social–sexual ideals of their 1950s setting. That closed world is made concrete through Carol's loveless marriage and Therese's dead-end department store job. The sexual freedoms that ensue in *Carol* are sporadic and brief, always located in the rare moments of privacy that the two women engineer for themselves: in hotel rooms or the closed world of Carole's car. The danger and fragility of those moments is often exposed to the film's audience using scale-based contrasts in the film's final edit, with extreme close-ups often juxtaposed with long-shot compositions in sequences (see Figure 3.3). These moments of visual juxtaposition alternately provoke intimacy and disconnection, paralleling the central character's relationship.

The film's sound editing also affects abrupt transitions. Carter Burwell's sombre string score, for example, often cuts suddenly to silence – a reminder, perhaps, that beneath Carol and Therese's relationship lurks an inevitably tragic outcome. Haynes, too, uses vivid palettes of reds and greens to depict the film's lead characters during their private exchanges. Colour use, here, signifying the life-giving energy of their relationship, but, again, jolting editing juxtaposes those vivid depictions with washed-out snow scenes and the desaturated world of conventional 1950s America. It is certainly true that Haynes rarely departs from a continuity-editing-based approach in the film, but, nonetheless, the abrupt shifts in sound and imagery in Hayne's editing adds a layer of expressive meaning to *Carol* that lifts the film beyond a conventional mainstream style.

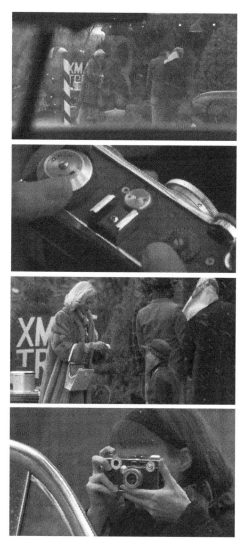

Figure 3.3 Carol: the deliberate juxtaposition of long-shots and extreme close-ups in *Carol* emphasises the physical distance between the two lead characters.

Montage edits

Montage edits are produced when unrelated shots follow each other in the same sequence. From the early history of cinema, filmmakers realised that editing didn't necessarily have to follow the logic of continuity editing. Early filmmakers realised that audiences, try to make sense of edits even if they contain disconnected or unrelated imagery. Soviet filmmakers in the 1920s were particularly interested in the potential effects of montage editing and readily experimented with new cutting strategies. Sergei Eisenstein in *Battleship Potemkin*, for example, famously intercut shots of marching soldiers with completely unrelated imagery of fleeing crowds to illustrate the terror of the Russian Revolution. Eisenstein further identified the following types of montage that filmmakers might use:

- **Metric montages** are time-based edits that sequence shots so that each shot lasts for the same amount of time regardless of content. Shots are cut to create an even, usually high tempo, editing pulse. Films often use fast-paced metric montage during narrative climaxes, for example, to inject energy and tension. Metric edits construct an even editing tempo.
- **Rhythmic montage** like metric edits, rhythmic montage is a time-oriented editing technique, but instead of cutting shots to a predefined shot length, rhythmic edits vary the duration of individual shots according to the action depicted. A scene, for example, that depicts a murder might start off with a slow editing tempo while the murderer stalks their victim, but then shifts abruptly to a high-tempo edit when the character launches their attack. Rhythmic edits vary editing tempo.
- **Tonal montages** are edited sequences that use disconnected imagery to build or concentrate one single meaning or emotion. Eisenstein famously demonstrated tonal montage in *Battleship Potemkin* by intercutting footage of a revolutionary soldier's heroic funeral with romantic shots of harbored ships at dusk. Eisenstein's use of montage during

the scene concentrates the sadness of the sailor's death by using imagery that invokes similar ideas or emotions. Tonal montages build emotional intensity.

- **Intellectual montages** include sequenced imagery that isn't immediately related, asking audiences to make connections between the contrasting subject matter of shots and to infer symbolic meanings that arise from those contrasts. Coppola's baptism scene at the end of *The Godfather* (Figure 3.4), for example, provides a prime example of intellectual montage, cross-cutting between the christening of Michael Corleone's godson and the graphic murders of rival gang leaders. The montage's juxtaposition of brutal executions with the christening of an innocent baby represents Michael Corleone's ascendancy as a mafia leader while also exposing the calculated cold logic that enables him to achieve his godfather status. Intellectual montages build symbolic or intellectual meanings rather than emotional effects.
- **Overtonal montage** combines two or more of the effects identified above.

Table 3.8 Montage-editing analysis questions

Identifying metric-montage effects	• Do sequences use shots that are the same length? • What editing tempo do those sequences affect? Fast or slow? • Why is metric montage used? Does it suggest an inevitable narrative event? Does it inject an upbeat editing rhythm? Does it create a sequence of abrupt cuts?
Identifying rhythmic montage	• Do sequences vary editing pace according to the content of the shot? • Does the editing pace slow or speed up? • What emotional effects do those changes have on the audience?

(*continued*)

Table 3.8 Cont.

Identifying tonal montage	• Are unrelated shots in sequences used to build a single emotion? • In what ways are the shots similar? • What emotion does the sequence emphasise?
Identifying intellectual montage	• Do editing sequences reference conflicting shots or cuts that force the audience to make symbolic connections? • What is symbolised by the montage? What are audiences forced to think about?

Exemplar: *The Hurt Locker* (OCR). Bigelow's use of overtonal montage at the start of *The Hurt Locker* constructs a sharp critique of the experiences of the Gulf War by demonstrating its corrosive mental effects on the film's central characters. Bigelow's phased use of tonal, metric and rhythmic montage provides an impressive scene opener for the film, with frenzied jump-cuts initially used to compress time and to inject a sense of urgency and panic. Bigelow here uses a tightly controlled metric edit alongside continuous 180-degree rule infringements to underline the soldiers' urgency in dealing with the chaotic situation in hand. Coupled with the film's documentary style camerawork, the cumulative effect of this initial sequence is to produce a frenetic and immersive viewing experience with no central-character viewpoint articulated.

Later shots in the sequence work as a tonal montage that depicts onlooking Iraqi citizens watching the soldiers from high vantage points, their accusatory oversight building an inescapable claustrophobic menace, also suggesting, perhaps, the underlying paranoia of the soldiers. The third phase of Bigelow's introductory sequence outlines the final realisation by the soldiers that they have been ambushed – a moment that is signalled to the audience using a rapid escalation in editing tempo (rhythmic montage) with a final slow-motion sequence used to exaggerate the force of the scene's climatic explosion.

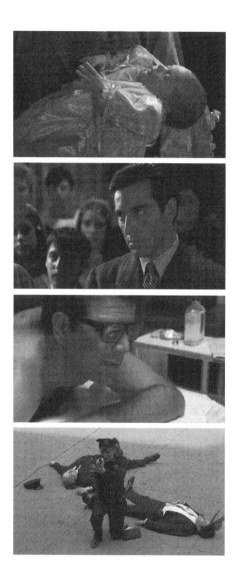

Figure 3.4 The Godfather. Coppola's use of intellectual montage in *The Godfather.*

Long-takes

It may seem strange, but the absence of editing cuts can also be used to construct expressive or dramatic effects. Edits that reduce scenes to one or two cuts immerse audiences or invite them to explore the film worlds presented to them. Long-takes, too, can be used to affect an extreme form realism with the removal of editor-oriented audience signposting sometimes used to suggest a film's lack of mediation. Long-takes can be categorised as follows:

- **Static long-takes** maintain a held vantage point that invites audiences to explore the interior of the frame. Static long-takes can be combined with actor movement or with various actor(s) entering or leaving the frame to effect variation. Director Roy Andersson, for example, uses static long-takes to affect a surreal dream-like aesthetic – most notably in *You, the Living* where his 'living paintings' editing style is most pronounced.
- **Circular long-takes** are a popular device, usually effected through Steadicam technology where the camera starts and ends the shot from the same vantage point or is used to circle a central point of reference. Circular long-shots can suggest repetition or be used to define a limited or enclosed location. Alfonso Cuarón's jaw dropping single-take car ambush scene in *Children of Men* provides a brilliant example of the use of long-takes to inject scene intensity.
- **Linear long-takes** are usually affected through horizontal tracking shots or track-ins. Linear long-shots can be used to suggest the expanse of a scene or to explore a film moment that deals with an epic event. The epic long-takes in the war film *Atonement*, for example, reveal the scale and desperation of the British army waiting to be rescued on the beaches of Dunkirk during the Second World War.

Table 3.9 Revise it: long-take analysis

Identify scenes in set texts where long-takes are used. Use these questions to explore the purpose and effects produced by such moments:

- What kind of camera movement is the long take combined with?
- Who or what is held in frame as the long take progresses?
- Is the long take used to define a poignant or important moment in the film's narrative?
- Is the long take used to define an expansive or confined setting?
- What kind of audience reaction does the long-take aim to produce?

Editing and auteur-based approaches

Traditional auteur theory suggests that a sign of a true auteur is the control that a director might exercise throughout the production process, not only during production shoots but also in the editor's cutting room. Editing analysis can be used to generate evidence that a director approached filmmaking using a defined or stylised approach.

Table 3.10 Revise it: identifying auteur-editing approaches

Diagnosing auteurial editing effects	• How does the editing style of your set text compare with other films made by the director? • How does the director control emotional meaning through editing tempo or scene set ups? • How does the editor treat dialogue or action-based sequences? What commonalities and differences are there between the set text you are studying and other films made by the same director?

(continued)

Table 3.10 Cont.

Exemplar: *Apocalypse Now* **(Eduqas).** The use of overtonal montage at the end *Apocalypse Now* is strikingly similar to Coppola's cross-cutting finale in *The Godfather* – both films using editing to alternate their narrative climaxes with secondary action. In *Apocalypse Now*, Kurtz's death is contrasted with the ritual slaughter of a bull by his tribal followers (Figure 3.5), with Coppola cross-cutting from Kurtz's murder to the bull sacrifice in an ever faster rhythmic climax. The visceral realism of the bull's death helps to underline the brutality of Kurtz's assassination, while also providing the film's audiences with an intellectual montage that suggests the renegade leader's death is a spiritual or ritualistic sacrifice.

A similar effect is produced when Michael Corleone's violent ascent to power is contrasted against the sacred solemnity of a Catholic christening in *The Godfather* (Figure 3.4). The death/birth symbolism here clearly echoes *Apocalypse Now* with Kurtz's death suggesting a new beginning for Willard and a new leader for Kurtz's renegade tribe in much the same way that Corleone's killing of his rivals allows him to become the new mafia figurehead. These editing similarities, perhaps, tease out a shared thematic subtext and cement Coppola's status as a film auteur. In both films, nonetheless, Coppola is clearly interested in cyclical ideas, and, moreover, in the notion that death inevitably leads to rebirth.

Figure 3.5 Apocalypse Now. The assassination of Kurtz is intercut with an animal sacrifice to symbolically infer the rogue commander's martyrdom.

Table 3.11 Editing: ten-minute revision

Essential background
• Editing helps to connect specific characters to audiences, helping them to identify with lead characters through increased screen time or by foregrounding their experiences and reactions in edits. • Editing plays a crucial role in constructing and resolving narrative enigmas. Films withhold and reveal information to maintain audience interest and to drive stories forward.
Essential knowledge: continuity editing
• Continuity editing is associated with mainstream film and Hollywood output. • Continuity editing produces chronologically ordered sequences. • Continuity editing creates a naturalistic feel for films and encourages, potentially, passive viewing. • Editing tempo affects emotional impact. • Continuity editing is increasingly used alongside expressive editing techniques in contemporary filmmaking.
Essential knowledge: expressive editing
• Jump-cuts are used to compress time or to disorientate viewing. • Filmmakers test the logic of continuity editing using editing juxtaposition. • Tonal montages build emotional effects using related imagery. • Intellectual montages produce symbolic meanings by sequencing discontinuous imagery. • Long-takes can invite prolonged interrogation of the screen and drive active audience engagement.

4   Sound

Table 4.1 What do you need to revise sound for?

> Study of sound is core to all aspects of Film Studies. Students should be able to identify the use and effects of ambient sound and dialogue control as well as the application of accompanying film scores.

Essential background

Sound has been applied to film from the outset of its invention. In the silent era actors were occasionally placed behind projection screens to speak dialogue – musical accompaniment was provided by full orchestras in the grand picture houses of the 1920s, while even smaller cinemas used solo pianists to improvise musical accompaniments while films were projected.

Today's digital multitrack surround sound experiences, of course, offer more complex soundscapes, and, as audio technologies have advanced, we might argue that the role that sound-based elements play in the meaning-making of contemporary films has increased significantly. Those technologies have also given filmmakers the tools to craft complex soundscapes in which scene ambience and bespoke musical scores work alongside dialogue and visual storytelling to create complex viewing experiences for contemporary audiences.

In general terms, we can break down the use of sound in film according to the following two categories:

- *Non-diegetic sound* refers to sounds that are not present in the world of the film, including key elements such as voice overs or film scores. Accompanying musical scores of films are hugely significant in that they offer a range of subtle connotative effects as a result of instrument choice, volume, tempo and pitch control, as well as the choice of musical keys that composers work within.
- *Diegetic sound* refers to sounds that belong to the world of the film depicted. These include aural cues that characters themselves might hear, including dialogue or noises that emanate from screen-based action – footsteps, the slamming of car doors and so on. The latter category of sounds – screen-based action effects – are usually applied in post-production by foley artists so that their connotative impact and volume levels can be carefully controlled. Foley artists use a variety of trade tricks to reproduce on-screen sound – the sound of combat punches, for example, are recreated by hitting meat, while rain is often mimicked by frying bacon. As a result of foley-artist applications, on-set sound recording usually focuses on capturing dialogue only.

We might further categorise diegetic sound into the following two groups:

- *On-screen sound* are those sounds that emanate from the depicted scene – principally those sounds that are connected to character action.
- *Off-screen sounds* includes background noise or ambient sounds that communicate subtle clues that reinforce where the action depicted is located: a background ambience, for example, that consists of the sounds of typewriters and telephone conversations could be used to convince an audience that action is taking place inside an office.

Capturing dialogue

Dialogue, of course, plays a vital role in communicating storylines. It defines character outlooks as well as the relationships that exist between characters. Actors, too, add meanings to the script of a film, delivering lines in ways that add emotional resonance to the raw dialogue of a script – adding what's called prosodic meaning to scripts through performances to suggest joy, sorrow or excitement, for example.

Similarly, the methods used to record dialogue and the post-production treatment of spoken speech by sound editors plays an equally crucial role in the meaning-making of dialogue within a film. Key factors to consider when analysing dialogue include the following:

- **Volume** the loudness or quietness of dialogue tells audiences a great deal. Voices that struggle to be heard against background sounds might infer a loss of control. Whispered dialogue might similarly suggest secrecy, intimacy or shyness. Character privilege can also be communicated if the volume of an actor's delivery in dialogue exchanges is given more presence than other characters.
- **Reverb** refers to the amount of echo applied to vocal components and is subtly applied to some degree in most films. Reducing voice reverb can suggest character confinement or can help to create a brittle or pointed voice tone. Conversely, excess reverb – the adding of subtle echo cues – can help to suggest the expanse or emptiness of a setting or can be used to give character delivery a hollow or distant feel.
- **Physical reproduction of sound** – panning – the process of placing sounds to the right, left, rear or front of audio mixes – reinforces on-screen character positioning. Voices, too, can be grouped to the left or right of soundtracks to infer character allegiances.

Table 4.2 Revise it: dialogue analysis

Dialogue sound analysis: top tips	
• Locate scenes in which key dialogue exchanges take place. • Listen carefully to dialogue exchanges, preferably using a surround sound audio system or headphones to help you identify panning and/or reverb effects. • Detecting reverb application requires careful listening – listen to sequences several times to gain a sense of reverb use.	
Volume effects	• Are some characters given more volume than others? Which characters are privileged as a result? • How does the volume of character dialogue change? How do volume changes support screen action? • Is dialogue dampened to suggest intimacy, powerlessness or character insecurity? • Is increased volume used to suggest character power or to reinforce the emotive undertones of the scene?
Reverb effects	• Is the level of reverb given to dialogue noticeably flat or roomy? • Is flat reverb applied to suggest an enclosed or busy space? Does flat reverb use emphasise a lack of character emotion? • Is increased reverb used to suggest an open or empty space? Does thick reverb suggest character isolation?
Dialogue physicality	• Are character voices placed to the left or right of sound mixes? how does the placement of sound help to reflect the physical positioning of characters in the scene? • Are characters' voices grouped to the left or right of audio mixes to suggest allegiance or conflict?
Challenge question: is sound reproduction in home-viewing conditions different to the experience of listening to a film in a cinema auditorium? Does that mean that the subtle meaning-making properties of sound control are lost on audiences watching films at home?	

Film ambience

As sound recording technologies have evolved, more finessed soundscapes have been authored by filmmakers. Certainly, ambience has become increasingly important in communicating subtle cues to audiences, and where pre-Second World War filmmakers struggled to reproduce satisfactory room tones, contemporary sound engineers can fashion complex sound mixes that can convey an artful presence. Ambient sound control in contemporary filmmaking can construct the following:

- **Concrete ambience:** sounds applied to underline a scene's location. Traffic noise for example, might be applied to suggest a city location. Nature-based ambience – bird calls or the rustle of trees – might be used to infer a rural setting.
- **Room tone effects:** ambience also plays a nuanced role in communicating the underlying emotion of a scene. Sound designers, for example, might dial up the emotional effect of a film moment by including harsher or more chaotic ambient treatments: traffic sounds, for example, might be made to feel more aggressive if they include the sounds of car horns. Likewise, a rural ambience might be given a more sinister feel if the mechanical sound of a tractor subtly disrupts the soundscape's rural harmony. Sound designers also use busy or high-tempo ambiences to suggest conflict or disorder, while the heightened use of bass/treble heavy ambiences can inject fear or emotional uplift.
- **Metaphorical ambient cues:** some soundscapes offer more direct auditory significance, with single sounds applied at crucial moments to reinforce on-screen action. An off-screen dog bark, for example, might be applied to underline a moment of impending danger, or rain sounds might fall harder when character dialogue increases in intensity. These subtle, and sometimes not so subtle, cues anchor narratives, pushing audiences towards a specific emotional reaction at key points in a film.
- **Silent ambience:** contemporary films rarely offer audiences moments of complete silence, but the dampening

of ambience can be just as significant as the presence of background noise. Little or no ambience might be used, for example, to suggest character isolation or to infer the presence of danger. Ambience might also be suppressed to foreground dialogue or to draw attention to a significant moment of character action. Likewise, ambience that fades into a scored soundtrack can signify scene changes or a narrative transition.

Table 4.3 Revise it: ambient sound analysis

A detailed discussion of ambient sound can be used to convince examiners you have considered in detail the effect of subtle sound cues in films. Locate key scenes in films and listen carefully to the layers of ambient sound that lie behind dialogue or any accompanying musical score.   **Ambient sound analysis: top tips**   • Turn off visual elements when analysing ambient sound to help you focus on the layers of sound that are present at any given moment in a film.   • Identify key sound personnel in exam responses to demonstrate your knowledge of the key filmmakers responsible for producing aural meaning in set texts.   • Consider how dialogue, ambience and scores work in sync with one another.   • Identify the use of room tone effects and metaphorical cues rather than the more general application of concrete ambience.

Diagnosing the significance of concrete ambience	• What background sounds do you hear in key scenes? What objects make those sounds? • What do the origins of off-screen sounds tell us about the physical location of depicted action? Do they suggest a specific environment? Do they suggest a specific city or place? Do they suggest a specific time period? • What do the sounds tell us about the location and time of scene action? Is it night or day? Is it busy or quiet?

Table 4.3 Cont.

Diagnosing the significance of room tone effects	• How do ambient sounds work to underline the emotional direction of a scene? • What are the connotative effects of the sounds presented? How do they make us feel? Are we given busy or sparse ambient soundscapes? • Does a film's ambience sound mechanical or natural? Dynamic or repetitive? Are sounds dominated by bass or treble frequencies? • Are ambient tracks allowed to dominate audio mixes or are they firmly held in the background? • What weather sounds are offered to us? Do these sounds offer the audience pathetic fallacy? Is ambience used to infer the emotions of lead characters?
Locating metaphorical ambient cues	• Are single symbolic sounds injected into the audio mix? What are the emotional connotation of those sounds? • Why do filmmakers use metaphorical ambience cues at particular points in the film? Do they offer warnings or foreground narrative events? Are sounds used to punctuate the effect of scene action?
Locating the significance of silence.	• Is ambience deliberately dampened at key points? With what effects? • What other sounds are allowed to dominate during these dampened moments?

Exemplar: *Apocalypse Now* **(Eduqas).** In *Apocalypse Now*, Walter Murch was one of the first sound editors to fully exploit the technical capacities of Dolby Surround Sound, with the film's carefully crafted soundscape used in the introduction to infer the physical and mental presence of the Vietnam war. Murch's use of panning helicopter sounds in the film's intro recreates the physical experience and chaotic immediacy of war-torn Saigon. Murch, too, cleverly fades that ambient backdrop into the chaotic hum of off-screen city traffic, with the noise of aggressive car horns carefully juxtaposed against Willard's whispered voice to highlight the character's isolation from the world outside. Murch also uses

(continued)

Table 4.3 Cont.

ambient noise for metaphorical purposes, inferring the collapsed emotional state of Willard through a subtle transition from city-based noises to jungle insects in a way that suggests Willard's inability to escape the trauma of jungle combat. The crescendoed buzzing of insects further connotes the overbearing nature of that trauma before receding into a reprise of the Doors countercultural anthem '*The End*'.

Links to exemplar film clips and exemplars for other OCR/Eduqas film texts can be found at www.essentialfilmrevision.com

Music and scores

Film scores, if present, work subtly within the sonic sound-scape of a film. Scores might affect a quiet presence, gently progressing beneath dialogue and other sound layers to signpost a range of meanings. Scores, too, are sometimes given centre-stage presences in films, replacing dialogue within audio mixes to punctuate action or to prompt a range of visceral effects for a film's audience. Film music performs the following six functions:

- **Emotional signification:** the choice of instruments as well as the volume or rhythm of accompanying music creates a sonic backdrop that helps to relay the emotional sub-text of scene action. A high-tempo piece might be used to construct drama or to signify the frantic inner-world of a character. Conversely, soft-paced tempos or lyrical accom-paniment might be used to underpin character connection or to signpost moments of narrative resolution. Music, in this sense, provides an invisible, yet hugely powerful effect on audiences by underscoring a narrative's lighter or darker moments.
- **Cultural signification:** not all films commission new compositions as accompaniment, using instead the ready-made significations of pre-existing songs. Using already-known tracks allows filmmakers to piggyback on pre-existing cultural meanings. In this sense, pre-existing tracks can create

nostalgia or help to construct a specific reference to an historical period. The Otis Redding soul-infused soundtrack of Selma, for example, neatly nurtures the film's historical setting, using politically resonant tracks to convey its Black-activist credentials.

- **Continuity effects:** music also plays a vital role in connecting scenes or locations to one another by smoothing out the transition from one scene to the next. Music might also help connect the emotional content of one scene to a scene that follows. A character might die, for example, in a scene that uses a lilting minor key score to underline the sadness of their death – the continuation of that score in subsequent scenes might be used to suggest the effect of the death on other characters.
- **Narrative cueing:** music plays an important role in helping audiences to orientate themselves within film storylines or can even be used to set up narrative expectations. Characters, for example, might be associated with specific musical phrases – the use of leitmotif, for example, is used to signal the entrance or presence of key characters within films. The instrumentation used to construct leitmotifs might also help to outline character traits: bass-driven timbres might suggest power or fear, lighter instrumentation – harps or pianos – might infer innocence or vulnerability. Similarly, film compositions can be used to signify narrative transitions: narrative disequilibrium, for example, might be suggested through discordant or clashing musical elements, story climaxes might similarly be conveyed through the presence of rising volume, while film openings might use solo instrumentation to infer enigma or to build narrative tension.
- **To parallel action:** sound can be described as empathetic when used to mirror or intensify scene action. Car chases or fight scenes, for example, might be augmented with scores that match screen movement in terms of tempo or volume. Similarly, character defeats might be reinforced using a score performed by a lone instrument.

- **To juxtapose scene action:** sound that contrasts with
  scene action, or anempathetic music, can be used to create
  ironic or sometimes deliberately comic effects. The rendition of '*O-o-h Child*' in *Guardians of the Galaxy*, for example,
  provides a comic counterpoint to Ronan's evil ascent. The
  use of Stealers Wheels '*Stuck in the Middle of You*' presents a
  similarly complex interaction of sound and action in *Reservoir
  Dogs* and is used to underline Blonde's casual sadism during
  the film's now infamous torture scene.

Table 4.4 Revise it: film score reference guide and analysis

Score component	Definition explanation	Key questions to ask during analysis
Instrumentation and timbre	Refers to the kinds of instruments used within musical sequences. Timbre alludes to the sound quality or tone that instruments convey – harps, for example, are often used to suggest innocence or delicateness, while brass instruments infer a much harder more powerful timbre.	• What musical instruments or voices dominate within the film's score? • What connotative or emotional effects do those instruments construct? • Does instrumentation change during the film? Why? • How many instruments are expressed at any one time? What connotative effect does this have?

Table 4.4 Cont.

Musical key	Refers to the key signature used to score music. Broadly speaking, music can be performed in either a major or minor key. Major keys produce brighter or more optimistic musical moments whereas scores written in a minor key produce discordant or pessimistic undertones.	• Does the score use a major key to create a bright or upbeat feel? • Does the score use a minor key to construct a sad or downbeat feel?
Sound motifs	Musical scores are often composed using repeated phrases. Some phrases are associated with specific characters (leitmotif) or suggest narrative themes. Sometimes musical phrases might be subtly adjusted as the film progresses, rewritten to mirror the narrative action of the film at that point.	• Are specific musical phrases attached to characters? What does the tone, key or instrumentation of those phrases suggest about the character? • Do musical phrases change or evolve as the film progresses? With what effect?
Volume	Refers to the loudness or quietness of music. Rising volume might inject drama or suggest an emotional climax, quieter moments might suggest a reflective or calmer narrative moment.	• How is volume used by the film's sound editor to create intrigue or to support moments of screen excitement?

(*continued*)

Table 4.4 Cont.

Score component	Definition explanation	Key questions to ask during analysis
Pitch	Refers to how high or low musical notes or phrases sound. We associate low-pitched notes with animals that have a big presence or with male voices. High-pitched notes sound lighter or more melodic and are associated with the female voice. Quite often films use low-pitched drones or pads to suggest fear or dread. Conversely high-pitched phrases can infer romance or a lighter tone.	• Are scores dominated by bass- or treble-driven motifs? • Are drones or pads added to construct an unsettling ambience? • What are the connotative effects of pitch-based decisions?
Tempo	Refers to the pace of a film score. Slow scores can construct a creeping or mysterious accompaniment, whereas a rising tempo might be used to accompany energised scene action or to infuse film sequences with energy.	• How fast or slow is the music used? • Is music beat-matched to action or to editing cuts? • Does score tempo reinforce the emotional impact of scene action?

Table 4.4 Cont.

> **Exemplar:** *Trainspotting* **(Eduqas).** The 'worst toilet in Scotland'
> scene exemplifies the complexity and subtlety of Boyle's Indie-
> pop infused soundtrack. Bizet's *Carmen Suite No. 2* initially offers
> a comedic counterpoint to Renton's drug experiences, before the
> soundtrack submerges into Brian Eno's sleepily paced *Deep Blue
> Day.* The track's slow melodic ambience dowses the audience in
> euphoric synth swells and an accompanying glissando of country
> guitar to signify the emotional high of Renton's drug find. The
> uplifting effect of the soundtrack is further emphasised as a result of
> its juxtaposition with the stomach-churning setting of the preceding
> scene. This juxtaposition, moreover, is symptomatic of Boyle's
> magical realist take on British social realism, transporting us from the
> gritty dirt of underclass Scotland to the imagined magical interior
> of Renton's drug world. Moreover, Boyle's use of Eno's obscure
> *Music for Film's* track alongside newer artists of the early 1990s, like
> Underworld, gave *Trainspotting* an indie kudos, enabling Boyle to
> repackage the outmoded social–realist output that had so dominated
> the British film industry of the period for a new culturally aware
> Brit Pop audience.

Table 4.5 Sound: ten-minute revision

Essential knowledge
• Diegetic sound refers to the sounds that belong to the world of film characters. Non-diegetic sounds are those that characters can't hear. • Off-screen sounds generally refer to the background noises or ambient sounds referenced in film soundscapes.
Voice and dialogue control
• Sound editors shape dialogue delivery in final edits by remixing volume and reverb levels. • Sound editors replicate real-world physicality using volume, reverb and panning.

(continued)

Table 4.5 Cont.

Ambience
• Sound can anchor the locations of scenes via the use of concrete ambience.
• Room tone can convey emotional connotations.
• Ambient sounds can infer metaphorical or symbolic meanings at key points in a narrative.

Sound scores
• Scores can construct or direct the emotional response of audiences via the use of instrumentation, key, pitch, tempo and volume.
• Scores or incidental music can construct meaning as a result of their cultural significance. The use of well-known music, for example, can provoke audience nostalgia or other intertextual meanings.
• Scores can be used to bridge scene transitions or to extend the emotional resonance of a film moment across several scenes.
• Scores can parallel screen action via matched tempos or volume control.
• Scores can provide a musical contrast with screen action for the purposes of comedy or dramatic irony.

5   Lighting

Table 5.1 What do you need to revise lighting for?

Study of lighting is core to all aspects of Film Studies. Students should be able to identify the use and effects of natural lighting, directional lighting, high- and low-key lighting ratios, diffusion effects as well as the application of colour lighting effects.

Essential background

Lighting control, often classified as an aspect of mise en scène, is a significant tool that filmmakers use to shape the aesthetic impact of their output. From the neon-lit colour washes of Nicolas Winding Refn to the desaturated naturalism of Ben Wheatley, the application of light in film alerts the audience to a host of ready-made meanings.

Lighting applications in film can be divided into the following two broad categories:

- **Naturalistic lighting** is used to construct a realistic or everyday film style, achieved, for the most part, using natural lighting and external shoots.
- **Expressive lighting** applies artificial lighting to add shadow, colour or focal points. Expressive lighting is usually controlled within a studio environment, using key lights to provide character illumination or backlighting to separate characters from sets. Expressive lighting can shape meaning

through a wide variety of techniques, adding drama or abstract layers of meaning to scenes.

Identifying the stylised application of lighting by filmmakers can help us to determine:

- **Auteurial markers:** directors often work with the same lighting crews on successive projects, and, in so doing, adopt techniques and styles that are unique to their output.
- **Character-oriented meanings:** character lighting applications generate important cues for audiences when watching films. The use of shadow, for example, tells us a great deal about the moral direction of a character, or can help to define a character's role within a narrative. Even the direction from which characters are lit can convey connotative clues that underline or supplement character actions.
- **Emotional impact:** lighting plays a crucial role in defining the emotional backdrop of a sequence. Film, for example, exploits our natural fear of darkness, using shadow or low-key lighting to construct horror, panic or alarm. Film also uses expressive lighting to paint compositions, using connotative colour palettes – golden-hour shoots, for example – to produce shots in which warming red and orange tones are prominent.
- **The application of genre:** specific kinds of lighting styles are associated with a range of genres. The use, or even the absence of those expectations, can help identify the class or subclass to which a film belongs. In horror, for example, we would expect to see heavy use of low-key or chiaroscuro lighting techniques, while comedies and romcoms would conventionally be lit using high-key set ups.

Natural lighting

The use of natural lighting produces ready-made realism for films. The choice, moreover, to film using natural light also minimises the need to set up expensive lighting rigs, and, as a result, enables filmmakers to shoot scenes without the need for studio set-ups. The use of natural lighting, however, requires detailed planning and careful location selection by filmmakers as a trade-off.

Approaches to filmmaking that use natural-lighting set ups tend to deploy one or more of the following strategies:

- **Golden-hour shoots:** often, filmmakers choose to shoot scenes just after sunrise or before sunset. The resulting red glow of golden-hour shoots produces warm tonal compositions. The sun's position during the golden hour also produces a low-angle or 'raking' lighting style that softens shadows while also producing attractive actor profiles.
- **Blue-hour shoots:** blue lighting shoots use natural lighting in the short window of time just before sunrise or just after sunset – the times of day when the sun lies below the horizon. Blue-hour shoots, much like golden-hour photography, produce a diffused or softened lighting effect, but, conversely, connote a much colder or darker feel as a result of the blue colour tones that the lighting style emphasises. In practice, blue lighting shoots provide filmmakers with a 20- to 40-minute window of opportunity for filming when the sun begins to set, and, much like golden-hour shoots, require both planning and patience if filmmakers are to make the most of the short period of time afforded by this shooting style.
- **Backlighting dominance:** filmmakers who use natural lighting often position characters with their backs to the sun so they don't squint during takes. Backlighting also produces a haloed effect that illuminates the edges of characters.
- **Use of 'practicals':** 'practicals' are light sources that are readily found in scenes – streetlamps, table lamps, car headlights and so on. Natural-lighting shoots will readily draw upon these props and light sources to provide lighting focal points or to add contrast or shadows during shoots.
- **Lens effects:** natural-light setups tend to favour the use of a wide-angle lens due to their increased ability to capture available light. As a result, shoots can be dominated by

wide-shot compositions, mid-shots or even long-shots to frame subjects. A lack of available light can also restrict a filmmaker's ability to capture shot depth, often resulting in the use of shallow depth-of-field compositions.

Table 5.2 Revise it: natural-lighting analysis

Natural-lighting analysis: top tips	
• Identify key scenes where the use of natural lighting has an unusual or pronounced effect. • Identify whether the filmmaker has used golden- or blue-hour shoots to film material. • Identify whether the filmmaker has used practicals to inject expressive lighting effects into key scenes.	
Golden/blue-hour shoots	• At what time of day has the filmmaker chosen to shoot material? What impact does that shooting time have on the tone or colour palettes that are emphasised? • How do blue/golden-hour shooting choices reinforce character portrayals or the narrative content of films?
Natural-lighting limitation effects	• Does the film contain backlit sequences as result of natural-lighting shooting? With what effect? • Is the film shot using a wide-angle lens? What effect does this have on the look or feel of the film?
Use of practicals	• What practical lighting sources does the film use in scenes that are shot using natural lighting? • What focal points are created by these sources? • How does the strength or the direction of the light source add to the scene?

Table 5.2 Cont.

Exemplar: *City of God* **(Eduqas).** The use of natural lighting dominates in Meirelles' brutal gangster/realist film, *City of God*, lending the text a docu-realist feel that, in turn, supports the film's credentials as a political commentary regarding the effects of social poverty in the favelas of Rio de Janeiro. The use of golden-hour shoots during the film's opening scenes (Figure 5.2) immerses the story with an initial sense of nostalgia and innocence, while later scenes – filmed using a more abrasive daytime shoot – help to outline the increasing brutality of the favelas via the harder shadows and high contrast lighting that this form of natural-lighting effects.

The film's darkening character morality is further suggested through the framing of actors using the claustrophobic backlit interiors of the favela slums, where the shapeless silhouetted forms of actors are used to suggest the eclipsing sense of humanity felt by lead protagonists. This is best exemplified by the compressed montage that explores the history of Blacky's turf, where extreme tilt-up compositions search hopelessly for the harsh overexposed glare of the sun in the heart of the slums, while the elliptical edit that charts the history of Blacky's room moves from the golden glow of the room's early history to a much harder light source when Rocket takes ownership of the space. Lighting, here, is used as a metaphorical tool by the director to suggest the tragic descent of the film's cast, and, moreover, to give presence to the favela as the prime source of character corruption in the film.

Links to exemplar film clips and exemplars for other OCR/Eduqas film texts can be found at www.essentialfilmrevision.com

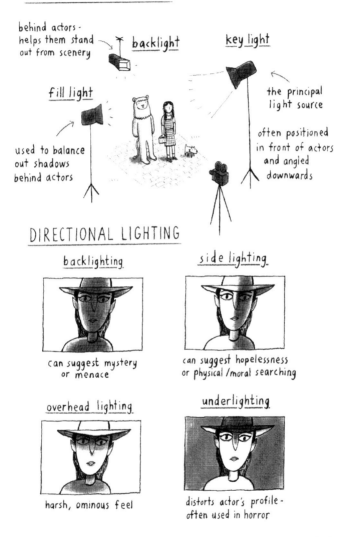

THREE POINT LIGHTING

behind actors -
helps them stand
out from scenery

backlight

key light

fill light

the principal
light source

often positioned
in front of actors
and angled
downwards

used to balance
out shadows
behind actors

DIRECTIONAL LIGHTING

backlighting

can suggest mystery
or menace

side lighting

can suggest hopelessness
or physical/moral searching

overhead lighting

harsh, ominous feel

underlighting

distorts actor's profile -
often used in horror

Figure 5.1 The three-point lighting set-up and directional lighting
effects. © Tom Zaino.

Artificial lighting

The move from natural lighting to artificial lighting is usually achieved using studio-based setups. In reality, those setups use complex lighting rigs with multiple light sources to create the desired result. The essential ingredients, however, of those set ups tend to deploy an adaptation of the three-point lighting system (see Figure 5.1). Three-point lighting is composed of the following types of light source:

- **Key lights** provide the principal source of light on film sets, usually illuminating actor profiles from a high angle to mimic natural sunlight. Key lights tend to create hard-lit subjects. If used without accompanying fill lighting, key lights will also project hard shadows behind subjects.
- **Fill lights** are used to balance out the shadows produced by key lights. Fill lights usually use a diffused light source to illuminate the set areas behind actors.
- **Backlights** – as the name suggests, backlights are positioned behind actors and are used to create a halo or rim of light around an actor's profile. Backlighting helps subjects to stand out from the surrounding scenery.

Directional lighting

Directing key lights from different angles produces a range of connotative effects (see Figure 5.1). Common techniques used include the following:

- **Backlighting:** extreme backlighting can reduce characters to shadowy profiles, while more subtle applications of backlighting can produce a spiritual glow around characters. The haloed glows that are produced by backlighting can sometimes be used to connote character innocence or vulnerability.

- **Underlighting:** directing key lights from beneath characters distorts an actor's profile and is usually avoided. Underlighting was traditionally applied to depict antagonists in horror films.
- **Overhead lighting:** aiming light sources at actors from above places an actor's eyes in shadow (Figure 5.2) – thus creating an ominous or serious portrait. Harsh top lighting can be used to portray villains or anti-heroes.
- **Side lighting:** side lighting creates actor profiles that are partially bathed in shadow and light. The use of side lighting without accompanying fill lights creates a chiaroscuro effect (Figure 5.3) – a dramatic lighting style where beams of light penetrate a dark scene. Chiaroscuro lighting produces scenes that suggest hopelessness or can sometimes be used to illustrate narrative moments where a physical or moral search is underway.

Figure 5.2 City of God (top): the use of natural lighting constructs a documentary realist aesthetic for the film. *Selma* (bottom): Overhead lighting can reinforce a somber or serious narrative subtext.

Figure 5.3 Pan's Labyrinth (top): the low-key lighting treatment of the Faun injects menace into Ofelia's dreamworld imaginings. *The Babadook* (bottom): chiaroscuro lighting creates beams of penetrating light, often used in films to depict moments when characters are surrounded by narrative darkness.

Low- and high-key lighting

The balance of key and filler lights dramatically affects the tonal qualities of a sequence. Two very general terms that are readily applied to the lighting style of films are those of high- and low-key lighting (see Figure 5.4):

- **Low-key lighting** predominantly uses backlights or key lights to illuminate tightly defined aspects of a scene.

Low-key lighting emphasises shadows and black tones and is usually associated with the horror, science fiction and thriller genres, but is also used to illustrate protagonist's during moments of crisis or to underline character hopelessness, suspicion or uncertainty. Low-key lighting might also be used during moments of narrative disequilibrium.

- **High-key lighting** refers to a brighter lighting style that reduces shadow while also emphasising colour. High-key lighting conveys a more optimistic feel and is readily used in comedies and romcoms. High-key lighting might also be used during narrative moments in which positive action is depicted or to reinforce moments of narrative harmony.

Diffusion: hard and soft lighting

Light sources can be softened by placing diffusion screens in front of them, in effect dampening the presence of shadows in a shot (see Figure 5.4). Conversely, a hard-lighting effect is produced when concentrated light sources are used to illuminate subjects – usually using spotlights or focused key lighting. Hard lighting produces defined shadows and a clean, clinical lighting ambience. In comparison, soft, or diffused lighting, is used to create dreamy, muted or subdued tonal effects (Figure 5.5).

Colour filters and colour temperature control

Much like the use of colour in costuming and set design, colour lighting filters or gels can be applied to produce colour decoration, and, moreover, can produce striking connotative effects as a result. Colour gels might be applied universally to scenes or just to key, fill or backlights to illuminate specific parts of a scene using a particular shade of colour. Contrasting coloured gels might also be applied to different aspects of a scene to construct a juxtaposed or jarring palette.

Colour can also be controlled by altering the temperature of film lighting, with low-temperature rigs highlighting red tones, while high-temperature lamps affect a much colder feel – subtly tinting white spaces with a blue or green hue. While most films aim to produce a balanced or natural-lighting feel, nudging colour balances by lowering or raising lighting temperatures can quietly adjust the warmth or coldness of a scene in a way that few viewers might consciously notice, but, nevertheless, has an enormous impact in guiding audience readings.

HIGH & LOW KEY LIGHTING

<u>low key lighting</u>

synonymous with horror, sci-fi & thrillers

can connote hopelessness, suspicion or uncertainty

<u>high key lighting</u>

omits shadow & emphasises colour

often suggests narrative harmony or resolution

DIFFUSION

<u>soft lighting</u>

light sources can be diffused or softened with diffusion screens

conversely, <u>hard lighting</u> can be achieved with concentrated light sources

shadows are dampened

dreamy, subtle or subdued effect

cold, clinical

Figure 5.4 High- and low-key lighting setups (top). Hard- and soft-lighting use (bottom). © Tom Zaino.

Figure 5.5 Room (top): a soft-lighting approach produces a muted or subdued aesthetic that helps to convey Jack's melancholy after his escape. *Captain Fantastic* (middle): high-key lighting in the film's early scenes reinforces the escapist ideals of the family's off-grid living. *Whiplash* (bottom): low-key lighting combined with hard-light sources helps to suggest the menace of the film's abrasive rehearsal sessions.

Table 5.3 Revise it: artificial lighting analysis

Lighting analysis: top tips	
• Identify scenes in relevant films where lighting is a significant ingredient in terms of the text's meaning-making capacity. • Namedrop key lighting personnel in analyses to demonstrate your film knowledge. • Think about the idiosyncratic approach that filmmakers take when lighting scenes.	
Key, filler and back light use	• Is three-point lighting used to replicate natural lighting? • Is three-point lighting used to produce expressive effects? • Are any sorts of lights – key lights, back lights or fills – allowed to dominate? Which ones and with what effect? • How does lighting change over the course of the film narrative? Why are these changes affected?
Directional lighting effects	• Which direction do key lights shine from? • What connotative effects does lighting direction produce? • How does the direction of lighting change in key scenes?
Low- and high-key lighting	• How does the use of high-key or low-key lighting affect the emotional thrust of the film? • Is the use of high-key or low-key lighting synonymous with the output of films in similar genres? • How does the use of high-key or low-key lighting change over the duration of the set text? • Is high-key or low-key lighting applied to specific characters within the film? Why?
Diffusion	• Does the scene use hard or soft lighting? • Does hard lighting emphasise shadows? Why is this lighting style used? • What connotative effects does the use of soft lighting produce? Does it flatten or subtly subdue scenes?

Table 5.3 Cont.

Colour filters and colour balance	• Are coloured filters applied? What elements of a scene are colour lit as a result? • What connotative effects does the use of colour produce? • How does colour affect characterisation or narrative themes? • Is lighting temperature adjusted to produce balanced colour correction? Is the film's colour balance slanted to enhance reds (low-temperature lighting) or blues/greens (high-temperature lighting)? What connotative effect does this have?

Pan's Labyrinth (**Eduqas**). *Pan's Labyrinth*'s director of photography, Guillermo Navarro, is recognised for his auteurial use of blue and yellow lighting, the application of which in *Pan's Labyrinth* helps to outline the film's realist/fantasy binary. Those scenes of the film that depict war-torn Spain, for example, are mostly shot using blue-hour natural lighting with high-temperature lighting rigs used to maximise the film's sombre treatment of the Civil War. The resulting blue-washed, low-key lit scenes help to outline the war's destructive impact on Ofelia.

Conversely, Ofelia's fantasy existence is affected through an oppositional lighting style, with high-key setups and yellow filters used to suggest the opulence, wonder and innocence of Ofelia's dreamworld existence. The exception to this approach occurs during Ofelia's encounters with the faun, with chiaroscuro side lighting, hard-lit shadow and minimal fill used to wrap the creature in darkness. Interestingly, Navarro's and del Toro's portrayal foregrounds the Faun's destructive potential and the idea that Ofelia's fantasy existence isn't simply an escape or a refuge but presents its own ambiguities: the world of the imagination, *Pan's Labyrinth* suggests, is a place that can amplify our anxieties with effects that can be just as destructive as those found in the real world.

Table 5.4 Lighting: ten-minute revision

Essential background
• Lighting can be used to produce a naturalistic feel – constructing realism for audiences. • Lighting can also be used for expressive or dramatic purposes. • Lighting is also a significant tool in determining the emotional tone of a film.
Essential knowledge: natural lighting
• Blue- and golden-hour shoots are used to emphasise cold and warm tonal compositions. • Natural-lighting shoots regularly use backlighting and wide-angle shots. • Practicals are used to add lighting focal points in natural-lighting shoots.
Essential knowledge: artificial lighting
• Artificial lighting setups use key, back and filler lights. Expressive depth can be created by enhancing or removing some of these lighting elements. • Directing key lights on subjects to create top lighting, side lighting, underlighting or back lighting produces a range of ready-made connotations. • Low-key lighting darkens film scenes and is usually used to illustrate character conflict. High-key lighting produces brighter compositions and can be used to suggest character harmony or emotional uplift. • Diffused lighting softens shadows. Concentrated light sources produce hard shadows. • Coloured filters can be used to paint scene details in specific colours. • High- and low-temperature setups can subtly offset colour balances to foreground red or blue/green tones in shoots.

Part II

Film theories

6 Theories of narrative

Eduqas
Component 1 section C: British film since 1995. Questions in this section of the exam ask students to evaluate how useful narrative-based approaches are in understanding the impact of set text films on audiences.
OCR
Paper 1 Section B: European cinema. Questions in this section of the exam might ask students to assess how narratives are constructed in selected films.
Paper 2: an understanding of narrative effects is required for all three sections of this exam.

Essential background

Traditional narrative structures

Exam questions that ask students to consider film narratives are concerned with the storytelling functions of film. They ask students to consider how film plots are structured, and, more importantly, to identify the messages and values that those story structures produce for audiences. Narrative-based analysis also focuses on the extent to which films use conventional story structures or genre-driven plot-based devices, or, indeed, whether they use more experimental narrative strategies.

The literary theorist Tzvetan Todorov provides a useful starting point to understand the significance of narrative. He identified the use of a staple storytelling structure in literature that is also widely employed across cinematic output with Todorov's narrative ideal using what has come to be known as the 'three-act narrative' – a structure that outlines a quest or journey, usually undertaken by a single heroic character. Three-act narratives, moreover, conventionally offer audiences resolved endings wherein the central character achieves the goals outlined at the beginning of their quest. Three-act narratives are traditionally organised as follows:

- **Act one (equilibrium):** opening sequences in three-act narratives tend to outline a world that is relatively harmonious, but, crucially, that world is usually inhabited by a flawed central hero. Importantly, the flaws attached to the central hero construct the underlying motivation(s) that propel the film forward. In *E.T.*, for example, the film's central character, Elliott, is emotionally vulnerable as a result of his parents' divorce. The film's narrative arc thereafter seeks to repair Elliott's loneliness and isolation via the arrival of an alien who, ultimately, heals the family's dysfunctional relationships.
- **Act two (disequilibrium):** the second act introduces narrative disharmony, usually via the appearance or actions of an antagonist character that the central hero is tasked to defeat via a quest or journey. Sometimes that quest asks the hero to negotiate internally oriented goals, requiring them to gain self-knowledge or a renewed sense of self-awareness. Invariably, the second act of the three-act narrative requires the hero to overcome a series of obstacles or tasks to restore the story's initial harmony. These tasks construct moments of character conflict or protagonist/antagonist flash points.
- **Act three (new equilibrium):** the third and final act of the three-act narrative usually works towards a final confrontation or obstacle that the lead character must overcome to fully achieve their quest. Once successfully completed,

the hero restores a sense of harmony, but, crucially, the harmony and order introduced at the beginning of the film is reshaped for the better: lead protagonists overcome their first-act vulnerabilities, transformed by the knowledge gained on their quest, they defeat the external barriers that prevented them from achieving self-fulfillment at the start of the story.

The essential effects and processes of three-act narratives

We might further argue that the essential qualities of the three-act narrative are conventionally affected through the following traits and devices:

- **Three-act narratives work through linear storytelling:** conventional film narratives usually progress using cause-and-effect storytelling, wherein character action produces a story event that, in turn, produces character action, and so on and so forth until the film ends. Plot events in three-act narratives also usually unfold chronologically, producing easy to understand stories that move forward in time. Linear narration also allows filmmakers to order events in a way that manufactures narrative suspense. We are often positioned, for example, to expect that the plot of a film will resolve in a final climactic moment wherein the film's hero finally overcomes the lead antagonist.

- **Three-act narratives traditionally produce single-character focalisations that audiences can easily align with:** traditionally, three-act narratives foreground the experiences of one central character. The repercussions, for example, of narrative events centre upon the effects they have on a lead protagonist. Similarly, the quests outlined in narratives tend to coalesce around the actions of those central figures. In *Trainspotting*, for example, the film squarely centres upon the experiences and actions of Renton – rarely does the film contain a scene in which that character isn't present. Importantly, the focus produced by single-character

focalisations prompts audiences to create connections with
lead protagonists – aligning their perceptions and emotional
reactions with film leads.

- **Character transformations reinforce social norms:**
  because the subplots of three-act narratives often involve
  themes of character repair, the resulting transformations
  that protagonists undergo provide audiences with a form of
  narrative instruction or a film template that they can use to
  perfect their own lives.
- **Narrative disequilibrium outlines 'otherness':** traditionally three-act narratives require a disruptive force to dis-
  turb the harmonious world depicted at the start of the film.
  Often, those disruptive forces produce ideological effects by
  outlining unacceptable social norms or by foregrounding
  social or cultural fears. In *This is England*, for example, disequilibrium is affected through the introduction of the character Combo who reflects the darker energies of English
  nationalism that found voice in 1980s Britain.

Table 6.2 Challenge it: subversion of three-act narrative

Visit Chapter 12 (Experimental film) to explore the use and
effects of narrative devices and film storytelling structures that
subvert the traditional three-act formula. Think about the
following questions to help you further explore the limits of three-
act storytelling:

- In what ways do three-act structures limit filmmakers? What kind
  of endings and beginnings do they force filmmakers to construct?
- Why do filmmakers use flash forwards and flashbacks? What
  effects does non-linear storytelling have on audiences?
- Do modern audiences demand more narrative complexity than is
  offered by the three-act narrative structure? Why?

Microcodes and three-act narratives

Three-act narratives offer audiences predictable storytelling, and,
more importantly, infer a range of equally predictable viewing
gratifications. Opening sequences, for example, might set up
intrigue, enigma or suspense, while later scenes offer audiences
action-based spectacle or emotional resolutions. Act transitions

in films, too, can signal a change in the emotional intensity or tone of a film. Key techniques that are used to communicate those transitions include the following:

- **Location changes:** transitions from one act to another might be inferred through location or setting changes. *Trainspotting*'s narrative resolution, for example, relocates the film's protagonists to cosmopolitan London to help convey Renton's escape from his drug addiction in Edinburgh. Geographical movement and narrative progression are similarly intertwined in Ben Wheatley's horror/social realism hybrid *Sightseers*, with Chris and Tina's serial-killing caravan tour terminating spectacularly at Ribblehead Viaduct. In *Skyfall* too the film's impending denouement or final climax is signaled to the audience when the action moves to the rain-soaked moors of Scotland (Figure 6.1).
- **Act transitions and costume changes:** costume change, too, infers important moments of narrative transition, with colour coding and costume styling used to connote character interiority during narrative stages. In *Skyfall*, for example, James Bond's suits darken when he arrives at his family home at the end of the film – thus inferring the hero's underlying sadness when confronting the impact of his parents' death. In *Under the Skin*, too, a narrative transition is clearly inferred by the alien's costume change and the shedding of her predatory fur coat that she wears during the film's opening acts.

The traditional function of dialogue in narratives

Film scripts are traditionally broken down into scenes wherein opening shots usually establish the scene's setting or location, with subsequent shots used to identify the key characters involved in the action of the scene. Scenes traditionally proceed to extended dialogue exchanges, with scripted dialogue used to reveal character thoughts and impending plot action. Scenes, in this sense, represent the heartbeat or pulse of a film, their arrangement and flow constructing the narrative arc or direction of a film's story.

Similarly, we might describe scene dialogue as the machinery that pulls and pushes a story into shape – that reveals or suggests the underlying emotions of a film's characters.

Dialogue, roughly speaking, provides the following four functions in film narratives:

- **Dialogue moves the story forward:** characters use dialogue to tell us where they are going or to give an indication of their future actions, thus signposting the cause-and-effect dynamic of film narratives to audiences.
- **Dialogue provides psychological insight:** scripts use speech to voice the thoughts of characters. Scriptwriters also relate character thoughts using a show-don't-tell technique – revealing character interiority through actions, symbolic expressions, and, importantly, via the use of subtle dialogue cues that provide hints and suggestions that audiences can use to decode a character's inner thinking.
- **Dialogue defines character relationships:** spoken exchanges in films also help audiences to decode the relationships that exist between characters, offering viewers moments that unify or disconnect key characters.
- **Dialogue privileges central characters:** lead-character dialogue is usually foregrounded as the first or last line of speech in scenes. Similarly, lead characters are privileged through the arrangement of dialogue that places protagonists at the centre of conversations – heroes, invariably, are spoken to and not spoken at.
- **Dialogue provides ideological alignment:** where audiences are aligned with central characters, the dialogue of those characters can affect a powerful presence. Dialogue replaces the thinking processes of audiences while watching a film and effect a subtle ideological presence by injecting the thoughts and ideas of filmmakers directly into the consciousness of the spectator.

Table 6.3 Revise it: dialogue analysis

Locate the scripts of relevant set text films – most can be found through internet searches. Using the scripts, locate key scenes in which important character details are revealed. While reading the dialogue exchanges in those scenes think about the following questions:

• Where is dialogue used to outline the kinds of relationships that exist between characters? Do exchanges suggest that the characters present in the scene are working together or against one another?
• How is dialogue used to outline the events of the film? Is dialogue used to foretell future narrative events or to provide recaps of the events in previous scenes?
• In what ways is the dialogue of the central character privileged? Do they speak first or last in a scene? Are they given more emotive lines? Are they spoken to or spoken at?
• Where does the screenwriter deploy 'show don't tell'? Where are the thoughts and feelings of characters hinted at in dialogue exchanges?

Table 6.4 Revise it: three-act narratives

Use the following questions to help you further diagnose the impact of traditional narrative structures:	
Effects of three-act narratives on spectator alignment	• Does the film use linear storytelling? Does the use of a linear narrative construct active or passive engagement? • Does the use of cause-and-effect narrative structure encourage active or passive spectatorship? • Are audiences encouraged to adopt the viewpoint of a single central character? • What ideals or norms do single-character focalisations encourage audiences to accept?
Effects of three-act narration on the subtextual meanings of films	• What transformations does the central character undergo in the film? What life lessons does that transformation outline for the audience?

(*continued*)

Table 6.4 Cont.

	• What character vulnerabilities are healed by the end of the film? What social norms or universal values are foregrounded as a result of that healing? • What or who injects narrative disequilibrium in the film? What ideas or norms are reinforced as a result of that narrative disequilibrium?
Act transition analysis	• How are narrative transitions signalled by sound or visual cues? • Are act transitions communicated through costume, setting or lighting changes? • How do those visual cues shift the tone of the film? • How do editing and cinematography styles change as the film progresses?

Exemplar: *Shaun of the Dead* (Eduqas). Despite *Shaun of the Dead*'s playful genre hybridity – realised through its black comedy take on the zombie horror genre – the film charts a traditional three-act narrative with a conventional single-character focalisation used to explore masculine identity. The opening of the film, for example, outlines Shaun's dysfunctional resistance to adult life: an equilibrium of sorts that is threatened by his girlfriend's desire to rehabilitate Shaun into an acceptable middle-class existence. Shaun's resistance to that rehabilitation is driven by his fear that he will become trapped in the same suburban zombie state as his parents – a fear that is fully realised by the zombie-apocalypse disequilibrium that appears later in the film.

A conventional survival-quest narrative ensues – a journey that helps Shaun to reconcile his fear of growing up with his love of Liz, while the end of the film delivers an equally predictable third-act climax wherein Shaun faces down the zombie hordes. Shaun, too, is forced to kill his own mother, symbolically slaying his fear of marriage and suburban living. As a result, the film establishes a new equilibrium for the central protagonist, an equilibrium wherein Ed's influence – Shaun's immature sidekick – is side-lined, thus enabling Shaun to fully assume the responsibilities of adult life.

Figure 6.1 Skyfall (top): the location change at the end of the film signals the film's impending climax. *Shaun of the Dead* (middle): *Shaun of the Dead* uses a conventional three-act narrative structure. *Under the Skin* (bottom): the alien's transition from predator to victim is visibly inferred when she sheds her fur-skin coat.

Propp's character archetypes

Another useful tool for analysing the impact of narrative is Vladimir Propp's character archetypes' model. Propp, a Russian literary theorist, systematically analysed hundreds of Russian folk stories in his highly influential 1929 book, *Morphology of the Folk Tale*, to discover whether those stories shared any underlying narrative similarities. Propp concluded that the stories he analysed were composed using a stable list of characters whose roles and narrative functions are defined below. Importantly, we can trace the presence of those character archetypes in contemporary films today:

- **The hero** is the central character with whom audiences align themselves with. Importantly, Propp differentiates between the seeker-hero (who demonstrates strength and courage to obtain new knowledge during their narrative quest) and the victim-hero (who must heal an internal weakness to complete their quest).
- **The villain** fights or pursues the hero of the story and often infers characteristics that audiences are positioned to reject.
- **The false hero** performs a largely villainous role by usurping the true hero's position. The false hero is usually unmasked in the last act of a story.
- **The helper** usually accompanies the hero on their quest, saving them from the struggles encountered on their journey. The helper plays a pivotal role in transforming the hero so that they might successfully conclude their quest.
- **The princess** represents the goal or reward obtained by the hero when their quest is successfully completed.
- **The princess' father** often sets the hero difficult tasks to prevent the hero from marrying the princess.

Table 6.5 Theory revision: Propp's character archetypes

- Does the use of Proppian archetypes create familiarity for film audiences?
- What gender, conventionally, are Proppian heroes? What gender, conventionally, are the Proppian Princesses in films? What norms or ideals do those gender-based archetypes suggest to male and female audiences? Do they suggest that males ought to be more active and females passive?
- Do your set text films use any Proppian character archetypes? With what ideological effect?
- Do your films subvert Proppian character archetypes?

Structuralist analysis of narratives

Another hugely significant analytical tool to use when analysing narrative is the Structuralist thinking of Claude Lévi-Strauss. Much like Propp, Strauss' anthropological writing concluded that cultural myths from across the world and from different time periods are composed using similar narrative structures. Indeed, Strauss tells us that stories are composed using binary opposites: oppositional characters, clashing narrative moments or juxtaposed elements. Strauss further argued that the use of these binary oppositions also convey ideological effects – that villainous actions, for example, are outlined as social taboos for audiences.

Although Strauss' writing was largely concerned with myths and fables, we can extend his ideas to the world of film. Films, we might similarly argue, work through the presentation of oppositional characters – heroes inevitably battle villains – while our alignment with heroic characters also infers ideological effects, and, consequently, encourages us to accept the norms and values of privileged characters. In the James Bond franchise, for example, 007 represents British middle-class values and protects British democracy against the evil tyranny of totalitarian villains. The privileging of 007 instead of his villainous counterparts consequently encourages us to accept hyper-masculine behaviours as a protective rather than destructive force, while Bond's quintessential Britishness further suggests the superiority of English values and outlooks.

Strauss' structuralist model suggest that the following sorts of oppositions might be present in a film text:

- **Character-based oppositions:** films produce oppositional characters, aligning audiences with some characters while others are positioned to be rejected. Sometimes oppositions are visible via the physical styling of characters (in terms of hair colour, costume, physical stature or even age). Oppositional characters might also be constructed via the use of juxtaposed outlooks, beliefs or behaviours.
- **Narrative oppositions:** film stories produce oppositional narrative moments – actions, for example, might be repeated or reframed using oppositional content. In narratives, events can also be oppositionally ordered using cross-cutting. In *Moon*, for example, the clashing fates of the Sam clones at the end of the film highlights both the destructive power of capitalism and a hope that we can escape exploitation.
- **Thematic oppositions:** films often convey themes using contradictory sets of ideas or ideals. *Captain Fantastic*, for example, continuously juxtaposes notions of freedom against responsibility. In *The Force Awakens*, the dark side of the force comes to represent totalitarian power and self-interest while the Rebel Alliance protects democracy via acts of self-sacrifice.
- **Stylistic oppositions:** films are often encoded using oppositional aesthetics or the use of juxtaposed aesthetic styles. Editing, for example, in Scorsese's *Raging Bull* swings from high-tempo, jump-cut fight scenes to the long-take observational style used to depict Jake's domestic life. Those stylistic clashes draw attention to LaMotta's instability and his inability to reconcile the violence of his boxing persona with the needs of his home life.
- **Genre-driven binary oppositions:** some binary oppositions are so deeply entrenched within genres that they are routinely served up as narrative ingredients in genre-driven products. Science-fiction films, for example, regularly offer audiences 'technology versus humanity'-oriented themes.

The ideological effects of oppositions

Determining the ideological effects of binary presentations requires an analysis that identifies which binary states are foregrounded or privileged to audiences. Such analysis might explore the characters, styles or thematic states that audiences are aligned to identify with. Such analysis might also identify moments in the film where those privileged binaries take precedence, and, more importantly, the values and ideals that those moments foreground for the film's audience.

Table 6.6 Revise it: binary oppositions analysis

Use the following questions to help you diagnose the meanings produced by binary oppositions in your films:	
Stylistic oppositions	• Are there moments where locations, props or costuming contrast? Why have they been styled this way? • Are colour contrasts offered in your set texts and to what effect? • How do editing, camera or lighting styles change across the timelines of your set texts? How do these stylistic oppositions support wider narrative themes? • Do sound elements offer significant moments of contrast in terms of volume, tone, key signatures or instrumentation? What effect do these aural contrasts have on audiences?
Character-based binaries	• Are characters constructed as opposites in terms of physical appearance, behaviour or outlooks? • Which characters are audiences positioned to like or prefer? Why and where? • Which oppositional characters triumph in the film and with what ideological effect? • Do characters learn anything from their paired opposites? • Does the narrative resist using binary pairings? Why?

(*continued*)

Table 6.6 Cont.

Narrative-based oppositions	• How do narratives end? Which oppositional moments, if any, are allowed to triumph? • Do the resolutions offered at the end of stories tell us anything about the ideological subtexts of the film? • Does the narrative produce more complicated assessments of the binaries present at the start of the film?
Thematic/ genre-based oppositions	• What thematic oppositions are presented in your film texts? Use Table 6.7 to help you identify the presence of thematic oppositions found within a number of contemporary film genres. • Does the film resist using the kinds of thematic binaries found in Table 6.7? Why?

Exemplar: *Under the Skin* **(Eduqas).** *Under the Skin* (UTS) uses a character-based binary presentation to articulate the corrosive effects of patriarchal power in society. UTS' initial presentation of Scarlett Johansson's nameless alien initially constructs a classic femme fatale – her red lipstick, black hair and animal print costume are a clear visual representation of the alien's predatory outlook. Glazer here produces a powerful version of femininity that, much like the classic film noir femme fatale stereotype, demonises female power as dangerous to the male characters of the film.

Glazer's ideological stance regarding gender is complicated, however, when the latter half of his narrative reverses the ideological thrusters – positioning Johansson as the victim to draw attention to the destructive power of female objectification within society. Johansson sheds her leopard skin print and red lipstick – her sexual allure replaced by a meeker characterisation that outlines the presence of female victimhood. The alien's brutal death at the end of the film also offers audiences a symbolic narrative opposition, her disrobing reversing the alien's initial entrance into the human world at the beginning of the film. These moments, coupled with the binary characterisation of the film, firmly help to cement the idea that female escape from patriarchal control is all but impossible.

Genre and narrative

The use of genre-based storytelling often guides filmmakers towards the use of predefined narrative themes, stock characters or story-structuring devices. Genre, in short, has the potential to generate ready-made templates that filmmakers apply and adapt. The use of repeated genre-driven motifs also provides audiences with a set of predefined narrative pleasures and story appeal. Genre-based audience gratifications might be constructed via the following:

- **Familiar story paths:** films within the same genre often share similar story structures or are ordered using similar narrative events. Thrillers, for example, routinely deliver enigma-based story structures with early narrative episodes used to outline a central mystery that the film's protagonist must solve. Similarly, horrors are identifiable through their use of survival-based narrative quests, wherein protagonists are subjected to ever increasing levels of threat from whatever form the film's antagonist takes.
- **Predefined narrative resolutions:** genre-driven labelling not only provides filmmakers with familiar route maps to use in film narratives, but also dictates story endings. We expect horror films, for example, to end when the antagonist is finally defeated, while thrillers usually outline the protagonist's solving of the mystery formulated at the start of the narrative.
- **Genre-driven subtexts:** genre-driven products often deal with similar subtextual themes or meanings. Thrillers, for example, often explore male-based identity issues: from Bruce Willis' divorce-ridden angst in *Die Hard* to Bond's exploration of his orphaned childhood in *Skyfall*, thrillers provide audiences with male-based identity reflection.
- **Genre subversion:** films construct meaning through the application of genre-based rules, but, even more significantly, the subversion of those rules delivers audience impact. A genre-driven film that resolves unconventionally, for example, can reposition the audience in uniquely interesting

ways: *No Country for Old Men* for example, refuses to resolve in the unequivocal triumph of the heroic lawman often seen in westerns, instead offering audiences an unsettling vision of a world in which immoral influences aren't extinguished.

Table 6.7 Know it: conventional thematic oppositions in common film genres

Genre	Science fiction	Crime	Horror
Common thematic binaries	Aliens/humans Exploitation/ freedom Knowledge/ ignorance Machine/man Man/nature Reality/ deception Technology/ humanity	Chaos/order Choice/necessity Corruption/ innocence Freedom/duty Guilt/innocence Law/justice Lawfulness/ lawlessness Morality/greed Power/weakness	Chaos/order Darkness/light Death/life Known/ unknown Past/present Reality/ supernatural Reason/madness Religion/ disbelief Repression/ acceptance
Emotional pleasures	Spectacle Exploring the unknown	Action Character conflict	Fear Suspense
Dominant narrative structures	Quest-based storytelling Survival-based narratives	Tragic downfalls Solving mysteries Revenge-based narratives	Decoding enigma Survival-based narratives
Genre	**Romance**	**War**	**Spy/thriller**
Common thematic binaries	Experience/ youth Family ties/ romance Friendship/ betrayal	Allies/enemies Duty/morality Experience/ innocence	Democracy/ tyranny Heroism/greed Hunter/hunted Intellect/action

Table 6.7 Cont.

Genre	Science fiction	Crime	Horror
	Loneliness/ belonging Masculinity/ femininity Relationships/ freedom Romance/ money	Family/duty Home front/the front line Honour/ self-interest Sacrifice/self interest Survival/ patriotism	Order/chaos Patriotism/ treachery State/individual Surveillance/ subterfuge
Emotional pleasures	Sentimentality Nostalgia	Action Patriotism/ nostalgia	Action Suspense
Dominant narrative structures	Love conquers all Unrequited love	Quest-based storytelling Survival-based narratives	Decoding enigma Revenge-based narratives

Table 6.8 Narrative theories: ten-minute revision

Essential background: the three-act structure
• Films traditionally used the three-act narrative as a storytelling template.   • Three-act films traditionally outline linear stories centred around one character.   • Three-act narratives outline characters who demonstrate weaknesses that are resolved during the film.
Structuralism and binary oppositions
• The ideas of Lévi-Strauss provide a hugely useful tool to analyse film meaning.   • Filmmakers order narratives using stylistic, character, narrative, thematic and genre-based binaries
Genre-based effects on narrative
• Filmmakers use genre-driven conventions as a template for filmmaking. Genre-based storytelling can shape characters, narrative structures or the underlying themes of a film.

7 Auteur-based approaches

Table 7.1 What do you need to revise auteur-based approaches for?

Eduqas
- **Component 1 section A: Hollywood 1930–90** asks students to evaluate the extent to which the creative decisions taken in key set text films are driven by studio, genre or author-based factors.
- **Component 2 section D: experimental film** asks students to evaluate experimental film practice and to identify the idiosyncratic approaches taken by auteur filmmakers.

OCR
- **Component 1 section B: European cinema** might ask students to assess the extent to which microcode usage in set text films is symptomatic of an auteur-based approach.
- **Component 2 section A: contemporary British and US cinema** requires students to evaluate how useful auteur-oriented approaches are in understanding set text films

Essential background: Truffaut and *Cahiers du Cinéma*

Initially outlined by the French film critics François Truffaut and André Bazin in the film journal *Cahiers du Cinéma*, auteur theory emerged in the 1950s as a cinematic call to arms. Bazin and Truffaut's celebration of auteur filmmaking advocated an alternative to the conservative output of the French film industry after the Second World War in which weighty adaptations of high-brow literary works dominated. Bazin and Truffaut suggested that the directors of such adaptations played a secondary function, fulfilling what Bazin called a metteurs en scène role – the chief responsibility of which was to translate scripts into cinematic end-products by applying dialogue-production routines or generic scene-ordering techniques to pre-existing story structures. Such an approach, Bazin argued, stifled the creative potential of film as a medium. Both Truffaut and Bazin, as such, advocated for a new wave of directors to take up the creative challenge and to inject some much-needed 'audacity' into French cinematic storytelling (Caughie, 1995, 39).

Truffaut's call for change championed those directors who were already producing films that demonstrated a personal vision or who managed to invest their films with a unique aesthetic style. Truffaut drew attention to filmmakers like Alfred Hitchcock, Orson Welles and John Huston, who, he argued, injected their own author-based hallmarks despite the restrictions imposed by the genre-based storytelling approach of Hollywood films made in the 1940s and 50s. The power of such auteur directors, Truffaut further argued, wasn't found in their ability to translate screenplays into a visual end product, but in the way that they shaped film meaning using mise en scène or cinematography.

Truffaut and the early Cahiers' proponents of auteur-based filmmaking further argued that:

- Film ought to be celebrated for its innovative or stylised use of mise en scène, cinematography or sound.
- That the director was a film's ultimate author, and that the films that excelled in terms of cinematic artistry were those where the director was allowed to apply their own authorial stamp.
- That an auteur's individual stamp was often visible in all the films made by that director.

Table 7.2 Discuss it: the director as the sole auteur

Investigate the combined output of the directors of the set text films that you are studying that demand an auteur-based analysis.

- What evidence can you locate that they deploy similar aesthetic styles?
- What evidence can be located that the director uses or defies conventional genre-driven storytelling?
- In what ways is Truffaut's auteur theory problematic?

Andrew Sarris' refinement of auteur theory

Truffaut's concept of the auteur was widely critiqued, both for its vagueness and its wide-ranging categorisation of film authorship. The crude metteurs en scène/auteur categories that Truffaut devised were criticised as overly broad, and, as a result, that a significant number of directors were questionably elevated to auteur status even though their film output was significantly flawed, technically poor or lacking in narrative depth.

In response, the American critic, Andrew Sarris, offered a refinement of the auteur definition, arguing that directors ought to meet the following three conditions before they could be labelled as authentic auteurs:

- **Technical competence.** To Sarris, some directors, including the much-lauded Billy Wilder, produced films that were worthy of merit in terms of screen craft but whose technical mastery was so poor that they didn't deserve to be labelled as true auteurs at all. Sarris argued that, 'if a director has no technical competence, no elementary flair ... he is automatically cast out from the pantheon of directors' (Caughie, 1995, 64).
- **A stylised approach to filmmaking.** Sarris further argued that directors needed to, 'exhibit certain recurring characteristics of style' to be considered true auteurs (Caughie, 1995, 64). Much like Truffaut, Sarris suggested that a director must deploy cinematography, lighting or

editing using their own artistic inflections to be considered as a potential candidate for inclusion in the auteur canon.

- **Interior meaning.** This, perhaps, is Sarris' most vague requirement – a term that he accorded to those directors who confidently injected layers of profound meaning into their films or who expressed something of their world view via their cinematic output.

Table 7.3 Discuss it: Sarris' auteur model

- Do you prefer Truffaut or Sarris' auteur definition? Why?
- Do you think that filmmakers must demonstrate technical competence to be labelled auteur directors?
- Is it possible to reach any objective agreement as to which films produce deeper meanings?
- Is it problematic that auteur critics like Truffaut and Sarris tend to celebrate white, male directors only?

Classical Hollywood production processes

Much criticism was aimed at Hollywood cinema by auteur theorists, many of whom drew attention to the mechanised practices of the seven major studios that dominated American cinema in the pre- and post-Second World War period. In the 1950s, most studios, for example, managed filmmaking using streamlined production units that were led by a handful of producer-managers. In the producer-unit system, moreover, creative decisions often took a secondary role to the overriding need for films to be completed on time and on budget, while the efficiency concerns of producer-managers were driven by the need to supply studio-owned cinemas with a steady stream of new releases. As such, the job of directors was to deliver producer-vetted projects on time, with very little scope left for creative invention or experimentation.

Director-driven experimentation was further limited by the following factors associated with the Classical Hollywood production model:

- **Ideas for new projects were controlled by producer-managers:** as a result, directors were often employed late in a film's conception and were largely tasked to execute the practicalities of a shoot after scripting and design processes had already been completed.

- **Films schedules and budgets were tightly controlled by studio managers:** some low-budget A-list projects were given as little as one month for directors to preplan shoots after scripts had been given a green light. Director involvement was also limited to cover the shooting phase of production only, with post-production work for most films – editing and sound treatments, for example – carried out by centralised studio-controlled departments.

- **Studios demanded the use of standardised production practices:** shoots were often organised using a studio-stamped approach that regulated production. Directors, as such, had no choice but to shoot scenes using routine set ups – establishing shots and stilted shot/reverse-shot dialogue, for example. Standardisation, in this sense, was driven by efficiency needs – so that a studio's editing department could quickly apply post-production processes. Standardisation of filming was also demanded to satisfy studio insurance regulations or other technical needs. For its Technicolor productions, for example, Paramount producers often supervised set and costume design to ensure that films affected maximum visual impact given the expense of colour film processing in the late 1930s and 40s.

- **Star power was central:** in the Classical Hollywood system, prestige film projects were often engineered as star vehicles for high profile actors on studio payrolls. Directors, as such, were often expected to shoot films that brought those stars to the forefront of the audience's viewing experience, with long-take close-ups and soft-focus photography routinely used to maximise a star's presence.

- **Access to resources:** studio executives also inhibited creativity by restricting access to equipment, posing a particular problem for directors who wanted to inject inventive moments of cinematography. MGM production manager Walter Strohm, for example, actively withheld camera booms from directors to limit the kinds of camera movement they could produce on sets. Equipment was rationed to make sure that prestige projects were given exclusive access, but rationing also prevented directors from using innovative cinematographic styles that editing departments might be unfamiliar with.

Auteur resistance in the Classical Hollywood period

Of course, there were directors who circumvented the standardised approach of the Classical Hollywood production model. Those exceptions – the directors who managed to wrestle control of their films away from producer-managers – are the very directors who auteur critics celebrated from the period. Nor did the factorylike manufacture of movies apply to all studios: RKO, for example, invested heavily in a special effects department, giving maverick directors like Orson Welles access to a whole range of cinematographic effects that he used during the production of his hugely innovative *Citizen Kane*.

Director's, too, circumvented studio control by shooting films so that they could only be edited in the way that they wanted. Studios usually demanded that directors shoot scenes from multiple angles to give editors increased leeway during post-production, but big-name directors circumvented that control by filming scenes with single-take shoots that ensured their version of the film would make the final edit. Directors who commanded significant audience appeal were also given increased control over the whole production process. Howard Hughes, for example, was elevated to the status of producer-director by Warner Bros in the 1940s – effectively granting him total control of his own productions. Similarly, John Ford was exempted from Darryl Zanuck's heavy-handed oversight of films at Twentieth Century Fox. Directors, too, were sometimes afforded an unusual degree of freedom when working on budget features – B movie productions, for example, often slipped under the managerial radar of producers who were often more preoccupied by the big-budget spends of their studio's A-list releases.

Table 7.4 Extend it: auteurs in Hollywood 1930–60

Visit Chapter 11 (Classical Hollywood 1930–60) to find out more about the **Classical Hollywood aesthetic** and the way that key auteurs adapted to the demands of the Classical style.

Table 7.5 Revise it: identify the effects of the studio-based production system on your Classical Hollywood set texts

Effects of studio production	• In what ways does the film privilege star power over innovation? Is there an excess of star-based close-ups? Does the star triumph in the narrative? • In what ways is the story like others in its genre? • Which film studio produced the set text? How much freedom did the studio extend to the film's director? Who is the named producer of the film? How much power did that individual effect over production?
Resistance to the Classical Hollywood process	• Detect a *stylised approach*: what moments in the film use cinematography or editing in an innovative way? • What aesthetic traits or markers are present in the movie that we see in other films made by the same director? • Detect *interior meaning*: does the set text deal with similar subtextual themes that we see in other films made by the same director? What are those themes? What world view does the director construct? • How much power did the director wield in the Classical Hollywood studio system? How did those freedoms enable a non-standardised approach?

Exemplar: *Vertigo* **(Eduqas).** Made in 1958, *Vertigo* (Figure 7.1) is emblematic of the Classical Hollywood production process. The film, much like other major Hollywood projects of the time, was a screen adaptation, using Pierre Boileau and Thomas Narcejac's 1954 psychological thriller, *The Living and the Dead,* as the source of the film's story. Equally conventional was the screen adaptation by a

Table 7.5 Cont.

studio employee, with Paramount contracted writer, Alec Coppell, providing the script blueprint for *Vertigo* as a film. The hugely contested final edit of the film was also overseen by Paramount's associate producer, Herbert Coleman, who insisted on the inclusion – much to Hitchcock's disapproval – of the pivotal flashback scene 40 minutes before the end of the film.

The Paramount-controlled script and final edit, coupled with the film noir romance-story structure of *Vertigo* initially suggests that Hitchcock's role in directing the film was limited to that of a 'metteurs en scène' director – a dismissive term coined by the film critic Truffaut to describe those filmmakers who translated fiction into screen-based action using limited creative cinematic input. *Vertigo*, we might conclude, operates within the stable parameters of the romance/thriller genre with an overriding intent to showcase the talents of its A-list stars: James Stewart and Kim Novak.

But Hitchcock's reputation as a prolific director of both film and television drama gave him a great deal more freedom than is suggested above. Indeed, Hitchcock's control of mise en scène within the film elevates *Vertigo* beyond the Hollywood-based conventions of the period, with the director's fascination with psychology and the internal worlds of his characters readily apparent in Scottie's mid-film dream sequence: a surrealist montage that looks and feels similar to the Hitchcock/Dali dream scene of his 1945 film, *Spellbound*. Hitchcock's ready use, moreover, of canted shots in the court scene and *Vertigo's* use of smashed zooms in his lighthouse-based climax testifies to the director's use of subjective camerawork to relate Scottie's experiences, while the attentive green/red colour coding used within the film's set design and costuming further suggests the kind of visual complexity that Truffaut celebrated in his early definition of the film auteur. Yes, Hitchcock worked within the producer-restricted production model of 1950s Hollywood, but the director's status and ingenuity means that a subtle range of mise en scène/cinematographic stylings periodically puncture the surface of the film's genre-driven frame.

Links to exemplar film clips and exemplars for other OCR/Eduqas film texts can be found at www.essentialfilmrevision.com

Figure 7.1 Daisies (top): Marie I & II construct transgressive femin-
          inity. *Vertigo* (middle): Hitchcock's iconic dream sequence
          elevates the film above Classical Hollywood conventions.
          Star Wars: The Force Awakens (bottom): Abram's reboot of
          Lucas' SF franchise was partially driven by fan power.

Auteur theory: Ian Cameron and multiple authorship

The call for an auteur-based approach to filmmaking wasn't restricted to France. In the early 1960s, the British film magazine *Movie* articulated a similar message under the editorship of Ian Cameron. *Movie*, for example, critiqued the British fad for social realism in the 1960s, arguing that UK cinema needed to move away from its concern to represent real life and to think more carefully about style and aesthetics.

Cameron, like Truffaut, celebrated those film authors who used the movie screen as a canvas on which they might shape film stories that resonated with artistic individuality. He particularly singled out those films in which direction and performance combined to elevate a film to a higher level, pointing to the 'remarkable' effects of films like *Casablanca* where both actor talent and directorial efficiency lifted the emotional intensity of the story (Caughie, 1995, 55).

Importantly, for Cameron, the concept of the auteur moves beyond Truffaut's identification of the director as the single source or authorship. He agrees that the director is the single most important authorial contributor, but he also acknowledges that there are, 'many films whose authors are not their directors' (Caughie, 1995, 54), thus opening up film analysis to consider the auteurial input of set designers, sound composers, actors, lighting directors, cinematographers and so on.

Cameron, importantly, made the argument that any single individual in the production process might apply a signature-based style that is detectable across the films that they have contributed to – that sound composers, for example, might apply the same sorts of scores, or that cinematographers might apply a trademark approach to shoots. Cameron, interestingly, resisted the suggestion that studios as a collective unit themselves might be considered for inclusion as auteurs, but it is important to note that films are often made using relatively stable production teams – that studio directors often employ the same directors of photography, lighting crews, set designers, sound composers and so on when planning and making new projects. Studios, old and new, use and reuse teams of personnel whose approach falls in line with the artistic vision of the producer. Studios, too, reuse the same teams because established working relationships allow crews to efficiently complete the job of making a film. We might suggest, as such, that the output of any one studio might evidence similar interests, themes or styles as a result of the collective artistry of such crews.

Table 7.6 Research it: multiple authorship in film

Investigate key personnel who worked alongside the director when producing key set text films. Investigate the key films that those practitioners are celebrated for. Key production presences that are worthy of investigation include the following:

- **Directors of photography:** perhaps the singularly most senior figure in the production process other than the director. DOP's take control of all aspects of cinematography and camera set-ups on set. They usually oversee set design and lighting setups too.
- **Lead actors:** actors are key auteurs in that they usually tackle roles using similar approaches and acting styles.
- **Sound composers** significantly shape the ultimate meanings of films and often approach film sound using similar processes, instrumentation or other stylistic devices.

Peter Wollen and auteur-structuralism

Another interesting auteur-based approach that departs significantly from Truffaut's director-based model is that of auteur-structuralists like Peter Wollen, who suggests that directors subconsciously revisit similar thematic structures and themes in their films. Wollen's contribution to the auteur debate dismisses Truffaut's idea that film auteurs are identifiable through their use of stylised mise en scène or other visual components. Wollen, instead, suggests that the detailed study of character, plot and narrative are key to unlocking author-based signatures.

Using Lévi-Strauss' structuralist arguments, Wollen argued that directors unknowingly shape their films using similar binary bundles – deploying similar characters, locations and plots to probe common themes across a director's filmic output.

In John Ford's westerns, for example, Wollen draws attention to the director's repeated use of a garden/wilderness binary in which the civilised comfort of the frontier small town is constantly threatened by the chaos of the American wilderness in the form of native Indian attacks or rogue bandit outlaws. Ford's garden/wilderness binary, Wollen argued, privileged a conservative inward-looking vision of America, while also supporting an authoritarian military-based patriotism that vigorously defended the American way of life.

Using detailed analysis of character and narrative, Wollen suggests that we might find similar binary motifs in the output of most auteur directors. Even when adapting pre-existing literary texts, Wollen suggests, directors select or refashion pre-existing storylines to give weight to their own interests and binary concerns. Wollen, interestingly, also argued that the binary concerns of directors might shift or adapt, opening auteur-based study to comparative analysis wherein the binaries of individual films might be compared or contrasted.

Wollen's arguments can be summed up as follows:

- Auteur-based analysis ought to be less concerned with stylistic components and more interested in narrative subtexts, themes and character.
- That directors are the primary authors of films, and, moreover, that they inject similar binary themes into films
- That the kinds of binaries constructed by directors are subject to change. We can identify how these binary bundles adapt over a director's life by comparing films they have made throughout their lifetime.

Table 7.7 Revise it: apply auteur-structuralist theory to set text films

• Do you think it possible that directors might subconsciously reuse similar conflicts or binaries in their movies? • Which filmmakers can you identify from your own viewing who play with the same themes and subtexts in their movies? • Wollen suggests that the hidden binaries in auteur-driven movies can only be revealed through detailed analysis and multiple screenings. Is it likely that ordinary film viewers will appreciate these subtleties? • In what other ways might Wollen's auteur structuralist theory be critiqued?
Exemplar: *Daisies* (Eduqas). Věra Chytilová's Czech New Wave film, *Daisies* (Figure 7.1), is hugely experimental – combining stop-motion montages, jump-cut psychedelia and colour filters to affect an anarchic visual aesthetic. The surrealist style of *Daisies* is similar to the director's 1969 film, *Fruit of Paradise*, with the thematic overlap of both films providing evidence that Chytilová was operating as a structuralist-auteur in the late 1960s. The female leads in both films, for example, are restricted by oppressive patriarchal expectations, with all three leads daring to transgress the boundaries of their respective worlds in a bid for personal freedom. The marionette movements of Marie I, Marie II and Eva in the opening sequences of both films underlines their puppeted presence in the world, with the Eden-like imagery of the early scenes used to further symbolise the moral fall of all three women. Chytilová here sets up a series of familiar narrative binaries in these early moments: freedom battles repression, restriction transforms into excess, masculine power is resisted by female cunning. But what is less clear in the symbolic workings of both films is whether female freedom is indeed possible. Marie I and II are left water-bound at the end of the film, both alienated, yet strangely reliant upon the world that they so overtly reject. Eva, too, is trapped at the end of *Fruit of Paradise*, when she is left with no option but to return to her loveless husband. The visual experimentation in *Daisies* in this sense is more than just anarchic playfulness, it exemplifies Chytilová's overarching struggle to reject the world as she saw it, and, perhaps also foretold the inability of future Czech's to forge any meaningful alternative to the totalitarian Soviet control of Czechoslovakia that began to take shape in the late 1960s.

Table 7.8 Revise it: applying auteur theory in exams

Auteur approach	Areas to think about
Truffaut: the auteur versus metteurs en scène distinction	• Truffaut suggests that only directors can be auteurs – explore other films made by the same directors as your set texts and look for stylistic similarities. • Truffaut is interested in the visual look of films – any Truffaut-based auteur analysis ought to concentrate on the director's use of cinematography, lighting, mise en scène and editing.
Andrew Sarris: the three conditions of auteurship	• To affect their own unique style directors must be technically competent. • Sarris also argues that directors must inject interior meaning into their films to construct stories that have deeper meanings or that have profound effects on their audiences. Use narrative-based analysis of films made by directors to detect those shared deeper meanings.
Ian Cameron: multiple authorship	• Cameron opens up auteur theory to the idea that films are authored by teams of creative personnel – with each individual member contributing their own ideas or stylings. • A Cameron-style auteur-based assessment would look at the key contributors to the film in addition to a film's director – directors of photography, score composers and actors, for example. Use Cameron's multiple authorship theory to explore how these personnel shape film set texts using an idiosyncratic approach.
Peter Wollen auteur-structuralism	• Unlike Truffaut, Wollen is interested in the underlying subtexts and binary oppositions that directors inject into their films. • A Wollen-style approach identifies the thematic or narrative conflicts a set text shares with other films made by the director.

(continued)

Table 7.8 Cont.

Exemplar: *Blade Runner* **(Eduqas).** Any assessment of director Ridley Scott's presence as an auteur is complicated by the lack of unity of auteur theory itself. Scott certainly fits Truffaut's 1950s auteur definition in that his *Blade Runner* reworking of Philip K. Dick's novella *Do Androids Dream of Electric Sheep?* significantly extends the original text, while Scott's attention to detail in terms of mise en scène and his use of a film noir science-fiction aesthetic clearly provides evidence to suggest that Scott is more than a metteur en scène. Indeed, Scott's epic cinematic style in *Blade Runner* is emblematic of the high-concept approach to filmmaking born in the 1980s – enabled through extended multi-camera shoots and the film's lush CGI-driven otherworldly escapism. The same high-concept styling overflows in Scott's other output – whether it be his work within the *Alien* franchise or the exacting historical verisimilitude of *Gladiator.*

In terms of narrative, too, *Blade Runner* reformulates Scott's fascination with corrupt corporations and their eclipsing effect on the individual. The post-apocalyptic world of *Blade Runner,* for example, is controlled by the omnipresent Tyrell Corporation, reworked as Weyland-Yutani Corp in the *Alien* cinematic universe, with both companies using advanced biotech and robotic technologies to explore ideas regarding human exploitation. Scott also uses technology-driven narrative themes to remind us of the essential qualities that make us human, and, as evidenced in *Blade Runner's* 'Tears in the Rain' monologue, being human, Roy reminds us, requires kinship, empathy and an understanding of our own human fragility – qualities similarly celebrated in the *2049 Blade Runner* reboot. For Peter Wollen, these repeated narrative binaries – technology versus humanity, corruption versus innocence, ruthless corporations versus the individual – signal a different form of auteurism – a form that confers an auteur status as a result of the underlying narrative similarities in Scott's output.

Criticism of auteur theory

Exam questions might prompt students to evaluate the useful-ness of auteur-based theory, and rightfully so – many of the leading proponents of author-oriented critical approaches were writing about film in the 1960s and 70s, and, unsurprisingly, film criticism has moved on from the debates waged during that period. Authorship, of course, is important, and an assessment of a film's meaning-making potential naturally leads us to think about the ideas that filmmakers want to impart. Comparative analysis of the output of filmmakers can also help to draw out thematic and stylistic similarities/differences, but concentrating on authorship alone potentially marginalises other influences that are important.

The following factors and processes might also be explored as a means of supplementing an auteur-based understanding of a film:

- **Institutional mediation:** as explored already, the commissioning studio or producers of films play an important role in shaping film narratives. In the case of the Classical Hollywood model, for example, considerable influence was affected by a studio-led approach. In terms of contemporary filmmaking, studios continue to exert a great deal of influence on the creative steer of products. Certainly, the penchant for franchise-based production evidences the degree of control that contemporary studios have in green-lighting certain types of projects.
- **Genre-based influences:** films work within genre-based templates, often borrowing or inflecting character archetypes, mise en scène conventions and narrative structures that are common to the genre or subgenre that a film is rooted in. Locating genre-based influences can throw into question the extent to which films might be regarded as author-driven.
- **Contextual influences:** films are also subject to the effects of their social and historical contexts – adapting or reshaping auteurial traits and genre-based conventions as a result of shifting social trends, values and norms. The current drive, for example, to make films that demonstrate diversity in terms of casting and story content are driven by the contextual effects of the #meetoo and Black Lives Matter movements.
- **Audience effects:** contemporary film production is profit-oriented, with the creative needs of films often sidelined by commercial imperatives. That single fact pushes directors

to prioritise the construction of audience appeal through focus-group-driven edits – an approach that places audience testing at the heart of the production process. Increasingly, commercial film releases also need to satisfy the needs of franchise-based fan communities whose disapproval can quickly orchestrate social media boycotts.

Table 7.9 Revise it: critiquing auteur theory

Questions that students can ask to evaluate the usefulness of auteur theory or that prompt identification of influences other than those of the director.	
Institutional context	• Which studio financed or commissioned the film? What kinds of audiences does that studio traditionally target? • Is the film made for global release? In what ways is the film crafted to sit within a global market? • What genres does the studio specialise in? In what ways does genre-based storytelling provide a template for the production? • What kinds of budgetary spends are enabled by the parent studio? In what ways does that budgetary spend hinder or liberate the film? • What specialist filmmaking capabilities does the studio offer? Does the studio, for example, offer extensive motion-caption filmmaking production technologies? How do those technologies affect the look, content or style of a film?
Genre-based influences	• In what genre/sub-genre is the film rooted? • What genre-based character archetypes are recycled in the film? • What genre-driven narrative structures/devices are used? • What sorts of genre-driven mise en scène, lighting, sound or cinematography-based conventions does the film use? • What genre-based conventions does the director subvert and with what effect?

Table 7.9 Cont.

Contextual effects	• In what ways does the film reflect contextual attitudes towards race, gender or sexuality? • Does the film reflect the social anxieties of its context? • What big historical events took place when the film was written?
Audience effects	• In terms of age, class and gender, identify the film's target audience. How is the set text tailored to fit the needs of that audience segment? • Does the film have an established fanbase? In what ways might that fanbase have channelled the look or narrative of the film?

Exemplar: *Star Wars: The Force Awakens* **(OCR).** Disney's selection of J.J. Abrams as director for its 2015 Star Wars reboot (Figure 7.1) produced, arguably, a highly stylised rendition of the longstanding science-fiction franchise. Abrams clearly deploys his trademark visual style in the film, using lens flares, snap zooms and handheld camera work to affect an energised feel to the story. But, arguably, that is all that Abrams brings to the film as a director auteur.

Instead, the production and creative steer of *The Force Awakens* is better evaluated as a product that exemplifies the high-spend, franchised approach that is very much a hallmark of contemporary Hollywood mainstream cinema. Disney's acquisition of LucasFilm, for example, exemplifies a studio-expansion strategy that seeks to build upon existing audience engagement using branded rather than original content. The LucasFilm purchase, in this sense, delivered a highly lucrative inherited audience to Disney for future film projects – an audience that expected those projects to deliver a range of familiar Star Wars-related gratifications. In this sense, Abram's director presence was limited from the outset in that he was working within the confines of both studio- and fan-oriented expectations.

The fact that the LucasFilm acquisition cost Disney \$4.3 billion, perhaps prompted a safety-first production strategy for the film. Lawrence Kasdan, screenwriter of *The Empire Strikes Back*, for example, was drafted in to co-write the film, while audience nostalgia and fan power were further appeased by the inclusion of

(continued)

Table 7.9 Cont.

longstanding characters, prompting George Lucas to suggest that
the film contained, 'nothing new'. We might, in response, point
to the addition of key new characters, to Rey in particular, who
defies the usual Proppian Princess stereotype of SF – and also to the
non-white presence of lead character Finn. But even here we might
question the extent to which these key character casting decisions
were director-led and suggest that their inclusion was more
influenced by the contextual effects of the #metoo movement,
BlackLivesMatter and the wider criticism bubbling during 2014
regarding the white-centric nature of Hollywood production.
Certainly, Abram's white-male led 2009 reboot of *Star Trek* offers
scant evidence that *The Force Awaken's* socially diverse cast might
have been an auteur-oriented decision.

Table 7.10 Auteur approaches: ten-minute revision

Essential background
• Auteur theory was an approach to film criticism that became popular from the 1950s.   • François Truffaut divided directors into two broad categories, firstly defining metteurs en scène as those directors who translated scripts into visual material with little cinematic creativity added, while *auteurs* were those directors who injected creativity through the stylised use of mise en scène, cinematography and editing.   • Andrew Sarris refined Truffaut's definition of the auteur, arguing that only those directors who demonstrated technical competence, a unique stylistic approach and who produced films that demonstrated interior meaning could be considered true auteurs.   • Ian Cameron further broadened the definition of the auteur to include production personnel other than directors.   • Peter Wollen further redefined auteur theory in the mid-1960s, using Lévi-Strauss' structuralist thinking to argue that auteurs repeatedly structure film narratives using similar themes and binary structures.

Table 7.10 Cont.

Evaluating auteur theory
• Auteur theory is hugely subjective. The varied definitions of what makes an auteur are often critiqued as vague. • Using auteur-based analysis alone ignores the effects of genre and the wider influences of the film's financers. • Filmmakers are influenced by their social and political contexts – they adapt stories to provide unique commentaries on those wider influences. • Auteur theory wrongly infers that all audiences react to films in the same way. Auteur theory also omits to take account of the effects that audiences and fans have on contemporary film-production processes.

8 Ideology

Table 8.1 What do you need to revise ideology for?

Eduqas
• **Component 1 sections B and C, British film since 1995 and American film since 2005.** Students are asked to apply ideological perspectives – structuralism, feminism and post-Marxian theories, for example – to better understand the meanings and messages created by set text films. Exam questions might also ask students to evaluate the usefulness of ideological perspectives as tools for understanding films.
OCR
• **Paper 2: section A Contemporary British and US cinema.** Requires analysis that identifies the representations of class, gender and race in chosen set text films.
• **Paper 2: section C Ideology.** Requires students to compare the influence of ideology on set text films in addition to the way that films themselves produce ideological effects for their spectators.

Essential exam knowledge: what is ideology?

Marx, hegemony and apparatus theory

The term ideology refers to the unwritten rules or norms that govern the attitudes, behaviours and outlooks of any given society. The study of ideology – or the unwritten rules that inform our culture – is embedded within Marxian thinking: the originator of which, Karl Marx, initially argued that the Victorian ruling class – the mine owners and industrial capitalists of the late nineteenth century – were able to exploit the working poor, not only through physical coercion, but also through more subtle ideological means. Marx tells us, for example, that religion in the Victorian era taught the poor to accept poverty as an inescapable fact of life, and that if the destitute miners and factory workers endured their impoverished conditions that they would be duly rewarded in heaven.

Marx's ideas have been reflected, in one form or another, in the thinking of various philosophers, economists and cultural theorists ever since. Antonio Gramsci, for example, suggested that subordinate classes are subconsciously controlled by the invisible grip of hegemony: a phrase Gramsci coined to describe the various sets of ideologies that unwittingly control our behaviours and ideas. Importantly, Gramsci tells us that hegemonies are subject to constant change with competing groups and ideas affecting control of the attitudes and beliefs that can dominate at any one time.

In the 1970s, post-Marxian sociologist, Theodor Adorno, further rekindled the spirit of Marx with his suggestion that culture played a vital role in hypnotising powerless sections of society into a blind acceptance of their social positions. Adorno acknowledged that the state ultimately affects control through physical means – by marshalling the police or army to quell riots or insurrections, for example – but Adorno also suggested that the state's ability to wield physical power is only used as a last resort. The more subtle and usual form of ideological control is affected through what he called ideological state apparatus (ISA) – education, religion, culture and so forth. Adorno's theory further tells us that a state's ISA is largely controlled by dominant social groups who use culture to align wider society to their world view. Those elites, importantly, might include privileged class, gender or ethnic groups.

Apparatus theorists further argue that film can have a particularly potent ideological effect as a result of its ability to 'suture' us into the fictional worlds of cinema-based narratives. Apparatus theorists deliberately use the term 'suture' to suggest that the psychological experience of watching a film 'stitches' audiences into the cinematic worlds they encounter – that point-of-view cinematography and character alignment, for example, have an immersive or profound effect on spectator thinking, or, indeed, that film narratives are able to subtly rewire subconscious thinking without audiences ever being aware that their outlooks or values are being reshaped.

Cinema and counter cinema

Apparatus theorists argue that film is an effective ideological persuader because it demands our undivided attention. Film also presents us with role models and ideals that can easily take root in the darkness of cinema auditoriums. Certainly, several regimes have openly attempted to harness cinema's capacity to persuade audiences. The fledgling Nazi government in 1934, for example, made a concerted move to control the German film industry, commissioning a slew of films that sought to convince the German people of the validity of their far-right racial ideals. To a lesser extent, Britain, too, established the Ministry of Information in 1939 to openly make and distribute propaganda films that sought to sustain Homefront morale during the Second World War.

In more general terms, apparatus theorists also suggest that mainstream film inadvertently reflects the dominant ideologies of their social or historical contexts. Apparatus theorists argue that films unwittingly absorb and reproduce the dominant ideologies that prevail at any given time, or that characters concentrate ideological ideas through action and dialogue. If, for example, we think about the changing role of female characters across the 60-year history of Bond movies we can clearly detect the emerging influence of feminism in framing the franchise's female leads.

The inadvertent ideological effect of mainstream cinema is also constructed through the character hierarchies presented by films – that the gender, class or race of lead characters reflect or reinforce the wider social inequalities. In Bond movies, for example, increasingly powerful female characters might be present within more recent films, but Bond as a white middle-class male retains the central lead role in films, and in so doing, reinforces the notion that white masculinity ought to dominate in the real world.

Of course, film is a place where prevailing attitudes and ideologies can also be challenged. A rich tradition, for example, of subversive filmmaking and countercultural film can be traced throughout the history of cinema, wherein directors, writers and other creatives have sought to use cinema to effect social change or to critique existing social norms. The British New Wave of the 1960s, for instance, delivered narratives that actively sought to counter the traditional ideologies that underpinned British society at the time, with film's like *A Taste of Honey*, *A Kind of Loving* and *Saturday Night and Sunday Morning* foregrounding issues of class-based injustice, racial prejudice and gender inequality. Indeed, that rich tradition of subversive British film-making continues today in the social realist output of Mike Leigh, Ken Loach and Shane Meadows.

Table 8.2 Think about it: ideology and your key set text films

To assess the presence of ideological messaging in relevant set texts think about the following questions: • Do your chosen films construct *intentional* ideological messaging?   • Do films deliberately ask us to rethink our attitudes to gender, race or class? Do films foreground issues of injustice? Do films challenge social norms, attitudes or beliefs?   • Do your chosen films *unintentionally* reflect the prevailing attitudes of their social or historical context? Do films present a problematic representation of gender, class or race? Do they reinforce the social power of elite groups?   • Which moments in films best illustrate any *intentional* or *unintentional* ideological effects?   • How does cinematography, mise en scène, editing, lighting and performance help to construct ideological effects?   • How does characterisation or narrative structure construct ideological effects?

Structuralism and ideology

One analytical tool that can be used to tease out the underlying ideological significance of media texts is Lévi-Strauss' structuralist analysis model. As discussed in Chapter 6, structuralists suggest that the themes, narratives and characters of films are composed using oppositional states. Importantly, those oppositions not only inject conflict, drama and excitement into film stories, but also produce ideological messaging through the privileged presentation of one oppositional state over another. In the fairy tale, Little Red Riding Hood, for example, drama and entertainment are created when the Big Bad Wolf meets the chaste female hero of the story. Riding Hood's innocence, charity and purity, of course, are positioned in opposition to the greed, cunning and menacing intent of the Wolf. Importantly, Lévi-Strauss' structuralist thinking suggests that binary oppositions also serve to outline the behavioural taboos that audiences are positioned to reject, and, moreover, those attitudinal ideals that we ought to embrace.

In Little Red Riding Hood, for example, the Wolf's death at the end of the story tells us that greed and cunning are taboo outlooks that society will punish, while Riding Hood's innocence and charity are held up as a behavioural model for little boys and girls everywhere. Film, we might argue, produces a similar effect in that most primary and secondary characters are arranged as opposites, with, ordinarily speaking, one set of characters prevailing during the course of a film story. Structuralist critics would suggest that those privileged characters foreground the attitudes, values, norms and behaviours that audiences ought to embrace, while the attitudes and outlooks of those characters who are defeated are outlined as taboo or non-ideal.

Table 8.3 Revise it: ideology and binary oppositions

- What character-based conflicts are offered in your set text films?
- What ideologies, outlooks or beliefs do characters represent?
- Which characters are privileged in narratives? Who wins and who loses?
- With which characters are audiences aligned with? How?
- Which characters are audiences positioned to reject? What are the ideological effects of rejection?

Exemplar: *Moon* (Eduqas). *Moon*'s use of the Sam-clone characters produces two deliberately contrasting representations of masculinity. An assertive newer clone is outlined who shares many of the hypermasculine derring-do attributes of a conventional science fiction (SF) hero. The older version of Sam is juxtaposed with this new twin – who yearns, not for adventure, but to return to Earth so that he can be reunited with his wife and child. Oppositional mise en scène is used to underline this contrasting characterisation, where old Sam tends his plant collection and delicately recreates his home town out of matchsticks, new Sam tests the confines of their Moon space station, training with a hypermasculine restlessness that original Sam can't match. Duncan Jones, however, consistently privileges original Sam's presence, using left-hand framing and close-up compositions to elicit audience empathy. Character privileging, signals Jones' ideological preference for a more feminised form of masculinity, and, moreover, that old Sam – although decayed and dying – offers audiences an outlook or set of behavioural ideals that are superior to those embodied by new Sam.

Links to exemplar film clips and exemplars for other OCR/Eduqas film texts can be found at www.essentialfilmrevision.com

Table 8.4 Challenge it: do all films produce clear-cut binaries?

- Do all film texts construct clear-cut binary conflicts?
- Do all films produce clear winners and losers?
- Do all audiences align themselves with heroic characters?
- Do privileged oppositions produce lasting ideological effects on audiences?

Tzvetan Todorov, formalism and the ideological effect of narrative transformation

The formalist ideas of the literary theorist Tzvetan Todorov also provide us with another useful framework to explore the ideological effects of narrative in film. As discussed in more detail in Chapter 6, Todorov argues that stories are conventionally structured using three identifiable movements or pulses of action. The ideal story structure, he suggests, initially outlines moments of equilibrium in which the world of the central character is outlined as harmonious and stable. The second pulse of Todorov's ideal injects conflict or disequilibrium into that world, usually activated by the entrance of an antagonist character. Todorov's third pulse – the new equilibrium stage – restores harmony, but crucially, also transforms the central character of the narrative through the discovery of newfound knowledge or a change in their attitude or behaviour.

Todorov tells us that each narrative stage – equilibrium, disequilibrium and new equilibrium – can convey ideological effects:

- **Ideologies constructed by the equilibrium stage:** in Todorov's 'ideal' narrative structure, the equilibrium stage represents a set of ideals that the central character often tries to recover during their narrative journey. Todorov, too, suggests that the harmony presented at the start of narratives is often flawed or defective, and, as a result, prompts central characters to seek change. Audiences can be aligned with those desires, prompting them to effect similar changes in their own lives.
- **Ideological effects constructed through narrative disequilibrium:** Todorov tells us that the use of transgression in the disequilibrium act can also convey a powerful ideological presence. Transgression occurs when rules or social norms are broken, prompting lead characters to seek to repair those moments of transgression by embarking on their narrative journey. Much like Strauss, narrative transgressions, Todorov

argues, outline taboo attitudes and undesirable behaviours that audiences are invited to reject.

- **Ideological effects constructed through new equilibrium narrative stages:** the last act of a narrative, Todorov tells us, is the most ideologically potent stage, largely driven as a result of the character-based transformations that occur during the new equilibrium stage. Restoring harmony in the new equilibrium stage, Todorov reminds us, requires central characters to change in some way – to acquire new knowledge or beliefs, or to modify their attitude towards the wider world in some way. Those transformations, he argues further, outline the beliefs, knowledge or attitudes that audiences are positioned to internalise as ideals.

Table 8.5 Revise it: detecting ideological effects produced by narrative stages.

Diagnose the way that set text narratives produce ideology by answering the following questions.

Questions to ask about equilibrium stages
- Does the start of the film provide an ideal world for the audience?
- Does the central character of the story attempt to restore the initial harmony outlined at the start of the film? What are the ingredients that make for that ideal world?

Disequilibrium effects
- What behaviours or ideals are audiences positioned to reject?
- Are disequilibrium stages constructed as a result of rule-breaking actions or other forms of transgressive behaviour?
- What negative traits or behaviours are embodied by the villains of stories?

New equilibrium effects
- In what ways do central characters change over the course of the film?
- Do characters undergo attitude, behaviour or knowledge-based transformations? What essential behaviours or knowledge do they acquire during the film?
- What life-lessons do character transformations communicate to audiences?

(*continued*)

Table 8.5 Cont.

Exemplar: *Selma* **(Eduqas).** An exploration of *Selma* that uses the formalist lens of Todorov's narrative theory provides an enormously useful tool to unpick the film's underlying ideological effects. DuVernay could have packaged the film using a conventional 'birth to death' narrative progression seen in other film-based biopics. That approach, interestingly, would have ended with King's assassination, and, as a result, have foregrounded the Civil Rights leader's martyrdom as another defeat in the fight for black equality. Instead, DuVernay steps back from that structure, replacing that story with a conventional three-act narrative that ends not in Luther's assassination in 1968, but in the victory he and others won in allowing voters to exercise their right to vote in the southern state of Alabama in 1965. DuVernay's packaging of the story in this way produces a more politically charged ending, and authors a new equilibrium ending in which Senator Wallace's whites-only power base is finally dismantled. The ending, too, magnifies the effects of black political action, while also suggesting that political solidarity in the face of overwhelming prejudice can result in significant social change. The film, in this sense, is directed at contemporary American audiences, with an ending that points to the ongoing work of groups such as Black Lives Matter and their continued fight to eradicate visible and invisible racism in the United States.

Stereotypes and ideology

Character-based analysis provides another powerful tool to explore the ideological effects of set text films. The cultural theorist Stuart Hall, for example, is particularly interested in the way that film and media products construct representations of powerless social groups. Hall argues, for example, that real-world social hierarchies are reflected by the characters of film products, and that the ready-made character traits of stereotypes reinforce entrenched negative perceptions of marginalised racial groups and other disempowered members of society.

Undoubtedly, stereotyped characters are widely used in film, usually to produce audience-based character recognition or to provide ready-made story frames for scriptwriters and directors to work within. In *Shaun of the Dead*, for example, a rich range of stereotypes is deployed for comic purposes: Ed, for instance, is the cliched unemployed stoner, Barbara is an archetypal overbearing mother figure, while Dianne provides a diluted version of the dumb-blonde stereotype. Importantly, Hall tells us, stereotypes usually construct negative perceptions of the social groups they represent. In *Shaun of the Dead*, for example, Ed's drug-based life-style might be seen to suggest that unemployed men are naturally lazy or stupid, and, as such, that Ed's powerless position in society is self-made (see Figure 8.1).

Hall suggests further that films tend to author stereotypes of powerless groups because filmmaking, in the main, is likely to be financed and produced by elite social groups who use their cultural influence to maintain their status in society. Conversely, powerless groups are presented with few opportunities to make films, and, therefore, are rarely able to challenge the stereotypical traits they are associated with. Hall, in this sense, suggests that stereotypes construct 'otherness' in that they exclude or demonise powerless groups.

Figure 8.1   Shaun of the Dead (top): Ed draws upon a problematic representation of unemployed masculinity. *Skyfall* (bottom): Raoul
Silva as the villainous gay in *Skyfall*.

Table 8.6 Revise it: identify negative stereotypes in film set texts

- Can any of the characters in your set texts be described as stereotypical? Use Table 8.8 to help you identify any potential character stereotypes in your film set texts.
- Which social groups are represented by the stereotypes of your films? Think in terms of ethnicity, social class or gender-based groups.
- In what ways does the physical appearance and/or behaviours of the character help to construct an exaggerated or negative representation of that social group?
- What negative traits are associated with the character's social group as a result of a stereotypical portrayal?
- Do stereotypes in your set text films construct social groups as outsiders or marginalise those groups as uncivilised 'others'?

Exemplar: *Skyfall* (OCR). *Skyfall*'s gender-blurred and facially disfigured Raoul Silva (Figure 8.1) provides the film with a classic Bond villain. Certainly, Silva's disability is an easy antagonist shortcut – delivering a genre-driven character that audiences will find difficulty in empathising with, while also providing easy motivation for the film's revenge-based narrative. Problematically, Skyfall's antagonist also produces a concerning representation of disability, recycling a well-worn disabled villain stereotype that might reinforce real-world discrimination. Silva's indiscriminate use of sadistic violence, for example, all too readily associates disability with fear or menace – constructing, Stuart Hall might argue, disabled groups as an 'other' to civilised behaviour. Equally problematically, Silva's character also recycles the gay-villain stereotype, clearly associating gender fluidity with deviant behaviour. Silva's caress of Bond while tied up, for example, reinforces an outmoded portrayal of gay masculinity as a predatory and sinister presence.

Table 8.7 Common negative stereotypes of key social groups

Racial stereotypes	• The menacing black male • The black best friend • Sassy black females • The Asian nerd • Martial-arts experts • The wise Asian	Racial stereotypes traditionally construct non-white groups as 'others' using sinister or threatening characteristics. The lower social status of non-white characters is also inferred through their positioning as secondary characters – the 'black best friend' stereotype provides an excellent example of this process. Non-white female characters are routinely presented as over sexualised – producing a heightened objectification of non-white femininity.
Disability-oriented stereotypes	• Burden or victim stereotypes • Superhuman representations • Evil disabled characters	Disability is often used to furnish antagonist characters with 'otherness'. Mental illness, disfigurement or physical disability, for example, are routinely used to repulse audiences. Victim-based stereotypes are also common – often used to elicit audience sympathy or to push tragic narrative arcs.
Gay stereotypes	• Butch lesbian • Effeminate gay • Sinister gay • Gay villains	Gay characters rarely feature as traditional story leads. When they are present in films they are often marginalised as comic characters or associated with exaggerated characteristics – gay men, for example, are constructed as abnormally effeminate.

Stereotype transcoding

Stuart Hall also reminds us that films are places where ideologies can be contested, and, by using what Hall calls transcoding, that cultural products construct representations that challenge racial, gender or ability-based stereotypes. Hall draws our attention to the following three transcoding mechanisms used by film and media products that test stereotyping effects:

- **Character countertypes** or counter-typical representations offer audiences characters who invert racial, gender or ability-based stereotypical traits. Black leads might, for example, deliberately reject violent action in favour of a more caring disposition. Disabled characters might play a lead role in rescuing others rather than working within the victim-based character conventions that are normally associated with disability.
- **Appropriated stereotypes** occur when films actively embrace the negative behaviours that are associated with a stereotype, but do so in a way that creates character appeal rather than 'otherness'. Jules, in *Pulp Fiction* for example, works within the menacing black-villain archetype seen across a great deal of mainstream film output. Tarantino's stylised rendition of Jules, however, is fashioned to construct character alignment rather than fear.
- **Deconstructed stereotypes** are produced when filmmakers effect simplistic or stereotypical representations of characters at the start of films but use the remaining narrative to explore the effects that stereotyping has on the character. Deconstructed stereotypes acknowledge the existence of narrative behaviours by key groups, but, importantly, also explain why such behaviours exist.

Table 8.8 Revise it: identify transcoding effects

Use the following questions to help you locate moments of
transcoding in your set text films and their corresponding
ideological effects:

- Does the use of transcoding shift perceptions of marginalised,
  demonised or powerless social groups? How?
- Do your set text films deploy *countertypes*? What stereotypical
  attributes are reversed by the presence of countertypes? What
  assumptions are challenged using countertypes?
- Do any of your set texts use *appropriated* stereotypes? What
  stereotypes are embraced by the film? Where is appropriation most
  visible and what effect might its use have on the film's audience?
- Do films explore stereotyping effects using *deconstructed*
  stereotypes? Which moments in the film narrative produce
  audience empathy for the social group depicted? What does
  the film teach us about the experience of the outsider group
  represented?

Exemplar: *Sweet Sixteen* (Eduqas). *Sweet Sixteen*'s anti-hero lead,
Liam, adheres to the kinds of conventional underclass stereotypes
that can be found in wider media products of the period. His
scruffy tracksuit and unkempt hair provide the visible signs to signal
his lower-class status. Liam too evidences many of the behaviours
and outlooks that are synonymous with lower-class character
stereotypes: criminality, single parenthood and drug use. Yet,
Loach does more than just reproduce the negative characteristics of
underclass culture, he offers audiences what Stuart Hall would call
a transcoded stereotype – using *Sweet Sixteen*'s tragic narrative arc to
outline the effects of Liam's underclass life rather than as a means of
demonising or marginalising lower-class groups.

Hints of that deconstruction are evidenced in the opening scene –
Liam's stargazing, for example, symbolises a yearning to escape,
while his regard to help the other children suggests a community-
minded outlook. Liam's tragic narrative arc after this moment
further reveals the role that social environment plays in his downfall,
a doomed and opportunity-free world that Liam tries to escape from
but is ultimately to remain a part of. Here, Loach's counter cinema –
his use of social realism – is clearly ideological in that it seeks to
outline the corrosive influence of economic inequalities on those
who try to do well, yet can't escape the insidious and criminalising
effects of poverty.

Absent representations

Films can also construct ideological effects as a result of the absence of social groups within narratives – that the lack of visibility of key social groups within mainstream films can help to marginalise such groups in the real world. Despite recent improvements, black representation in mainstream film, for example, continues to be problematic. The UCLA 2019 Hollywood Diversity Report, for example, identifies that just 27.6% of lead roles were played by Black, Asian and minority ethnic (BAME) actors in 2019 – significantly up from the 13.9% return of 2016, but still much lower than the 72.4% of lead roles played by white actors. In terms of film direction, too, diversity is hugely problematic, with just 15.1% of Hollywood films directed by BAME filmmakers in 2019, and while females accounted for 44.1% of lead roles in 2019, women were significantly underrepresented in terms of their directorial presence – with just over 15% of films made in 2019 naming a female director.

The annual Gay & Lesbian Alliance Against Defamation (GLAAD) survey of Hollywood paints a similarly depressing picture with just 18.6% of films made by the Hollywood majors in 2019 featuring lesbian, gay, bisexual, transgender and queer or questioning (LGBTQ) characters in 2019. GLAAD point also to the huge number of very minor roles that contribute to that figure, with 56% of the gay characters featured in major film output receiving no more than three minutes of screen time in the films in which they appeared. Even more shockingly, none of the major Hollywood releases in 2019 featured a transgender character.

Table 8.9 Revise it: identify the ideological effect of absent representations

• Do set text films construct a problematic representation of the real world as a result of absent social groups? • If non-white or LGBTQ characters are present in the film, are they given equal screen time? • As a result of absence, do your chosen films construct a world view that is largely white or male-oriented?
Exemplar: *La La Land* **(Eduqas).** For all its editing and lighting artistry, *La La Land* has drawn considerable criticism for its white-centric story arc (see Figure 8.2). Unmistakably, the film's idealised romance narrative is heteronormatively aligned, with its use of white protagonist leads mirroring wider Hollywood diversity trends that many view as deeply problematic. Further criticism is directed towards the underlying story of the film in which a white male character tries to save jazz – a music genre that is universally seen as synonymous with black culture. The film's inclusion of band leader Keith perhaps acknowledges something of the jazz genre's black heritage, but the character's two-dimensional role as the instigator for Seb's and Mia breakup and his minimal screen presence does very little to shore up the film's diversity credentials. Cultural theorists would argue that the absence of a diverse cast affects a powerful ideological narrative presence – marginalising key social groups in the real world as a result of their narrative exclusion.

Feminist ideological approaches

Where Stuart Hall's development of apparatus theory was interested in the way that cultural products used stereotyping, Laura Mulvey draws upon Althusser's approach and Freudian psychoanalytic theory to explore the ideological effects of film in terms of gender. Mulvey's approach is outlined in her hugely influential 1973 essay, *Visual Pleasure and Narrative Cinema*, in which she outlines a feminist analysis methodology that can still be applied to today's contemporary film output. Mulvey's key argument suggest that:

• **Film-based representations of gender are largely constructed by men:** Mulvey points to the practical impact of masculine domination of the film industry, reminding us that film producers, scriptwriters and directors are mostly male and that the cinematic worlds, characters and stories offered to audiences reflect, in the main, a masculine perspective.

- **Cinema viewers are aligned to masculine viewpoints via the male gaze:** Mulvey further argues that the cinema experience principally offers audiences what Freud called scopophilic pleasures – that the dark world of the cinema auditorium constructs voyeuristic or sexual viewing pleasures – and because filmmaking is dominated largely by males, film narratives predominantly work to satisfy male-oriented fantasies.

- **That the male gaze objectifies femininity:** as a result, females in film are constructed as passive and objectified – as objects that male characters pursue with sexual intent, or who might be offered up to the gaze of a film's male lead without a female character's objection. Mulvey, too, discusses the way that women are routinely filmed in films and points to the ubiquitous use of soft-focus tilt-down compositions in Classical Hollywood output to frame female actors. Mulvey argues that this widely used shot composition constructs a passive representation of femininity.

- **That the male gaze is internalised by audiences:** Mulvey further tells us that the male gaze aligns both male and female spectators with passive female ideals. As a result, female objectification is internalised as a social norm.

Table 8.10 Revise it: identify gender-based representations

• Do your set text films reproduce a passive or objectified representation of femininity?   • Are female characters framed differently to their male counterparts? Are soft-focus shots or tilt-downs used to suggest female passivity?   • Are female characters constructed as erotic spectacle?   • Are male characters constructed as more active than their female counterparts?   • Are male presences encoded as stronger than females in your set text films?
Exemplar: *Jurassic World* (OCR). *Jurassic World*'s reboot of the dinosaur-based franchise initially seems to break with Hollywood's tradition of passive female leads (see Figure 8.2). Claire's no-nonsense intro as the first primary character of the movie places her firmly in the world of business – a sharp contrast to her family-oriented sister. Yet even here, the director's ankle-to-head crane shot produces an objectified female representation, while Claire's red lipstick and revealing blouse suggest the character's sexual availability and provides audiences with a representation that is moulded for the male gaze – a male gaze that Chris Pratt's later introduction in the plot actively models. A later scene similarly provides evidence of a problematic representation, where Claire's lead in explaining the park's manufacture of the Dominus Rex, is interrupted by a secondary male who abruptly interjects to explain the more complicated science behind the invention. This objectified passivity contrasts sharply with Owen's backlit tilt-up intro that clearly depicts him as the alpha-male lead of his velociraptor pack. *Jurassic World* might offer initial hints of a strong and independent female lead, but ultimately that independence is constructed as inadequate when Claire finally accepts her true place as a maternal caregiver to her two nephews, and, moreover, acquiesces to Owen's romantic affections. In this sense, we can firmly conclude that the film presents a traditional representation of family life – a representation that clearly provides ample evidence of Mulvey's male-gaze theory.

Figure 8.2 Jurassic World (top): the 2015 reboot of the franchise reinforces active male and passive female stereotypes. *La La Land* (bottom): Critics argued that the film reinforces a white-centric heteronormative worldview.

Table 8.11 Challenge it: do spectators align themselves with the male gaze?

- Do filmmakers still frame females as passive or secondary characters in contemporary film texts?
- Do contemporary filmmakers encode more active representations of femininity?
- Do female characters continue to be objectified in contemporary cinema?
- Is the cinema industry still dominated by male filmmakers? Are the key authors – directors, producers and scriptwriters – of your set text films female?
- Is it problematic that Mulvey thinks all spectators react to film-based representations in the same way?

Challenging ideological approaches

Exam questions for both OCR and Eduqas can require students to evaluate the application of the ideological approaches outlined above. Certainly, a more nuanced assessment of the effects of film has been proposed since the 1970s vogue for feminist, structuralist and post-Marxian analysis, with a range of theoretical assessments developed that suggests that audiences read films as active rather than passive spectators (for a full discussion see Chapter 9). Key criticisms of post-Marxian, formalist, structuralist and feminist approaches might include the following objections:

- **Audiences don't decode films in the same way.** Most of the ideological approaches outlined above assume that spectators decode films using universally applicable processes. Mulvey, for example, suggests that all audiences internalise the male gaze without question. Apparatus theory, too, suggests that audiences are passive recipients of cinema's ideological messaging and that individual spectators can offer little or no resistance to the hypnotic thrall of a film's hidden ideologies. Of course, individual audience members interpret films using their own perspectives/outlooks in a way that might lead them to accept or reject the ideological effects of a film narrative.

- **Audiences don't readily align with characters of the same gender**. We might further critique Mulvey's arguments, by pointing to the idea that female viewers can just as easily align with male protagonists, and, as a result, internalise the male gaze as an active rather than passive participants. Of course, the opposite is true, in that men might identify with the objectifying hold of female representations in cinema. Audiences might also align themselves with secondary characters or even antagonists, and, as such internalise values that aren't obviously privileged or foregrounded by narratives.

- **Counter cinema effects limited viewership.** The ideological effect that counter cinema might produce is constricted as a result of its limited distribution to independent cinemas. As a result, counter cinema is watched, almost exclusively, by educated middle-class audiences who are probably already predisposed to the political messaging that such films might offer.

- **Contemporary character-construction is complex.** The notion that films deliver simplified binaries is highly questionable. Lead characters deliver complex and often contradictory ideals. Ideological effects might also be diluted through the use of constructed irony – in *Jurassic World*, for example, Chris Pratt's objectifying hypermasculine representation is more comedic than serious, potentially leading audiences to reject the traditional ideals that the film offers through this character.

Table 8.12 Ideology: ten-minute revision

Essential background
• Post-Marxian theorists like Louis Althusser suggest that cultural products have an ideological effect on audiences and that culture plays a crucial role in reinforcing the economic and political status of those who hold power. • Counter cinema can work to challenge the dominant ideologies that exist in society.
Essential knowledge: ideological effects of character and narrative
• Structuralist film theorists suggest that films create ideology via the use of binary oppositions. • Formalist film theorists suggest that films routinely create stories using predefined narrative patterns. • Cultural theorists like Stuart Hall emphasise the power that character stereotypes play in films. • Stuart Hall also tells us that cultural products can use transcoding to shift assumptions normally inferred by character stereotypes.
Feminist analysis and ideology
• Feminist film theorists like Laura Mulvey argue that films privilege a masculine viewpoint and that the routine objectification of women in film is internalised as a social norm by both men and women.
Challenges to ideological approaches
• Most ideological approaches are problematic in their assertion that audiences are passive film watchers who can't resist the ideological effects of the films they consume. • Audiences might not align themselves with lead characters. As such, films don't necessarily produce predictable ideological effects.

9   Spectatorship

Table 9.1 What do you need to revise spectatorship for?

Eduqas • **Component 1 section C, American film since 2005:** students are asked to think about the different sorts of responses that film viewers might take when watching films. **OCR** • **Paper 2: sections A and C, contemporary British and US cinema, and ideology:** responses to questions in paper 2 might benefit from a knowledge of how spectators' interpretation of films are affected by social and cultural factors as well as an understanding of how films position audiences to be active or passive viewers.

Essential background: problematic ideological approaches

The vast range of film theories that have formed over the past 80 years point to a dizzying array of ways that films can be assessed or analysed. The narrative and character-driven ingredients of film, for instance, have invited the application of literary theorists such as Barthes or Propp, while the commercial nature of the film industry has solicited commentary from post-Marxian theorists such as Louis Althusser and Theodor Adorno. Perhaps what links a huge swathe of theory (until the 1970s at least) was an intention to produce a single unifying explanation for the kinds of meanings that film produced. The following four approaches vied to provide an overriding explanation pre-1970:

- **Formalist and linguistic frameworks:** these conceived of film as a kind of language – that certain shot types or arrangements of shots created a universally understood range of effects that viewers absorb during spectatorship. In many ways, the first part of this revision guide follows a similar approach in its suggestion that cinematography, sound, editing and so on produce a fixed range of meanings.
- **Structuralist theorists:** these suggest that films construct narratives and characters that draw from a fixed range of storytelling structures. Levi-Strauss' ideas, for instance, have been used to suggest that films work through the presentation of oppositional characters or conflicting stylistic features. Similarly, Propp's ideas regarding character archetypes have also been applied to suggest that films universally draw upon a fixed range of character types whose narrative functions are predetermined.
- **Marxian/post-Marxian theoretical frameworks:** central to Marxian thinking lies the assumption that a specific set of ideas or ideologies are nurtured by society and that those ideas usually reinforce the power of social elites. Some Marxists argue that films, as produced by the financial might of Hollywood, produce stories that demonise or marginalise key social groups. Filmmaking, they suggest, is conventionally controlled by those social elites who are rich enough to finance production. As such, elite views tend to be represented by film narratives.
- **Psychoanalytic film criticism:** these focuses on the links between film spectatorship and the workings of the subconscious. One aspect of the psychoanalytic approach suggests that film viewing produces the same sorts of states we experience while dreaming. Other psychoanalytic critics focus attention on film as an expression of the subconscious desires of their directors and writers. Psychoanalytic theorists argue that films compel audiences to experience those desires and wish fulfilments in a way that aligns the spectator with the inner world of the film's author. We are positioned as voyeurs, they suggest: we don't watch films – we interpolate their subconscious meanderings – that is to say we align

ourselves with the subconscious desires of a film's creators as expressed through the storylines and characters they construct for the cinematic screen.

Table 9.2 Know it: Jacques Lacan, spectatorship and the mirror stage

Alignment and desire

The impact of Jacques Lacan's theoretical work on film theory is particularly significant when addressing issues of film spectatorship and is worth considering in more detail. Lacan's psychoanalytic approach outlined what he called the 'mirror stage' – a crucial moment in the development of infants where children initially comprehend that they are independent and separate from the wider world. Importantly, for Lacan, it is during this pre-language stage of development that we start to develop our sense of self-identity. For Lacan, the mirror stage also expels us from the preconscious warmth of babydom. Lacan, moreover, further suggests that we experience that transition as a disruptive loss. The mirror stage, as such, prompts:

- An unconscious yearning to return to the cozy world of dormant infancy.
- It leads us to perceive ourselves as incomplete, or that we lack the power or purpose of those older adults who control our day-to-day existence.
- Lacan argues further that we experience an overwhelming desire to copy or replicate the adult role models who are prominent in our childhood years. Crucially for Lacan we never manage to fulfil those desires.

Psychoanalytic film theorists suggest cinema operates much like the mirror stage, in that films nurture the same sorts of desires that we experience during infancy. The hypnotic power of cinema induces the following two specific pleasures according to the Lacan inspired film theorist Christian Metz:

- **Voyeurism:** the cinema screen facilitates the pleasure of watching from the comfort and safety of the cinema auditorium. Much like the cozy pre-conscious world of the new-born infant, we become lost in the hypnotic pulse of cinematic imagery and that we lose our sense of self during these moments.

(continued)

Table 9.2 Cont.

> • **Identification:** we simultaneously and subconsciously align ourselves with the characters depicted on screen. In the darkness of the cinema, Metz argues, spectators are lulled into a subconscious dreamlike state in which we inhabit the actions, desires and motivations of our onscreen heroes. Cinema spectatorship is, he suggests, a process of wish fulfilment in which the characters depicted provide us with moments where our dreams or ideals can be finally realised.
>
> Crucially, the theoretical thinking of both Lacan and Metz suggests that cinema spectatorship is underscored by a desire to bridge those gaps that exist between our real and ideal selves. In short, cinema allows us to assume a perfected version of our less than perfect real-world lives through character alignment.

Post-structuralism and the death of the author

Much film writing in the 1980s and beyond sought to fore-ground a more nuanced and flexible set of arguments regarding film viewing to those linguistic, Marxian and psychoanalytic frameworks identified above. Prompted in part by the work of Roland Barthes and Jacques Derrida, the post-structuralist film theorists of the period overturned the generalised analysis provided by pre-1980s film writers.

Post-structuralist critiques of Lacan, Levi-Strauss, formalism and Marxism centre around the following observations:

• **That structuralist, linguistic, psychoanalytic and Marxian approaches are overly deterministic:** all approaches assume that spectators read films in the same way. Neither the experiences of the spectator nor the gender, race or class of individual audience members are accounted for by pre-1980s writers when assessing the impact of a film. Post-structuralists, conversely, suggest that our individual experiences – our backgrounds, political biases and life experiences – play a significant role in helping us to decode the meanings of cinema stories.

- **Psychoanalytic and Marxist thinking focuses on authorship rather than spectatorship:** the analytical force of much pre-1980s film theory centred on the authors of films as the ultimate creators of meaning. Psychoanalytic analysis, for example, often focused on the biographies of directors in a bid to understand the hidden meanings that those authors encoded when making films. Of course, authors shape film meaning, but, post-structuralists argue, not all film spectators decode those meanings in the ways that directors or script writers intend.

- **The style and content of filmmaking is too varied to support a unified film theory:** pre-1980s film theory sought to locate a grand unifying explanation that could be applied to all films. The application of those ideas to the real output of the film world is hugely problematic in that real films vary enormously in terms of style and content. The aesthetics and story styles of mainstream and independent cinema, for example, are incredibly different in terms of their effect or even in the way they are consumed. To apply the same analytical models to all films inevitably misses much of the distinctiveness of individual products.

- **Pre-1980s approaches emphasise intellectual analysis over emotional engagement:** the act of film spectatorship is an emotional experience – the moments of joy, fear or surprise that cinema spectatorship induces are often side-lined by the various theoretical schools that flourished pre-1980 in favour of complex intellectual assessments. Such approaches don't readily reflect the way that ordinary viewers interact with cinema narratives.

Stuart Hall: the reception theory revolution

Perhaps, one of the most important critiques of structuralism was authored by the Jamaican-born British cultural theorist, Stuart Hall, who, in his highly influential 1973 essay *Encoding and Decoding in the Television Discourse*, dared to suggest that audience engagement is hugely varied and complex.

Of course, filmmakers encode their work in a carefully controlled way – they want to create ideas and messages for audiences to read, but, Stuart Hall told us, that doesn't necessarily mean that all viewers will interpret those messages in identical ways. Similarly, filmmakers might subconsciously reproduce problematic ideologies in their work, but, again, some audiences, Stuart Hall argues, are able to resist those ideas as a result of their contextual knowledge and beliefs.

Hall, for example, draws attention to the problematic and widespread use of stereotypes in the media. The routine use of black characters as film criminals, for example, is a staple feature of crime-driven narratives. Hall argues, controversially, that such stereotypes exist because black people don't have the economic power to control film production, and, as a result, have limited capacity to offer alternative models to negative criminalised representations. The effect of such depictions, Hall tells us, works to demonise black masculinity in the real world.

Yet, Hall also tells us that audiences can resist the ideological pull of these representations. Audience readings, Hall tells us, are influenced by the experiences and beliefs of the individual spectator. The 'situated logics' of individual readers play a vital role in guiding audience interpretations of any film. A spectator, for example, who has had positive experiences of black communities can resist the negative framing of criminalised black characters, while audiences with little or no experience might be more prone to accept the idea that black males are socially deviant.

Hall suggests, as a result, that audiences can produce the following types of film readings:

- **Dominant readings:** audiences knowingly decode films as intended by the author and accept the ideological messages produced. Audiences are passive when making a dominant reading.
- **Negotiated readings:** audiences produce a negotiated reading if the author's message is acknowledged in general terms, but the experiences of readers also lead them to question or resist some aspects of a text. Audiences are both passive and active when making negotiated readings.

- **Oppositional readings:** audiences understand the author's message but also challenge the ideas produced as a result of their experiences or beliefs. Audiences are active when they resist the ideological thrust of a text.

Table 9.3 Write it: using reception theory to answer spectatorship-oriented questions

Hall's ideas, if applied carefully, can help students generate detailed answers. Close analysis that carefully examines how different audiences might read a particular screen moment in diverse ways can produce high-level responses. Some top tips:

Strategy one
- Construct a detailed reading of a film moment using a formalist, psychoanalytic, Marxist or structuralist theoretical approach.
- Construct an oppositional reading of the same sequence identifying how some readers might produce alternative readings to those identified above.
- Identify the types of audience who could construct oppositional readings, explaining why they fail to engage with the text as expected.

Strategy two
- Identify the intentions of the film's director, actors or scriptwriters in key sequences.
- Explore key moments where those authorial intentions might be decoded using oppositional readings.
- Identify the audiences or groups that might offer oppositional readings and explain why.

Exemplar: *Captain Fantastic* **(Eduqas).** The countercultural thrust of *Captain Fantastic* is clearly outlined during the Noam Chomsky Day scene. Significantly, this plot point follows the family's 'free the food mission' and is used to underscore their economic and political resistance to the mainstream values of consumerist America. That resistance is reinforced via a five-second jump-cut montage. Here, the film's audience is passively aligned with that countercultural impulse via a series of quick-fire tilt-ups of the family devouring the cake. Yet, potentially, the alignment of the

(*continued*)

Table 9.3 Cont.

spectator with the ideologies of the iconic left-wing Chomsky is undercut if they don't know who Chomsky is. Without this knowledge, Stuart Hall would suggest that a spectator would most likely construct a textual misreading at this point of the film. The film, however, accounts for this potential knowledge gap with a 'tell don't show' moment in which Ben explicitly explains Chomsky's left-leaning credentials for those audiences who lack the necessary cultural knowledge needed to accurately decode this sequence.

Importantly, the slower editing tempo and subsequent central framing of Rellian offers a counterpoint to the celebration; a moment where the audience are invited to critique the naive idealism of Ben. This depiction is crucial within the film in that it positions the audience to question Ben's morality. A politically biased left-wing audience, however, might not be entirely convinced of the way that Chomsky's ideas are so easily dismissed. Importantly, the audience is asked at this point in the film to abandon an intellectual assessment of the family and to embrace an emotionally driven response. The director, too, asks the audience to realign themselves with Rellian rather than the previously dominant presence of Ben. The potential for audiences to engage in an oppositional reading during this sequence is significant given these layered shifts in narrative direction.

Links to exemplar film clips and exemplars for other OCR/Eduqas film texts can be found at www.essentialfilmrevision.com

Beyond Lacan and psychoanalysis: intellectual versus emotional engagement

Explicit and extensive criticism has also been directed at the psychoanalytic approach, particularly those ideas forwarded by Lacan and Metz that cinema spectatorship always aligns audiences with screen-based leads who make good our real-world human failings. The idea that film provides a compensatory pleasure, some writers argue, provides an overly pessimistic view of the way we interact with film.

Taking his cue from the philosophical writing of Gilles Deleuze, the film theorist Steven Shaviro, for example, reminds us that spectatorship offers us more than just compensatory character alignments. Cinema, he tells us, might indeed bewitch us with moments of desire and fantasy, yet film is also attractive and hugely successful because it provokes a rainbow of emotional responses. Shaviro's view of film spectatorship recognises that cinema goers engage with films because they provoke and resolve fears, because they provide us with moments of romantic excess or comedic release. The 'images of film' Shaviro writes, 'are the raw contents of sensation' (Shaviro, 2000, 30). To explain the effects of cinema as an experience of compensatory wish fulfilment, he argues, misses much of the varied emotional gratifications that film spectatorship provides.

Table 9.4 Think about it: which of your set texts provoke emotional rather than identity-based responses?

• Which scenes of your film set texts provoked strong emotional responses when you watched them? • Which other films beyond your set texts do you remember as a result of their emotional impact? • Is character identification or emotional positioning more important to you when watching a film?

Passive and active spectator positioning

Where Shaviro and Hall argue that film spectators respond to narratives in a variety of unpredictable ways, other writers have picked up on the notion that some contemporary film authors use a range of storytelling devices that deliberately orchestrate spectator ambiguity. Jill Nelmes, for example, differentiates between the passive viewing experience induced by mainstream cinema and the more nuanced experiences of independent film spectatorship.

Mainstream film, Nelmes argues, offers us, 'ever more spectacular forms of visual and aural cinema' (Nelmes, 2012, 138). Best exemplified by the franchise-based offerings of Marvel, the must-see movie events of the contemporary period are rich in CGI otherworldliness, their core appeal constructed using visual spectacle.

Films of this kind, Nelmes argues further, produce what Richard Wollheim calls 'central imagining' experiences in which the spectator is passively locked into a cinematic roller coaster ride of fast-paced, action-based direction. The intensity of 'central imagining' films tend to produce a uniform response for all viewers.

Conversely, what might loosely be described as 'independent cinema' is more likely to produce spectator ambiguity and 'a-central imagining effects'. Independent cinema, for example, often places film viewers in morally liminal spaces, asking audiences to evaluate character action across more complex narrative arcs. Independent films also routinely resist the easy resolutions of mainstream cinema via the use of complex antagonists or flawed lead characters.

Other narrative devices found in independent products that prompt active spectatorship might include the following:

- **Anti-hero protagonists:** these repulse film spectators while also inviting audiences to align themselves with the actions of those characters. The morally ambiguous world of anti-heroes is variously embraced or rejected by audiences.
- **Narrative irony:** directors can construct actions that aren't meant to be taken seriously by audiences. The use of irony, however, requires audiences to be able to decode film moments in a sophisticated manner. Samuel L. Jackson's delivery of the Ezekiel biblical verse in *Pulp Fiction*, for instance, isn't used to enhance Jules as a spiritual character – if anything, its use ironically underscores Jules cold-blooded violence. Whether audiences fully embrace the emptiness of its meaning when delivered is less than straightforward.
- **Multi-protagonist casts:** narratives that focus attention on the action of a single heroic character are often resisted in independent cinema, replaced instead with narrative action that dissipates across multi-protagonist ensembles. The lack of focus on singular heroes produces complex character alignments, and, when watching such films, audiences might find that they align with secondary characters or identify with those characters whose age, gender or behavioural qualities mirror their own.

- **Unresolved narratives:** where mainstream cinema produces clear-cut resolutions, the narratives of independent films can produce muddied moral meanings.

- **Character backstory and deconstructed characterisation:** the separation of protagonist and antagonist moralities is more clearly evidenced in mainstream cinema than in independent film. Characters are often realigned, morally speaking, by the narrative events of independent film – whether those realignments force a similar adjustment on the part of the audience is less than straightforward.

- **Bricolage, pastiche or intertextuality:** the use of postmodern narrative devices are not unique to independent cinema, but their sustained presence in non-mainstream film also helps to construct varied audience responses. Intertextuality – the referencing of other media texts inside of a film – rewards knowing audiences who can spot the inclusion of elements from other media forms. Bricolage and pastiche (the referencing of aesthetic styles from other genres or time periods) is often used to prompt audience nostalgia – to create connections based on memory, but without the necessary knowledge to understand or decode these moments of bricolage audiences can construct misunderstandings or become distanced from the product.

Table 9.5 Challenge it: do mainstream films produce central imagining spectatorship?

• To what extent is it true that mainstream cinema produces passive consumption? Can you think of any exceptions to this argument? • What is problematic about the term 'independent' cinema?

Table 9.6 Revise it: passive and active narrative effects

- Do your film set texts use any of the narrative strategies described above? At what points do those effects surface in the film?
- What knowledge or experiences do audiences need to have to be able to successfully decode those moments?
- What kinds of viewers might be most likely to succeed or fail to understand those moments?

Exemplar: *Boyhood, Richard Linklater* **(Eduqas).** The realist pull of Linklater's ageing actors in *Boyhood* helps to construct spectator intimacy. Watching the film's actors grow up on screen compresses their fictional presence into carefully choreographed sequences that defy the narrative simplicity of mainstream cinema. Linklater engages his post-millennial primary target audience with nostalgia hooks – scenes that position viewers with POV shots of Wii games or snatches of Britney Spears. But to suggest that all of *Boyhood*'s spectators will align or interpellate themselves with Mason through the use of these cultural references misses much of the film's complexity.

Boyhood, perhaps, is constructed to create appeal for a much wider range of spectators, with the weight of the narrative deliberately dissipated across its multi-protagonist cast to effect identification for a wide range of genders and ages. The bowling scene provides an excellent example of how Linklater's cinematography helps spectators of all hues to align, where Linklater's even presentation of character eyeline (hugely unconventional when filming parents and children) invites audiences of all ages to connect with Mason and Mason Snr. as equals.

Equal weight is also given to each character in the editing of the scene, with Mason and Mason Senior's shifting screen position calling on audiences to resist the pull of a single-character alignment. Similarly, the resolution of the parents' argument towards the end of this sequence resolves in not one but two POV shots – again calling upon the audience to actively select from the brother's or sister's vantage point. Linklater's concern, as such, isn't to present the morally compromised world of *Boyhood* from a single perspective, but to deliberately invite active viewers, both young and old, to make connections with the film's richly observed multi-protagonist cast.

Table 9.7 Spectatorship: ten-minute revision

Structuralist, Marxist and psychoanalytic perspectives
• Early film criticism sought to produce single unifying explanations for how audiences engaged with film texts.
• Psychoanalytic film theory suggested that film spectators align themselves with characters while watching, using those character alignments to explore perfected versions of their real-world selves.
Post-structuralist responses
• Spectators use their individual knowledge and beliefs to challenge the ideas that filmmakers construct.
• Some films are constructed to encourage an active or ambiguous response from spectators.

Part III

Contexts and forms

10 Silent cinema

Table 10.1 What do you need to revise silent cinema for?

Eduqas
• **Component 2 Section C, film movements – silent cinema:** this section asks students to consider the use and purposes of realist/experimental filmmaking during the silent period.
OCR
• **Paper 1: Section A: film form in US cinema from the silent era to 1990 (Classical Hollywood cinema only):** it requires students to discuss the use and function of cinematography, mise en scene and editing during the silent era.
• **Paper 2: Section B: European cinema history (German Expressionism option only):** asks students to consider the contextual influences that underpin German Expressionism and to discuss the extent to which the narrative features of the movement were unique.

Essential background: early silent cinema – realist and expressionist storytelling modes

Film Studies is perhaps one of the few academic subjects in which it is possible to explicitly locate its origins. Of course, there were a number of prototypes that preceded the Lumière Brothers cinématographe projector, but their 25-minute programme of films projected in the Grand Cafe in Paris on 28 December 1895 is generally accepted as the first public screening of a moving image film.

To the total astonishment of their well-heeled French audience, the Lumière Brothers screening consisted of a range of one-shot shorts that variously depicted seascapes, a mother feeding her baby and a comic vignette of a young boy playing with a garden hose. Just a year later, the first film screening in England was made when Birt Acres introduced the Royal Photographic Society to his 39-second self-made short, *Rough Sea at Dover*. Acres' 1896 audience were similarly incredulous that a Dover harbour scene could be captured and replayed – that the real world could somehow be made to repeat itself with a degree of visual accuracy that had never been seen before.

Just six years later and the pioneer filmmaker Georges Méliès had built a purpose-built studio, complete with interchangeable painted backdrops that he used to film his 13-minute fantasy short *A Trip to the Moon*. Méliès' 1902 science fiction story charts the journey of a group of astronomers who are captured by an alien race when their space capsule crash lands on the lunar surface. Méliès' genius pushed the boundaries of filmmaking to extraordinary lengths – using stop motion photography and carefully crafted mise en scène to transport his audience to the furthest reaches of their imagination.

Acres' realism and Méliès' out of this world fantasy films encapsulate a debate that has been fought ever since regarding the purpose and function of filmic storytelling. Acre's early attempts at uninterrupted realism – his one-shot show reels of the natural world – exemplifies a brand of cinema that seeks to re-present the world we know, while Méliès' expressive films transport us to cinematic spaces that lie beyond our known reality. In many ways, the various film movements that followed Acres and Méliès in the early twentieth century – Soviet Montage, German Expressionism and American Hollywood – progressed those divergent visions of what film ought to do.

American Classical cinema

The American film industry quickly expanded in the early part of the 1900s, with, importantly, the vertically integrated ownership patterns of the seven major Hollywood players enabling them to reap huge profits. The major Hollywood studios, owned not just production studios but also the movie theatres where films were exhibited, allowing them to maximise their profits and to minimise competition by preventing more minor producers from screening their films in their theatres. Nor was Hollywood cinema of the silent era successful in America alone. The financial might of the industry enabled the production of high-quality films that dominated the international market.

The overriding stylistic direction of Hollywood output centred on:

- **An entertainment-driven focus:** importantly the output of Hollywood firmly centred around the production of content that was entertainment driven.
- **Realism and naturalism:** silent film from the period used a continuity-based aesthetic that looked and felt like Acres' representation of the real world – an aesthetic that has influenced mainstream cinema ever since.

Soviet Montage

In the wake of the 1917 revolution, the Soviet film industry was isolated from international influence, and where American filmmakers sought to entertain audiences with high-quality continuity led narratives, the purpose of Soviet Montage was overtly political, using jarring editing techniques to channel audience thinking to accept the communist-based ideologies of the newly formed Bolshevik State.

Soviet Montage foregrounds:

- **Editing as the principle means of producing meaning:** using montage and quick-fire editing tempos to inject abstract or symbolic meanings into film narratives.
- **Using film to construct overt ideological messaging:** where American Hollywood was driven by commercial imperatives, Soviet cinema was effectively placed under the total control of the Bolshevik state, producing a distinct film form that was hugely different from the Hollywood mode.

German Expressionism

Much like Soviet Russia, Germany's defeat in the First World War resulted in its cultural isolation and the development of an equally idiosyncratic style of filmmaking. Using German Romanticism as its starting point, the movement sought to explore human extremes, and, in so doing, produced an aesthetic that provided an interesting contrast to Hollywood realism.

German Expressionism gives weight to the following elements:

- **Expressive mise en scène:** as a result of Germany's post-war economic crisis, its domestic film industry had scant resources compared to their counterparts in Hollywood. Filmmakers compensated for their lack of production equipment and studio resources by using an approach that emphasised creative set design and performance-driven elements.
- **Liminal narrative content:** German Expressionism sought out narrative subjects that dealt with human extremes: madness, criminality or the supernatural. Where American film effected a largely reassuring narrative experience, German Expressionists sought to unsettle their viewers with low-key lighting, canted angles and untameable antagonist presences.

Table 10.2 Discuss it: André Bazin's celebration of realism

André Bazin founded the French cinema magazine *Cahiers du Cinéma* in 1951 and was a hugely influential figure in the world of film journalism and film theory from the 1940s onwards. He championed realist cinematic narratives, claiming that the true value of film lay in its ability to reflect the reality and beauty of our lived experiences. He advocated that films use long-takes and deep focus photography to reflect as accurately as possible the world around us.

Conversely, Soviet Montage for Bazin represented an approach that destroyed the continuity of the real world – its high-tempo editing style dissecting rather than reconstructing the beauty of lived reality. The importance of German Expressionism, too, was marginalised by Bazin, for whom the movement's manipulation of imagery offered audiences a coarsened or secondary cinematic aesthetic.

Table 10.2 Cont.

> Bazin's appraisal has been the subject of much criticism, with many commentators arguing that his celebration of realism offered an overly narrow assessment of expressive cinema forms. Expressionism, for example, might not mirror external reality, but it does reveal something important regarding our hidden psychologies.

- Do you prefer films that deal with the real world or stories that transport us to worlds that are fantastical or imagined?
- Do you prefer mainstream cinema or more experimental film forms?
- Are modern audiences less tolerant of films that use long-takes and straightforward editing strategies? Why or why not?

American silent cinema in the post-war years

Film historian, Kristin Thompson, suggests that American silent cinema by 1917 had fully transitioned from its primitive beginnings to assume – albeit in an embryonic form – the classical style that has so influenced Hollywood ever since. That development starts with the one-shot shorts and Vitascope films of the late 1890s which were exhibited in circus tents or Vaudeville theatres, and that used simple subject matter as content – mostly factual subject matter: boxing matches and seascapes, for example – or, less commonly, projected one-take recordings of established Vaudeville performers and dancers. The early novelty of such films quickly wore thin with audiences demanding longer films and more complex content, that, Thompson argues, prompted filmmakers to assemble films that were composed of multiple shots.

Crucially, the crude early use of multi-shot films invited filmmakers to tell fictional stories – stories that imported, albeit crudely, the strategies and narrative ordering devices of theatre and literature. Factual content, as such, was replaced by comedies, romances and westerns that were played by charismatic actors, many of whom started their acting careers in the popular Vaudeville theatres of the period.

Fast forward to 1917 and the Hollywood studio system, Thompson tells us, had fully fleshed out the storytelling conventions associated with Classical Hollywood film. The speed with which the American film industry progressed is partly attributed to the studio system that adhered in the United States, wherein the techniques forged by innovative individuals and forward-thinking film auteurs were quickly shared and reproduced by the big Hollywood studios.

Key conventions of the Classical Hollywood style that had been developed by 1917 include the following:

- **Continuity storytelling:** the classical style of filmmaking affects a natural or realistic feel, constructing smooth flowing stories that are audience-friendly and entertainment driven. The classical style, in this sense, lies at the opposite end of the filmmaking spectrum to Soviet Montage with its use of elliptical editing and graphic contrasts. The continuity style of Hollywood is affected through multiple shots that are edited together to give the impression that action is continuous. Multi-shot edits deployed ever faster editing tempos using intercuts, eyeline matches and, increasingly, match-on-action edits. Importantly, those editing techniques are routinely used by 1917 to produce seamless continuity edits. 180-degree shooting set ups, too, were adopted as a cinematic standard so that viewer's perspectives were kept stable, while scene endings were signified via standardised transition effects like iris fades.

- **Personal storytelling and cause and effect narratives:** where 1920s Soviet Montage sought to use film to narrate epic historical moments, American cinema of the period focused on character-driven stories that attended to the action of individual protagonists. Storytelling is personalised in American film – indeed, even those stories that sought to depict epic moments of history were narrated in terms of the effects of such events on individual characters. D. W. Griffith's deeply problematic *The Birth of a Nation*, for example, charts the aftermath of the American Civil War and the wider anxieties of black emancipation through the lead character of Ben Cameron – using a single lead protagonist to affect a personal portrait.

- **Star power:** the character-led storytelling of Classical cinema helps to drive the presence of star power in early silent films made in America. The character-driven approach of Classical cinema thrust successful actors into the public realm in a way that hadn't been seen before, with some actors repeatedly used by Hollywood producers who were keen to capitalise on their audience appeal. As such the character-driven quirks, movements, costume stylings and performance idiosyncrasies of successful actors were used as repeated motifs that audiences might instantly identify. Charlie Chaplin's little tramp persona is immediately recognisable, for example, through the character's trademark bowler hat, bow-legged walk and Chaplin's childlike innocence. Star personas, as such, were carefully cultivated as bankable film commodities, providing studios with ready-made plot expositions that audiences would readily engage with. Chaplin's tramp character, for example, invariably provided audiences with comedy-driven plot paths and misadventure-driven narratives wherein the star's underdog status could be used to manufacture instant audience empathy.
- **Genre-driven production:** American cinema's use of writers from the world of literature helped to nurture Classical Hollywood's genre-driven approach, and much like the popular fiction of the period, cinema stories were styled as westerns, romances, historical dramas or comedies. Genre-based styling also provided audiences with a marketable promise of specific filmic pleasures, while also yielding filmmakers a stable list of ingredients, character types, narrative structures and mise en scène decisions that helped films to be made quickly.
- **High production values:** investment in the American film industry during the 1920s was such that the industry rapidly expanded in terms of production facilities. Importantly, purpose-built studios enabled filmmakers to control production where innovative techniques like three-point lighting were applied as a standardised approach. High-key lighting techniques also helped to produce Hollywood's shadow free naturalistic feel, with key lighting used to inject lead protagonist star appeal via the use of key lighting strategies.

Table 10.3 Analyse it: Identify the use of American silent cinema
conventions

Continuity editing	• Identify the use and prevalence of continuity editing techniques such as intercuts, eyeline matches or match on action editing. • Identify moments of innovative continuity editing. These could include: over-the-shoulder shot exchanges, cross-cutting or the use of varied shot distances. • Identify the use of innovative camera movement to produce immersive experiences for audiences.
Character-driven storytelling	• Identify the use and prevalence of storytelling devices that enable single-character alignment, including eyeline matches and POV shots. • Identify the use of conventional narrative structures, three-act narratives and protagonist/antagonist-centred conflicts. • Where applicable, identify the use of character-driven stories as used to explore historical events.
Star power	• Identify the presence of stars where applicable. • Provide analysis of star motifs: gestures, acting styles, costume or associated story content. • Explore the marketing appeal of star power. • Identify the emerging use of director power during the period to market films.
Genre-driven approaches	• Identify the genre of the film and the use of any conventional ingredients. • Explore the ways that genre rules are tested or extended by your silent film set texts.

Table 10.3 Cont.

High production values	• Identify the use of multiple locations in shoots. • Explore the use of studio-based shoots and the level of control studio shoots enabled films to achieve. • Identify the use, prevalence and effect of three-point lighting – think how lighting produced a natural feel, yet also created a glamorous representation of lead actors.

Exemplar: *One Week* **(Eduqas).** The naturalistic continuity editing style of Classical Hollywood affects a firm grip on the aesthetic style of Keaton's films. In *One Week* (Figure 10.1), for example, the film's vaudevillian emphasis on physical comedy forms a central part of the actor's mass appeal, but even here eyeline matches are used to connect characters, invisibly binding multiple shoots as a cohesive whole; and where intertitles once provided jarring moments of exposition in silent film, Keaton uses them to articulate dialogue rather than to provide story direction – a sign of continuity editing's ability to carry audience interest without unnecessary exposition. The growing confidence of Hollywood continuity editing is also evidenced in the film's use of cross-cutting and the presentation of the villainous Hank as a distanced antagonist to Keaton's little guy hero. The match-on-action editing of the piano delivery, too, affects a seamless sense of continuity and demonstrates the maturation of cinema from its one-shot long-take origins just 20 years earlier.

The film also affects a Hollywood styled star presence through Keaton's straightlaced slapstick performance and his underdog ineffectuality; his star presence in *One Week* quickly eliciting sympathy from young cinema goers who were struggling to build their own family homes in the shadow of 1920s poverty.

Links to exemplar film clips and exemplars for other OCR/Eduqas film texts can be found at www.essentialfilmrevision.com

Figure 10.1 One Week (top): Buster Keaton's star-driven appeal was
realised through his strait-laced comic persona. *The Cabinet
of Dr. Caligari* (bottom): used ornately designed sets to
create visual interest with shadows painted directly onto
scenery to create added atmosphere.

German Expressionism

Initially, Expressionism was an early twentieth-century art movement that was principally interested in the idea of 'Sturm and Drang'. Literally translated as 'storm and stress', it was a term that encapsulates the Expressionist's fascination with the darker forces of nature and the idea that nature's terrors – storms, natural disasters or epic mountain ranges – evidence the raw power of God as the supreme creator. Expressionism was also interested in the terrors that could be found within – Norwegian painter Edvard Munch, for example, is often touted as the poster boy of Expressionism, his famous *Scream* paintings depicting the movement's fascination with the psychological horrors of modern life. Expressionism, in this sense, scoped the dehumanising effects of mass industrialisation on the individual – of factory production, urban living and the increasing mechanisation of everyday life in the early 1900s. The Die Brücke artist Ernst Kirchner's depiction, for example, of emaciated greyed out soldiers in his 1915 painting *The Artillerymen* exemplifies the movement's concerns that humankind was enduring a collective moral breakdown.

Expressionism, however, was largely over by the end of the First World War – its participants either dead or suffering from shell-shock as a result of the trauma of trench warfare. The movement's resurrection as a cinematic force is partly explained as a result of the migration of a few key practitioners from German Expressionist theatre into the rapidly expanding industry of filmmaking in the 1920s. Some critics further suggest that the ornate visual styles of Expressionist cinema were deployed as a deliberate attempt to elevate the status of films during the period and to invest them with the same kudos that had been attached to Expressionist art in the pre-war years. Other arguments are forwarded to suggest that Expressionist set design was used to compensate for the crude levels of technical production that German cinema makers faced in the years after the country's defeat in the First World War.

The economic woes of Germany in the 1920s also afforded the German film industry a commercial opportunity – largely driven by the industry's enforced insulation from the influence of foreign film imports. Hyperinflation in the German economy, crucially, prevented imported films from making substantial profits. The domestic German film industry, as a result, was afforded fewer competitors than other countries, and, as a result, was granted creative and commercial space to produce a form of cinema that was idiosyncratically German in terms of its style and narrative content.

1920s German Expressionism is readily identifiable as a result of its use of the following ingredients:

- **Chiaroscuro lighting styles:** shadow rich mise en scène is a vital component of the German Expressionist style, with contrasts of dark and light used to foreground the movement's interest in the extremes of human emotion. The shadowy worlds depicted in Expressionist cinema were not just achieved through lighting alone – in *Dr. Caligari's Cabinet*, for example, shadows were applied to sets to help concentrate the film's gloomy and foreboding presence (Figure 10.1).

- **An emphasis on set/design and other mise en scène elements over editing:** set designers were clearly influenced by the geometric aesthetic of Expressionist artists, using heavy patterns, diagonals and art nouveau-based motifs to invest films with visual interest. Canted objects also helped to sustain the off-centre depictions of Expressionist films, while ornately painted sets trapped actors inside of frames to help suggest their human frailty. Sets also suggested off-screen space in a way that hadn't been achieved before: staircases, for example, wind upwards to imagined spaces in Weine's 1920 German Expressionist masterpiece, *Dr. Caligari's Cabinet*, while *Nosferatu* emerges from the black interior of his castle, helping Murnau to imaginatively suggest that his limited set extended beyond what the filmmaker was able to show.

- **Actor/set blending:** Kristin Thompson and David Bordwell point, too, to the use of actor 'blending' (Thompson & Bordwell, 1994) as a deliberate strategy that was used to suggest the idea that characters could be readily absorbed by the worlds in which they were placed – that, in short, humans effect an insignificant presence in the world. Actor costumes, as such, are often styled so that they match or blend in with set designs, while actor poses were often held to mimic key shapes in scene settings.

- **Melodramatic acting styles:** German Expressionism is synonymous with a purposefully overplayed acting style in which exaggerated facial expressions were held – often in close-up – to communicate emotional extremes or to convey overplayed emotional reactions. Expressive subtleties are replaced by wide-eyed fear or uncontained fury. Realism is replaced by melodrama.

- **Repetitive actor movement:** was also imported from Expressionist German theatre and used to suggest human mechanisation. Some critics further suggest that exaggerated acting styles were encouraged to help actors stand out from the busy set decoration used by German Expressionist filmmakers.

- **Slow editing tempos:** German Expressionist cinema progresses at a much slower pace than that of wider silent cinema, principally to give time for viewers to appreciate and register the level of detail invested in mise en scène components. Expressionism too resists the emerging American-led fad for continuity editing, instead using long-takes and intertitles to advance plotlines.

In terms of story content and narrative direction, German Expressionism is also associated with the following traits:

- **An interest in the 'unheimlich':** translated as the 'uncanny', unheimlich plots – much like those of literary German Romanticism were interested in stories that centred around liminal subject matter, whether it be the supernatural world of Murnau's *Nosferatu* (Figure 10.2), the lunatic asylum of *Dr. Caligari* or the gambling dens of *Dr. Mabuse*. The locations of Expressionist films allow their stories to engage dark characters and plotlines that explore the outer limits of human reality, whether it be haunted castles, funfairs or the hidden lairs of master criminals. A range of supernatural plot devices and character traits are also associated with the unheimlich, with the use of character doubles, moments of coincidence or the interplay of unseen spiritual forces featuring heavily in Expressionist plotting.

- **An interest in the dehumanising effects of mechanisation:** Expressionism, too, routinely points an accusing finger at the strictures of modern living as seen in the early twentieth century, often using storylines as a thinly veiled criticism of industrialisation. In *Metropolis*, Lang's dystopian cinematic vision, an army of subterranean workers toil in life-threatening squalor while the social elites in the city above lead a carefree hedonistic lifestyle. Lang's *Spies* banker villain, Haghi, also hints at the shadowy control effected by the social elites of Germany in the Weimar Republic.

- **Rural/urban binaries:** Expressionist films also contrast the evils of modern life with rural ideals. In Murnau's 1927 *Sunrise*, for example, the film's rural hero is led astray by a city slicking femme fatale, with Murnau's montage of neon-lit city living persuading the film's anti-hero husband to murder his wife so that he might escape the humdrum poverty of his rural existence.

Context effects

The end of the First World War elicited economic, political and social chaos for the fledgling Weimar Republic. The fascination with corrupt or dangerous authoritarian figures in German Expressionism would certainly have struck a chord with German audiences who were mindful of the disastrous role played by Kaiser Wilhelm II in taking Germany into the war. The Kaiser's abdication in 1918, moreover, created a power vacuum, with groups of armed militias or Freikorps seizing control of major cities across Germany.

The Freikorps were often led by charismatic officers returning from the front. Freikorps' leaders also exploited the loyalty of demobilised men to form dangerous militias who engaged in organised crime, with some estimates suggesting that upwards of 1.5 million returning troops were co-opted into Freikorps groups in the early 1920s. Over 350 assassinations of politicians were attributed to Freikorps activity by 1922 alone. Certainly, *Dr. Caligari's* maniacal characterisation might be interpreted as a symbolic representation of the anarchy that German society experienced in the years following the country's 1918 defeat. Similarly, *Dr. Mabuse's* thuggish underlings provide further hints of the dark social forces that existed in Germany during the period.

German Expressionism: a unified cinematic movement?

Exam questions might ask students to assess the extent to which films solely exhibit the stylistic, aesthetic and narrative conventions of German Expressionism alone. The following arguments could be used in responses to suggest that films of the period offered audiences hybridised narrative stylings:

- **Kammerspiel and street film influences:** Expressionism wasn't the only film genre to emerge from Germany in the 1920s, what became known as Kammerspiel cinema provided a sharp contrast to the fantasy-based excesses of Expressionism. Kammerspiel settings were located in the dreary real world of poverty-stricken Germany of the period, and where Expressionism focused on the presentation of extreme human emotions, Kammerspiel effected slow-burn psychological portraits of the effects of poverty on lead characters. Murnau's 1924 film *Last Laugh* provides an excellent example of this 'street film' approach in its narration of the gutter bound descent of a hotel doorman after he's fired from his job. Murnau's 1927 *Sunrise* further evidences the director's fondness for realism with its location-led depiction of rural poverty. Fritz Lang, too, uses something of the 'street film' aesthetic in his depiction of his hobo operative in *Spies* – named only as no. 326 – who provides viewers with tender moments of poverty charged realism amidst the canted excesses of the film's celebrated chase scenes.

- **Films selectively apply the stylistics of German Expressionism to create export appeal:** the unexpected international success of *Dr. Caligari* in 1920 played a hugely significant role in shaping German cinema in the decade that followed. Caligari, much to Wiene's surprise, was hugely successful outside of the domestic German cinema market. Some critics argue that subsequent directors selectively applied the aesthetic nuances of Expressionism as a means to emulate the success of *Dr. Caligari* – applying the fantasy-based mise en scène and melodramatic excesses of Expressionism to add marketable flavour to what were, in essence, conventional genre-based narratives. Undoubtedly, films like Murnau's 1922 *Nosferatu* or Wegener's folk 1920 folk horror *The Golem* revel in the uncanny, exuding Expressionism's trademark sense of the unheimlich, yet as the movement progresses those moments punctuate rather than permeate, with canted cinematography and Expressive acting applied as stylistic adornments rather than as integral storytelling features.

- **The influence of conventional editing and narration:** the distinctive long-take mise en scène rich aesthetic of Expressionism is further diluted as a result of the increased use of Hollywood-driven stylistics. Subjective POVs, continuity editing, faster editing tempos and diffused lighting are as likely to be found in Lang's later work as Expressionist stylings.

Table 10.4 Analyse it: identify German Expressionist conventions

Lighting	• Identify the use and prevalence of low-key lighting. • Explore the effects of chiaroscuro lighting. How does lighting underscore the tone of the film? Where is lighting used to maximum dramatic effect in the film?

Table 10.4 Cont.

Set design	• Identify the use and prevalence of ornate sets. • Explore the effect that set design has on audiences. What connotations are achieved using painted backdrops? What functions do props serve? What do sets suggest about film characters? What do sets suggest about the world of the film?
Acting style	• Identify the use and prevalence of Expressive acting: repetitive movements, melodramatic poses, mirroring of set-based features. • Explore the effect that Expressive acting styles create. What extreme human emotions are produced? What does the actor's style suggest about human experience? How does acting work in conjunction with other elements?
Editing and cinematography	• Identify the use and prevalence of the editing and camera traits that are associated with German Expressionism: long-takes, canted angles and static camera shoots, for example. • Identify why those traits adhered: think about the technical equipment constraints and the concern to focus attention on elaborate set designs.
Narrative conventions	• Identify the use and prevalence of narrative concerns associated with German Expressionism: references to the unheimlich or the uncanny, tragic narrative structures, character doubles and narrative coincidence. • Identify the use of narrative subtexts associated with German Expressionism: rural/urban binaries, a fear of mechanisation, the dehumanising effects of modernisation.

(continued)

Table 10.4 Cont.

Contextual effects	• Identify the effect of historical contexts on film narratives. Think about the economic poverty of the Weimar Republic and the levels of social disorder that were prevalent in German society at the time.
Other aesthetic markers	• Identify the influences of other cinematic movements: the use of Kammerspiel ingredients and street films, or the increasing influence of Classical Hollywood ingredients.

Exemplar: *Sunrise* **(Eduqas).** Much like Murnau's *Nosferatu*, *Sunrise* provides audiences with a doomed romance that is undercut by a foreboding sense of darkness. The twilight scene of the male hero's temptation in the foggy marshes particularly suggests something akin to the German Romantic notion of Sturm and Drang – injecting a sense of terror and elation in the hero's decision to murder his wife. Exaggerated facial gestures also vent the film's emotional intensity at this point, while the lumbering zombie-like gait of the hypnotised hero thereafter echoes the stalking evil of Murnau's Nosferatu vampire (see Figure 10.2).

Narratively, *Sunrise* further echoes the anti-modern sentiments of German Expressionism and the movement's anxieties regarding the dehumanising effects of industrialised life in the early twentieth century. The banker femme fatale of the film symbolises the invidious effects of capitalism in her bid to lure the hero away from his life of rural simplicity – a theme that is reinforced through the fast-cut frenzy of the film's urban scenes later on.

Yet, to describe *Sunrise* as solely offering audiences an Expressionist aesthetic would be hugely controversial. The film was funded and made by the fledgling Fox studio in Hollywood, wherein American cinema's influences can be traced in the films use of continuity editing – in its use of match-on action cuts and the technical prowess evidenced within the special effects of the temptation scene. Similarly, the psychological intensity of the film's lovers when faced with poverty echoes the intense drama of films made by the German Kammerspiel movement, while the chaos of the film's street scenes, perhaps, owe more to the realism of Murnau's *Last Laugh* than to the use of the unheimlich narrative themes that permeate Nosferatu's unsettling horror earlier in the decade.

Figure 10.2 Nosferatu (top): Murnau's unheimlich vampire narrative as realised by the Expressive acting style of Max Schreck. *Man with a Movie Camera* (bottom): Vertov's portrait of Soviet industry places man and machine in perfect harmony.

Soviet Montage

Soviet Montage was the by-product of the Russian revolutions of 1917 and 1918 which saw the overthrow of the authoritarian Tsarist regime, replacing the monarchy with a people's government organised around Marxian principles. From the outset, the newly formed Bolshevik revolutionary government foresaw the potential for film to be used to convince the Russian masses of the worth of their communist agenda, initially setting up the Narkompros filmmaking unit in 1918 to produce pro-Communist newsreels and other low-budget agitprop films that toured rural Russia in mobile projection units.

By 1919, the newly formed Bolshevik government took complete control of both the production and distribution of Soviet cinema, nationalising all film production as well as establishing the centralised State Film School, overseen by the fledgling agitprop filmmaker Lev Kuleshov. Kuleshov's influence was huge, his montage-based approach to filmmaking emphasising the role of editing as the principal focus of film production. Kuleshov's approach and the resulting Soviet Montage aesthetic are marked by the following ideas:

- **Filmmaking is both science and art:** filmmakers were encouraged to think of the underlying scientific principles that allowed cinema to control the psychologies of viewers. Kuleshov argued, for example, that imagery in edits could be arranged in carefully controlled montages to build emotion or to communicate complex or abstract ideas. Kuleshov, too, considered editing tempo to be important in controlling the emotional reactions of audiences, with scenes in Montage films often working towards faster cuts as they progress to stimulate viewer excitement. Eisenstein's further refinement of montage, and in particular his use of intellectual montage, sought to build meaning using contrasting or disconnected imagery in sequences.
- **Revolutionary representations:** where Hollywood films sought to produce stories that were naturalistic or that reflected wider reality, Soviet Montage tried to project

a utopian version of Bolshevik life. Vertov's celebration, for example, of Russian life in *Man with a Movie Camera* underscores the state's drive to modernise production in the late 1920s, positioning Russian society as a harmonious and socially cohesive machine (Figure 10.2). Montage films also centred around moments of symbolic conflict, idealising, for example, the perpetrators of the failed 1905 revolution in Eisenstein's *Battleship Potemkin* or the celebration of the Bolshevik revolution in his 1928 film *October*.

• **Decentred subjects and epic narratives:** importantly, the Russian revolution of 1917 sought to emphasise community and collective responsibility: farms and factories, for example, were placed under communal ownership so that all society could reap the benefits wrought from what were once privately owned enterprises. Similarly, Soviet Montage withdraws from storytelling that focuses on the stories of individuals or that traces the personal plights of single protagonists. Montage substitutes single-character depictions with stories that narrate the experiences of the masses. Editing, of course, picks out individuals from those masses, spotlighting their role or their emotional reaction in the epic events Montage films depicted, but, crucially, that spotlight rarely lingers long enough for audiences to identify with any one single protagonist.

Where Expressionism advanced cinema as an art form through lighting and mise en scène, the innovative, highly stylised approach of Soviet Montage is affected largely through editing. Key Soviet Montage techniques include the following:

• **Rhythmic edits:** Soviet Montage routinely uses editing tempo to inject emotional energy into sequences. The crescendoed cutting of *Strike* and *October* reach peak tempo during crucial moments of conflict, often with shots lasting no longer than the length of a single frame to emulate the staccato fire of machine guns or to echo the chaos of street battles.
• **Overlapping editing:** this occurs where shots are repeated in sequences, usually from a different viewpoint or perspective –

used to emphasise the importance of a particular moment. At the start of Eisenstein's *October*, for example, the counter-revolutionaries' victory is symbolised through the repeated shot of a falling white horse.

- **Elliptical editing:** Montage filmmakers further subverted filmic realism by cutting films so that they compress time. In Eisenstein's *Strike*, for example, preparations for the workers' uprising is compressed into a short sequence, with shots of secret rendezvous meetings crossfading from full to empty spaces to signify the passing of time. Contemporary audiences, of course, are used to time compression treatments, but their invention and use by Montage filmmakers presents an interesting contrast with the cause and effect editing style that underscored Hollywood produced silent cinema of the period.

- **Intellectual montage:** Eisenstein is largely credited with the introduction of intellectual montage in Russian films of the 1920s, combining dissociated imagery to produce symbolic effects or to infer abstract ideas that realism alone couldn't produce. Perhaps, the most famous example is Eisenstein's cow slaughter reference during the climax of *Strike* that is used to underscore the inhumane treatment of the striking workers at the hands of their factory bosses in the wake of their failed uprising.

- **Graphic contrasts:** juxtaposition was also achieved through the sequencing of oppositional compositional effects, with montage sequences progressing via the use of shots that offer compositional contrasts – sometimes even mirroring imagery – to excite or confuse spectators with quick-fire sequences that dramatically shift viewer focal points. In *October*, for example, trains, tanks and the revolutionary masses march left then right in montages to create exciting and dynamic visual sequences.

Soviet Montage: more than an editing tour de force

Exam questions might ask students to assess the extent to which Soviet Montage films are driven by factors other than editing. The following arguments could be used in responses to suggest that film set texts experimented with a wide range of film codes:

- **Dynamic camera compositions:** it is easy to overlook the significance of composition given the rapid-fire nature of Soviet Montage, but individual shots also mattered in early Soviet cinema, with canted angles and extreme tilt used to reinforce power-based connotations across a great deal of Montage output. Similarly, *Strike's* repetitive use of closed framing loads later scenes of the film with a sense of cinematic peril.

- **Typage characters:** despite the lack of single-character narratives in Montage it would be wrong to suggest that Bolshevik cinema of the period cared little for character-based representations or that filmmakers merely reflected the reality of real-world Russia. The Soviet Montage approach advocated the use of what were called 'typages', using actors whose looks or physical appearance suggested a particular class or profession (Figure 10.3). An interesting example occurs when Eisenstein depicts the spies who are sent to infiltrate the workers at the beginning of *Strike*: the lowly animal nature of the counterrevolutionaries is exposed when their faces cross-fade into shots of their named animal counterparts – the monkey, fox, owl and bulldog.

- **Lyrical lighting:** much experimentation existed with regard to lighting too – a lack of fill lighting enabled villainous generals, policemen and other pre-revolutionary authority figures to be framed by an inky blackness, while Vertov's backlit steelworkers in *Man with a Movie Camera* affect a lyrical and romanticised portrait of heavy industry.

Table 10.5 Analyse it: Identifying the use of the Soviet Montage style

Narrative subtexts	• Identify the ideological role of Soviet Montage and its support for the post-revolutionary Bolshevik government. Think about Montage film's depictions of epic events and the reasons why filmmakers sought out these subjects. • Identify the use of decentred character-based narratives.
Editing techniques	• Identify the use and prevalence of key Soviet Montage editing techniques: rhythmic edits, overlapping editing, elliptical editing, intellectual montage and graphic contrasts.
Other conventions	• Identify the use of other stylistic conventions of the Montage movement: dynamic camera compositions, character stereotypes and lyrical lighting.

Exemplar: *Man with a Movie Camera* (Eduqas). *Man with a Movie Camera* clearly exemplifies the experimental editing of Soviet Montage. The film's high-energy rhythmic editing echoes that of other Soviet Montage directors in its use of rapid-fire montage. Vertov's editing also builds montages in ever faster rhythmic edits – his intention to convince audiences of the capacity and productivity of industrial Russia, while also depicting the harmonious machine-like cohesion of Russian society in its newly formed communist enterprise.

Yet, Vertov's film gives us more than just rhythmic or intellectual montage. Time reversed sequences of unfolding chairs and split-screen post-production effects paint reality rather than objectively revealing Soviet Russia through Vertov's notion of the Kino eye. Similarly, Vertov's carefully orchestrated montage of graphic matched sleepers at the start of the film suggests a lyrical concern to make cinema that celebrated the patterns and textures of Soviet society in addition to the ideological necessities of state-funded movie making (see Figure 10.2). Horse trap mounted cameras, canted compositions and tilt-up freeze frames of athletes further suggest Vertov's experimental use of camera movement and composition in addition to the editing strategies commonly linked with Soviet Montage.

Figure 10.3 *Strike* (top): the use of backlighting constructs a romanticised view of worker resistance. *Battleship Potemkin* (bottom): an archetypal Russian mother figure demonstrates Eisenstein's use of typage.

Table 10.6 Silent cinema: ten–minute revision

American silent cinema
• American cinema developed a distinctive continuity editing style. The studio-driven system deployed a naturalistic aesthetic, using realism rather than expressive experimentation. • Star power becomes a staple feature of American cinema in addition to a character-driven cause and effect narration style. • Exacting production values are evidenced as a result of Hollywood's vertically integrated organisation and its heavily commercialised approach. Films, as such, are produced using studio-based shoots and technically advanced lighting set ups.
German Expressionism
• German cinema was insulated from wider global influences as a result of Germany's isolation at the end of the First World War. • Expressionism is synonymous with dramatic lighting, highly Expressive acting styles and a focus on mise en scène elements. • After the wider success of early Expressionist films like *Dr. Caligari*, the German Expressionist aesthetic was applied to films to add marketing appeal for international audiences. • Towards the end of the 1920s, German Expressionism fused with other German storytelling styles – Kammerspiel, German street films and the continuity style of Hollywood.
Soviet Montage
• The Soviet film industry was insulated from global influences as a result of Russia's isolation in the wake of the 1917 Communist revolution. • The Soviet film industry was nationalised, effectively placed under the control of the Soviet authorities. Cinema was used for political and ideological purposes. • Soviet Montage under the steer of Lev Kuleshov placed emphasis on editing as a means of constructing meaning. • Editing techniques used by Soviet Montage filmmakers include: rhythmic edits, overlapping editing, elliptical editing, intellectual montage and graphic contrasts.

11 Classical Hollywood 1930–60

Table 11.1 What do you need to revise Classical Hollywood for?

Eduqas
• **Component 1 Section A, Hollywood 1930–1990 (comparative study):** students are asked to compare a set text film made during the Classical era with another film from 1961 to 1990. Students are asked to consider the contextual effects of the two periods and/or to consider the extent to which films evidence an auteur-based approach.
OCR
• **Paper 1: Section A film form in US cinema from the silent era to 1990:** focuses on the use and development of microelements to create meaning in set text films of the period.

Essential background: the Classical Hollywood style

Producer-led film control

The 1929 Wall Street Crash heralded an economic downturn that gripped America up until the outbreak of the Second World War in 1939. Mass unemployment and wage suppression during the period hit the film industry hard – reducing audience numbers, and, as a result, forcing the Hollywood majors to exact efficiency squeezes to maintain profitability.

At the same time, technological developments meant that the film production process was more complicated and labour intensive than ever before. The introduction of sound in the 1920s, for example, meant that dialogue had to be written by scriptwriters and recorded by new teams of audio specialist production personnel. Whole new departments of music-based personnel were also created to oversee the application of film scores and other non-diegetic sound treatments. The introduction of colour in the 1930s presented further challenges and expenses, with costly colour processing treatments necessitating the use of technical specialists on set as well as increased investment in set and costume design.

The major studios responded to the twin-threat of squeezed budgets and the expenses prompted by technological change by reorganising the management of film production, using producer-managers who oversaw the development, staffing, production and post-production of films from conception to completion. These producer-managers often specialised in a specific genre or type of film, and, more importantly, were tasked to control production spends so that films could be delivered on budget. The hugely successful Arthur Freed, for example, oversaw production of MGM's musical output during the 1940s and 1950s – effecting his own aesthetic stamp on the films constructed during his tenure.

The cost-based challenges of the period also prompted the major studios to reorganise key aspects of production into centralised teams. Make-up and costuming functions, for example, were often delivered by centralised departments for all films made inside of the same studio, while pre-production personnel – casting scouts, story researchers and scriptwriters – worked in bespoke divisions, sourcing story ideas that producer-managers were later tasked to oversee.

The Classical Hollywood style

The growth of producer-manager oversight and centralised production teams created a uniformity of style across studio outputs during the Classical Hollywood period. Importantly, the producer-managers tasked to oversee production were often more concerned with making risk-free films that were completed on budget rather than creating films that pushed experimental aesthetics. As a result, films were story-driven rather than exuding any stylistic experimentation, with camerawork, lighting and mise en scène used to serve storytelling functions rather than as expressive tools. Much like the Hollywood silent cinema of the preceding period, a common aesthetic is identifiable, that includes the following:

- **Quick-fire dialogue:** it comes as no surprise that the arrival of sound in film resulted in a focus on dialogue-driven storytelling. Hollywood films of the period certainly feel more dialogue heavy than contemporary cinema, using speech to narrate film story in a way that modern audiences might find staid or too heavy.
- **Character-driven cause and effect narration:** partly as a result of the heavy presence of dialogue, classical Hollywood films deploy a conventional storytelling style where plot progression is driven by character actions and reactions.
- **Three-track sound treatments:** by 1932 sound had advanced so that simple multitrack recording could be applied to films. Movies thereafter applied a rudimentary three-track system that allowed music, dialogue and simple ambient sounds to be heard at the same time.
- **Symphonic scores:** the use of fully scored musical accompaniments compensated in part for the rudimentary ambiences that could be achieved using the three-track system. Musical accompaniments were often lavish, using symphonic orchestras and lush string swells to underpin the emotional sentiment of accompanying action and dialogue. Longer musical interludes also began to be used to underline scene changes or to signify narrative transitions.
- **Grouped actor blocking:** the primitive nature of microphones during the period produced a staging style where actors had to be tightly grouped around concealed microphones on sets (Figure 11.1). Actors moved into or away from these huddled groups when scripts prompted

them to deliver dialogue. As a result, camera movement is often minimised during scenes that were dialogue heavy.

- **Soft-focus femininity:** a standardised approach to the shooting of female stars deployed low contrast, soft-focus camerawork to overlay a sense of glamour during romantic narrative moments (Figure 11.1). The soft-focus style froze female stars in moments of exalted romantic joy.

- **Limited camera movement:** the 1940s saw the development of some crane-based technologies that enabled limited horizontal and vertical camera movement. However, cameras were still bulky and unwieldy, and where crane or track-based technologies were available, they were often noisy and couldn't be deployed during dialogue delivery. As a result, elaborate camera movements were often reserved for scene intros where dialogue wasn't present – musical interludes were often applied during scene transitions to disguise the lack of diegetic sound.

- **The introduction of colour:** colour recording was introduced in the 1930s and was initially used to add exotic flavour to big-budget fantasy epics like *The Wizard of Oz*. Colour production, however, required specialist personnel, and, as a result was substantially more expensive than black and white film processing. The expense of colour production often prompted set designs and costuming that were colour rich to maximise the spectacle and expense of costly Technicolor applications. Of course, some directors saw the introduction of colour as an opportunity to explore new aesthetic directions – Hitchcock's red/green symbolism in *Vertigo*, for example, provides an interesting example of the early use of expressive colour.

- **Spectacle-oriented narratives:** the introduction of sound and colour resulted in an explosion of films that exploited sound or audio-based spectacle. Musicals were particularly popular, with the high-energy song and dance routines of the genre providing studios with the means to showcase new sound recording technologies.

- **Widescreen treatments:** another significant technological development was the introduction of widescreen projection, enabling the use of letterbox screen projection formats like Cinemascope. The larger screen widths were used to maximum effect in epic cinematic offerings like 20th Century Fox's biblical story of *The Robe* in 1953 where the film's epic use of extras and exotic filming locations could be fully showcased using widescreen projection.
- **Rear projection, mattes and optical printing:** a range of cinematic special effects began to be woven into cinematic offerings, enabling studio-based shoots to affect a bigger feel to films. Rear projection, for example, placed actors in front of pre-recorded material to suggest that action was taking place on location, while matte's used masks so that painted scenery could be added to scenes in post-production. Optical edits were often used to create montages that suggested the passing of time by superimposing newspaper headlines on top of footage.

Figure 11.1 Singin' in the Rain (top): the rudimentary microphones of the period required actors to deliver dialogue exchanges in blocked groups. *Casablanca* (bottom): the use of soft-focus compositions to frame female leads produced a dreamy depiction of femininity.

Table 11.2 Analyse it: identify key Classical traits in set texts

Character and narrative	• *Personalised storytelling:* does the film revolve around one or two central protagonists? • Is the plot of the film revealed through a cause and effect storytelling style? • Is the plot of the film easy to follow? Which moments of the film help to make the plot obvious for the audience?
Sound use	• How does the set text showcase sound as a film feature? • Does the film use dialogue-heavy sequences to drive stories forward? Where? • Does the film use a three-track soundtrack? What layers of sound are applied? • Does the film use a symphonic score as musical accompaniment? • Does the score affect a romantic or emotionally intense tone? • Does the score guide the audience's emotional response during the film? Where is this particularly evident? • Does the film use grouped actor blocking to record dialogue? How does this affect the editing tempo and the filming style of the set text?
Mise en scene	• Does the film use a high-key lighting set up? What is the impact of this lighting style? • How does the film showcase colour? Do sets and costuming deploy vibrant colour schemes?
Cinematography	• Does the film lack the use of expressive camerawork? • Does the film affect limited camera movement? Why? • During what moments in the film is camera movement deployed? • Are camera movements disguised by musical scores? • Does the lack of technology result in the use of a static camera style?

(continued)

Table 11.2 Cont.

	• Are female leads composed using soft-focus cinematography? What effect does this have on the representation of women in the film?
Other technological developments	• Does the film use widescreen technology? How is composition shaped to accommodate this new frame size? • Does the film use mattes, optical printing or rear projection? Do these features help the film to be made without the need for location shoots? How do these effects help filmmakers control sound and lighting?

Exemplar: *Singin' in the Rain* **(OCR).** It is a sign of Hollywood's maturity as an industry that MGM's 1952 *Singin' in the Rain* uses the 1920s invention of talkies as its backdrop to the film's performance-based extravaganza (Figure 11.1). Overseen by MGM's specialist in musicals, Arthur Freed, the film exemplifies much of the Classical Hollywood style of the period. It delights in the relatively new discovery of film sound, effecting a dialogue-heavy narrative and a jaunty orchestral score to construct escapist pleasures for its post-war audience. Built as a big-budget star-driven offering, *Singin' in the Rain* also uses performance and spectacle as ingredients to lure suburban audiences away from television-based competition. The deployment of Technicolor, too, adds additional visual presence with vivid costume colouring deployed to maximise the additional spend incurred as a result of colour processing.

The film's deployment of female-based soft-focus cinematography and its cause and effect narrative also suggests a conventional Classical Hollywood storytelling product. Don's 'rags to riches' tale, of course, provides audiences with a Hollywood compliant happy ending, while carefully choreographed actor blocking injects the energy of the popular screwball comedy genre. However, as a result of its frenzied stage blocking, the camera remains largely static with mid-shots mostly used to capture both the dialogue-driven performances of the film as well as its highly choreographed dance routines.

Scene entrances, however, provide an exception to the film's static shooting style, with a limited range of cranes and tracks enabled via the new crane technologies that were available by 1950. Camera movement, here, injects further energy and is most evident in scene openers as a means to showcase the film's elaborate and extensive

Table 11.2 Cont.

studio sets. The limited camera movements evidenced in the film, perhaps, also testify to the primitive nature of equipment in the early 1950s and the noise made when operated – in effect limiting the use of expressive camera movements to those scenes where diegetic sound could be omitted or disguised by score accompaniment. The film too takes advantage of other technological innovations of the period – its upbeat tone constructed through a Classical Hollywood high-key lighting style: the result of studio-based shoots that took full advantage of the relatively new innovation of back projection.

Ultimately, *Singin' in the Rain* exemplifies the formulaic big-spend producer-led approach of the period, while also offering us an example of the effects of technology in shaping cinema as a distinct artistic medium in the early 1950s.

Links to exemplar film clips and exemplars for other OCR/Eduqas film texts can be found at www.essentialfilmrevision.com

Table 11.3 Know it: film regulation during the Classical period

The growth and influence of the film industry in America during the 1920s drew considerable attention from a range of groups who were concerned by the immoral effects that cinema going might produce. Organisations like the Catholic Legion of Decency, for example, publicly condemned films that promoted lifestyles that were incompatible with the Catholic faith. In a bid to stop mandatory regulation by the Republican government, Hollywood also convened the Motion Picture Producers and Distributors Association (MPPDA) in 1922, which outlined a self-regulatory code that prevented producers from showing sexual content, criminal activity or profanity.

By 1934, the MPPDA'a regulations were consolidated as the Hays Code, a more rigidly enforced set of rules that if contravened could result in a profit crippling $25,000 fine. The subsequent effect on the moral content of films was enormous, with most filmmakers avoiding sexual depictions of any kind. However, filmmakers, especially towards the end of the 1950s, tested the code, using ingenious cinematic devices to infer moments of adult activity. Hitchcock, for example, cuts to crashing waves to infer Scottie and Madeleine's sexual union in Vertigo, while Billy Wilder's 1959 hit *Some Like it Hot* subdues the immoral import of its cross-dressing leads with a veil of slapstick comedy, beneath which are buried a myriad of gender blurring nods and winks.

Hollywood auteurs: challenges to the Classical Hollywood style

Genre-based production and the influence of emigre directors

The use of the producer-manager production model channelled film narratives in the direction of genre-driven storytelling – partially because of the various specialisms of individual producers but also because genre-driven productions were easily marketable. In the late 1950s, musicals, westerns and melodramas might have dominated film releases, but there also existed a growing number of directors whose working methods and stylistic nuances challenged the genre-driven conventions of the period.

The turbulence, for example, of Europe in the 1930s and the relative affluence and safety of the American film industry attracted a number of emigre filmmakers to the United States who invested their work with the aesthetic flourishes and narrative concerns of European cinema. Those directors had to work within the confines of the producer-led studio system, but they sometimes applied a sense of individuality to their films that later earned them the title of auteur filmmaker.

Key features of films produced by such directors included the following:

- **German Expressionist ingredients:** the Nazi's rise to power in 1933 and the glamour of big-budget Hollywood filmmaking lured directors like Fritz Lang and Robert Murnau to the Unites States who invested their films with a German Expressionist aesthetic, using low-key lighting, canted cinematography and a visceral film style that foregrounded emotion at the expense of naturalism. Alfred Hitchcock, too, stands out as an Expressionist influenced auteur – his experience of the German film industry during the 1920s, clearly reflected in his post-Second World War Hollywood output.

- **Film noir obsessions:** importantly, film noir was one of the only genres to buck the naturalist cause and effect narratives of Classical Hollywood, offering audiences flawed anti-heroes who often suffered tragic narrative resolutions – a distinctly different mode of storytelling to the feelgood resolutions of conventional Classical Hollywood. Film noir offerings also experimented with narrative storytelling, deploying voice overs and flashbacks, while also replacing the colour rich settings of escapist Classical Hollywood with the drab city worlds of urban America. Billy Wilder's B-movie hit *Double Indemnity*, perhaps, best reflects the low-key lit style of film noir during the period.

- **Experimental editing:** auteur filmmakers are notable not only for their use of innovative cinematography, but also for the remarkable degree of control they sometimes affected over editing. Studio controlled productions conventionally demanded that directors shot scenes according to a standardised approach – an approach that enabled post-production teams to assemble stories with relative ease. Cause and effect narratives were enabled, predominantly, using master shots, dialogue-driven mid-shots and the occasional use of a cutaway when crucial props were needed to be shown. In contrast, filmmakers, like the Soviet Montage influenced Hitchcock, storyboarded shoots to construct rhythmic editing effects or to deploy Kuleshov-styled montages.

- **Innovative use of new technologies:** one of the key commonalities of auteur directors of the period lies in their willingness to use new production technologies to provide alternative stylings. From Orson Welles' use of deep focus photography in *Citizen Kane* to Hitchcock's smash zooms in *Vertigo*, auteur directors pushed visual storytelling in new directions as a result of equipment experimentation.

Table 11.4 Revisit it: auteur theory

Revisit Chapter 7 (Auteur-based approaches) to read more about the competing theories film critics use to define auteurs.

Table 11.5 Revise it: auteur trends in Classical Hollywood

Auteurs of the period worked within the producer-controlled studio system. Use the following questions to help you identify key auteur effects in set texts:	
Expressionist aesthetic	• Do filmmakers use cinematography, sound or mise en scène for expressive purposes? Where and for what reason? • Do filmmakers use cinematography, sound or editing in subtle ways to reveal ideas or emotions that were unconventional within the Classical Hollywood style?
Film noir influences	• Do films use the experimental narrative strategies of film noir? Are, for example, flashbacks, voiceovers, unresolved or tragic endings deployed? In what ways do these devices defy the linear/resolved storytelling styles of conventional films of the period? • Do films use the character conventions of film noir? For example, are femme fatales, powerful females or anti-heroes used? In what ways do these devices defy the heroic male and passive female leads of conventional films of the period? • Are the stylistic features of film noir deployed? For example, is low key-lighting, urban settings, realism or expressive camera work used to style the film? In what ways do these stylistic flourishes construct an aesthetic that is radically different from conventional Hollywood films of the period?
Editing innovations	• Do films use montage, rhythmic edits or editing tempo in an unusual or interesting way? • Did filmmakers control the editing of their films? In what ways was this unusual for the period?
Innovative technology use	• What innovations in filmmaking were used by the authors of your set texts? What are the effects of those new techniques? How do they change audience perceptions of characters or the worlds of their films? • What techniques did the makers of your set text create or innovate?

Table 11.5 Cont.

Exemplar: *Lady of Shanghai* **(Eduqas).** Welles was one of the few directors who managed to affect some control of the post-production process – largely as a result of the kudos gained via his 1941 hit *Citizen Kane*. Yet even Welles struggled to find financial backing for projects, his reputation for overshooting during production marking him out as a director who was difficult to control and whose films weren't always commercially viable. Welles finally gained financial backing for *Lady of Shanghai* (Figure 11.2) from Columbia Pictures, and, in many senses, the film's soft-focus cinematography of Rita Hayworth and it's melody-driven soundtrack conformed to many of the expectations of films during the period. Yet Welles, unusually, oversaw both the production and post-production phases of the film, overlaying layers of expressive meaning during both stages that look and feel distinctly out of place within the mainstream Hollywood aesthetic of the 1940s.

Welles' use of film noir elements, for example, gave the director license to exercise narrative experimentation. The film's *in media res* opening, O'Hara's voiceover and Rita Hayworth's femme fatale antagonist characterisation offer audiences a number of film noir tropes, while the unconventionally tragic ending of the film – hugely different to the happy veneer of Hollywood resolutions – offers further significant narrative subversion.

In terms of technical control, too, Welles' low-key, shadow-rich canted photography is suggestive of a German Expressionist aesthetic; indeed, the film's highly experimental mirror scene pays homage to Wiene's *Dr. Caligari's* funfair setting, while Welles' trademark deep-focus cinematography helps to convince us of the immoral nature of O'Hara's world through the distorted profiles the shooting style produces. In terms of editing, *Lady of Shanghai* takes inspiration from the expressive styles of Soviet Montage: the film's introduction of Grisby, for example, offers audiences a jump-cut rhythmic montage that ends in a series of claustrophobic compositionally juxtaposed close-ups of O'Hara and Grisby that underscore their combative relationship.

Figure 11.2 The Lady from Shanghai (top): Welles' canted film noir approach owed much to German Expressionism (bottom). A more subversive version of femininity was constructed via the use of femme fatale stereotypes.

Contextual effects

The HUAC hearings

US paranoia regarding the influence and spread of Soviet communism prompted the setting up of the Congress-led House of Un-American Activities Committee (HUAC) in 1947. The government-sponsored HUAC hearings singled out individuals in the film industry that they suspected were left-wing sympathisers or were thought to harbour Communist leanings. Actors, producers, directors and screenwriters were called to the hearings and asked to denounce their colleagues and co-workers who they thought were left-wing sympathisers.

Ultimately, the hearings resulted in the blanket blacklisting of upwards of 300 filmmakers and creatives throughout the 1950s. The witch hunt mentality that took hold of Hollywood is reflected, perhaps, in a number of key films: Nicholas Ray's 1954 film *Johnny Guitar*, for example, suggests something of the paranoia of the period in the film's depiction of a town posse whose pursuit of the innocent Vienha mirrors the haranguing tone of the HUAC interrogations. The presence of Philip Yordan as the screenwriter of *Johnny Guitar* gives further credence to the film's pro-left sentiments in that Yordan was widely suspected to have anonymously employed blacklisted screenwriters during the 1950s. Hitchcock, too, reflects something of the period in the trial scene of *Vertigo* in which Scottie is subjected to a relentless interrogation, complete with canted reaction shots of the trial's jurors that lends the film an air of paranoia that is highly reminiscent of the HUAC hearings' abrasive interrogation style.

Subverted femininity and masculinity

Most directors deployed films that reinforced the rigid gender roles of the period – hyper-masculine gun-toting heroes often took central roles, while female leads were relegated to a soft-focus passivity. Film noir, however, provided filmmakers with a female character template that reversed the expectations through the all-powerful allure of the femme fatale. Again, *Johnny Guitar* provides an interesting use of that subverted female character type via the film's twin female leads of Joan Crawford and Mercedes McCambridge, both of whom affect a gender-defying control of the menfolk of the film. Crawford's balcony entrance in black-clad chaps, for example, provides a shockingly delicious spectacle of female empowerment for the period. *Some Like it Hot* also subverts gender expectations, using comedic cross-dressing to test the norms of straightlaced American society during the post-war years, while Maddie's duplicity in *Vertigo* offers audiences a version of passive femininity that camouflages a more active intent.

Table 11.6 Analyse it: auteur treatments and contextual forces

Auteur filmmakers used their output to outline subtle challenges to the hugely restricted social norms of post-war America. Use the following questions to help you identify key historical factors that filmmakers explored in their work:	
HUAC	• Do films reference American paranoia of Communism?
Subversive gender treatments	• Do films challenge or reinforce the traditional outlooks of the period in terms of gender? • Is comedy used to present gender transgression in a non-threatening way? Are subversive characters presented as villains or femme fatales?

Table 11.7 Classical Hollywood 1930–60: ten-minute revision

Essential background: the Classical Hollywood style
• Hollywood films of the period were controlled by a producer-manager led system. • The producer–manager led system resulted in the production of entertainment-driven films that minimised expressive or experimental filmmaking content. • The introduction of sound channelled films to include fast-paced dialogue and symphonic musical accompaniment. • Colour film was introduced, but was reserved, initially at least, for big-budget films. • Films often deployed a straightforward cause and effect storytelling style.

Table 11.7 Cont.

Hollywood auteurs: challenges to the Classical Hollywood style
• Auteurs often incorporated the aesthetic or editing styles of European cinema: Soviet Montage, German Expressionism or French poetic realism. • Auteurs often worked within the film noir genre. Film noir afforded some creative space to make films that subverted the Classical Hollywood aesthetic. • Auteurs often pioneered new production technologies. • Auteurs used films to challenge the norms and conservative political outlooks of the period.

12 Experimental film

Table 12.1 What do you need to revise experimental film for?

Eduqas
Component 1 Section C, British film since 1995: questions in this section of the exam ask students to evaluate how useful narrative-based approaches are in understanding the impact of set text films on audiences. An understanding of the use of more experimental storytelling structures could prove hugely useful when answering these questions.

Component 2 Section D, experimental film: requires students to discuss the extent to which set text films are experimental.

OCR
Paper 1 Section B, European cinema: might ask students to evaluate the extent to which chosen surrealist films (and to a lesser extent other European film movements) use experimental narrative structures or alternative stylistic presentations. Students might also be asked to consider the significance of the use of non-traditional narrative structures.

Paper 2: the specification does not explicitly refer to experimental filmmaking in this exam, but an understanding of genre hybridity and alternative narrative forms could be used when tackling exam questions across the paper. Areas that this chapter might be useful for include:
• **Section a:** an understanding of how non-traditional narratives are used to position spectators in contemporary US and British film.
• **Section c:** an understanding of the role that alternative narrative structures play in constructing ideology and representations.

Essential exam knowledge: moving beyond traditional narrative structures

Subversions of the three-act structure

Both independent cinema and contemporary filmmaking routinely test the classic three-act structure, offering audiences more experimental forms of storytelling by fragmenting or reordering timelines or by telling stories that shift character perspective across the arc of the film. Breaking the rules of three-act storytelling can engage contemporary audiences who, arguably, are overly familiar with the predictable rhythms of equilibrium, disequilibrium and new equilibrium storytelling. Contemporary audiences, as such, are more cine-literate than ever before. Those audiences, moreover, are suitably equipped to decode complex narrative arcs.

The three-act formula, too, presents filmmakers with an overly rigid storytelling schematic – a schematic that invariably produces narratives in which flawed protagonist characters are magically healed. If filmmakers want to tell stories that narrate tragedy or that outline doomed protagonists, they need to find alternative narrative mechanisms to work within.

Table 12.2 Revisit it: traditional three-act narratives

Visit Chapter 6 (Theories of narrative) to remind yourself of the core structure and function of traditional three-act storytelling.

Narrative restructuring

Filmmakers – particularly independent filmmakers – depart from traditional three-act structures by adapting or altering conventional storytelling formulas. Common strategies include the following:

- **Unresolved timelines:** indie narratives often produce stories that don't end with the happy resolution of a new equilibrium. Instead, they create characters who fail to complete their quests or offer us storylines that leave audiences with unresolved endings. Those unresolved endings can be used to infer tragedy, or, alternatively, to produce ambiguous meanings. Narrative ambiguity also prompts active spectatorship – forcing the audience to imagine how stories might end for themselves via the information supplied during the film's narrative. Other stories might end with ambiguous resolutions to assert the complexity of the character's film existence.

- **Circular narratives:** occur when stories refuse to end with a new equilibrium transformation, finishing instead with the suggestion that central characters are trapped within a cycle of repeated action. Circular narratives are often used to underline character tragedy through their suggestion that protagonists are unable to transform their self-destructive behaviours or escape the tragic circumstances of their lives. In the *Hurt Locker*, for example, Sergeant James' return to the front to repeat another tour of duty foregrounds his continued self-destructive behaviour, while the alien's death at the end of *Under the Skin* presents her existence as part of a wider cyclical pattern of female exploitation.

- **Condensed equilibriums:** contemporary audiences increasingly demand that film narratives deliver action or disruption from the outset. Filmmakers respond by providing narrative hooks or by condensing initial act one equilibriums – using what's called 'in media res' to immediately engage audience attention with a moment of crisis at the start of a film. The frenzied jump-cut opening of *The Hurt Locker*, for example, inserts audiences into the chaos of the Iraq war at the very start of the movie, with the sequence's disorienting energy reflecting the realities of the war arena from the get-go of the film.

- **Frame stories:** these are stories that are told within a wider story, using complex layers of narrative to place the main action of the film within a wider context. Frame narratives often start and end with action that is displaced from the main body of the film. *Pulp Fiction*, loosely speaking, provides a good example of the strategy in its use of the diner hold-up sequence to bookend the film. Frame stories use narrative layers to immerse audiences in cinematic universes. They can also be deployed as devices to reveal secondary stories before returning to the main action of a film.

- **Disjointed prologues:** a distinct strand of film storytelling exists in which filmmakers preface action with narrative sequences that don't fit with the cause-and-effect logic of the rest of the movie. Kubrick's introductory ape scene, for example, in *2001: A Space Odyssey* and Terrence Malick's strangely abstract prehistoric prologue in *The Tree of Life* locate the human actions of their central stories within a wider evolutionary context.
- **Anachronic devices (flash forward/flashback):** anachronic devices test the linear storytelling expectations of conventional narration, reordering scenes or sequences so that they appear out of order. Films generally use anachronic devices to inject enigma, suspense or anticipation. Flash forwards, for example, might be used to relate story endings before they have occurred – to give enigmatic hints of future events that lie within the film's storyline. Flashbacks, conversely, might be used to outline character backstories or to revisit screen action from an alternative perspective.
- **Smashed timelines:** some films super-charge anachronic storytelling to the extent that any semblance of a linear timeline is minimised – literally smashing the timeline of a film. Because smashed timelines can easily confuse or disorientate viewers, their use is usually restricted to Avant Garde or surrealist film output (see below for further explanation).

Character-driven narrative subversions

The charm and simplicity of the three-act structure's use of single-character protagonists is increasingly tested by contemporary cinematic output. Perhaps the long-format multi-protagonist box sets of on-demand television have helped more than anything else to test the simplicity of the single hero story structure. Certainly, contemporary audiences can now track multiple character arcs with greater ease. Common character-driven subversions include the following:

- **Multi-focalisation narratives:** tell the same story using a range of character perspectives. Films with multi-character protagonists often crosscut from one character's experience to another, switching story arcs at narrative climaxes in order to maintain audience interest. Narratives that use multi-protagonist plots also help to broaden audience appeal by offering viewers a range of identities that they can align themselves with. Multiple character arcs can also be used as narrative counterpoints or for oppositional effects: the twin tracked narrative of *Carol*, for example, compares the experiences of upper- and lower-class gay women via the parallel revelations of Carol and Therese's stories.

- **Unreliable narration:** is created when films are related from the point of view of a dishonest or unreliable character. Films can use unreliable narration to reflect the experience of a character who has a limited world view. *Room*, for example, proceeds via the viewpoint of five-year-old Jack to shield the audience from the grotesque horror of his mother's kidnapping. Unreliable narration might also be used to deliberately disorient the audience. In Duncan Jones' dystopian sci-fi film, *Moon*, for example, the memories of Sam are revealed as fake implants, aligning the audience with the horror of Sam's dawning realisation that his Earthbound dreams are a lie.

Postmodern stylistics

Films have also adapted a variety of narrative and aesthetic idiosyncrasies that further challenge the three-act storytelling model. These include the following:

- **Metanarrative and intertextuality:** these provide audiences with moments that knowingly draw attention to the idea that they are watching a story. Metanarration might knowingly refer to a film as a media construct or speak directly to audiences through fourth wall breaks. Also known as reflexive filmmaking, this postmodern device begins to circulate after film becomes an established cultural presence and where its historical back catalogue of output can be referenced through moments of intertextuality. Directors of the French New Wave, for example, integrated reflexive moments as a result of their shared interest in pre-Second World War filmmaking: Godard's anti-hero lead Michel in *À Bout de Souffle*, for instance, models himself on the screen-based persona of Humphrey Bogart. Intertextual references of this kind make use of sequences that reference other films and visual media forms. Intertextuality, as such, rewards knowing audiences who can spot potential links to other products or can prompt questions regarding the social/psychological effects of film as a cultural force. Intertextuality, too, can be deployed to provoke audience nostalgia or to piggyback on the emotional resonance of the scenes that are reproduced.

- **Parody and homage:** parody and homage provide extended moments of intertextuality wherein filmmakers provide extended references to other artforms. Homage invariably celebrates the influence of other artists and filmmakers. Parody, conversely, references external media for the purposes of humour or to offer a critique.
- **Bricolage:** films can also offer experimentation by collaging the styles of several different film aesthetics. Czech New Wave Director, Věra Chytilová, for example, incorporates a range of aesthetic styles in *Daisies*, where moments of dreamlike surrealism give way to a more sombre documentary aesthetic or the psychedelic excesses of stop motion animation. Tarantino, too, builds films using bricolage – his costume and sets in *Pulp Fiction* borrowing elements of film noir, Rock and Roll and 1960s hippy culture in a way that makes it difficult to be totally sure as to the exact historical setting of the movie.

Table 12.3 Discuss it: do contemporary audiences expect films to experiment?

The extent to which the subversive strategies outlined above are experimental is debatable.
• Are contemporary audiences more able to negotiate narrative complexity? Why? • Can a film that uses a simple three-act structure still engage audience interest? Why not? • Can you think of any successful films that have recently applied a traditional narrative structure?

Table 12.4 Three-act subversion narratives: essential revision questions

Use the following questions to help you diagnose the effects of narrative subversion in your set text films:	
Narrative restructuring	• **Flashback use.** Are flashbacks used to convey important backstory? Do flashbacks reorientate the viewer or reveal important information? • **Flash forwards**. Are flash forwards used to tease audiences or to promise specific viewing pleasures later in the film? • **Unresolved endings.** In what ways does irresolution promote active spectatorship? • **Circular narratives**. In what ways do circular narratives, if used, suggest that a character might be trapped or incapable of transformation? What actions or behaviours are repeated? • **Frame stories and disjointed prologues**. Is the story framed within another story? What is the relationship between these narrative layers? How do frame stories disorientate the spectator?
Character-driven subversions	• **Multi-character focalisations**. Does the story resist the use of a single-character focalisation? Does this lack of clear character alignment prompt active spectatorship? • **Unreliable narration.** Can we trust the viewpoint of the film's central character? What are the effects of unreliable narration on the audience?

Table 12.4 Cont.

Postmodern stylistics	• **Intertextuality**. Does the text reference other films or media products? Does this create nostalgia? Does intertextuality create comedy? Does it reward spectators who can identify these moments? Does intertextuality promote an intellectual assessment of the film? • **Metanarrative**. Does the film contain moments where the story acknowledges its status as a film? Do these moments suspend passive viewing? Are these moments used to promote active spectatorship? • **Bricolage**. What visual styles or forms does the film combine? What emotional or tonal effects do those borrowings enable the film to produce?

Exemplar: *Pulp Fiction* (Eduqas). *Pulp Fiction's* smashed timeline offers audiences some semblance of experimental film storytelling. From the outset, the diner flash forward, for example, delivers a promise that the film will provide delayed narrative pleasures. That initial promise of action-based pleasure is delivered when we return to the diner at the end of the film. But, importantly, Tarantino also uses his frame narrative to outline a moral reappraisal of Jules, and, in this sense, we might suggest that the film returns to the kind of single-character transformation storytelling that we associate with more traditional three-act narratives. Jules' changing outlook – his transformation from the apathetic bible preaching hitman in earlier sequences to the forgiving ex-gangster at the end of the movie – ultimately underlines the positive moral subtext of the film. Importantly, Vince Vega's smashed narrative death scene in the middle of the film further helps audiences to make sense of the film's redemption subtext in that our knowledge of his future death tells us that Vega's unchanging outlook at the end of the film ultimately leads to his death. Yes, Tarantino provides us with experimental narrative motifs, but, ultimately, they are packaged within a traditional quest narrative in which the central hero's weaknesses are clearly resolved.

Links to exemplar film clips and exemplars for other OCR/Eduqas film texts can be found at www.essentialfilmrevision.com

Genre subversion and genre hybridity

Table 12.5 Revise it: genre basics

Visit Chapter 6 (Theories of narrative) to remind yourself of the functions and viewing pleasures derived from genre-driven storytelling.

Assessing the impact of genre in individual films requires analysis that explores how genre-based rules are both applied and adapted. As explored further in Chapter 7, genre-driven conventions are selectively used or bypassed as a result of the approaches that individual filmmakers adopt during production. Auteur filmmakers apply and break genre-based conventions to shape stories using their own artistic direction. Genre-driven output, in this sense, does not offer us a static classification system, but presents us with an ever-changing set of rules that individual filmmakers continuously bend and reshape.

Genres, too, can be fused or hybridised, sometimes spawning entirely new subgenres of film. The ever-changing nature of audience tastes plays a pivotal role in sustaining or even reviving commercially successful genres, while those film types that fail to attract box office success are casually forgotten.

Some film academics further suggest that most contemporary filmmaking exhibits a hybridised approach in which narratives combine elements from across several established genre forms to help nurture audience appeal. Genre hybridisation as a narrative formatting strategy appeals to contemporary filmmakers for the following additional reasons:

- **Hybridity enables quick tonal shifts:** film stories can quickly change emotional effects using hybridisation. *Guardians of the Galaxy*, for example, neatly switches emotional gears as a result of its hybridised approach, alternating from moments of humour to the more serious and escapist pleasures invoked by it's science fiction based elements.
- **Audience appeal is expanded:** films need to garner widespread appeal to be successful. Combining ingredients from

several genres is one way that films can grow their audiences. Many commentators suggest that British cinema output in the 1990s used hybridisation to nurture mass audiences for UK-produced films. Edgar Wright's zombie/black comedy hybrid *Shaun of the Dead* perhaps exemplifies the economic benefits that this form of hybridisation delivered.

- **Nostalgia:** hybrid narratives can invoke audience nostalgia by referencing genre-based character or narrative tropes. *Pride's* social realist/comedy-driven approach, for example, charted a narrative course that invoked much earlier UK-based hits like *Billy Elliot* (2000) and *The Full Monty* (1997).
- **Knowing audience rewards:** the sheer weight and scope of film/media consumption in the contemporary era means that contemporary audiences are far more knowledgeable. Hybrid products both acknowledge and reward knowing spectatorship by including intertextual references to products from across a range of genres. *Shaun of the Dead*, for example, is saturated with intertextual references that pay homage to zombie films and their directors, partly to encourage multiple viewings but also to nurture fan engagement for the film.

Table 12.6 Revise it: diagnose genre hybridity effects

Think about the following questions to help you diagnose the effects of genre hybridity:

- What genres/subgenres does the film incorporate?
- In what ways does the use of genre hybridity expand the film's audience reach?
- What narrative pleasures does the use of genre hybridity enable?
- What emotional pleasures does the use of genre hybridity construct?

Exemplar: *Ex Machina* (OCR). *Ex Machina's* use of genre hybridity enables the film to access several genre-driven narrative pleasures while also maximising its box office potential. The narrative sets up a conventional 'corporate greed versus the individual' thematic binary, a theme extensively explored within contemporary US-oriented science fiction output and that is particularly evident across the hugely successful and contextually relevant *Alien* franchise.

(continued)

Table 12.6 Cont.

We might argue that the inclusion of this universally recognisable thematic binary in *Ex Machina* also helps to generate much needed global box office appeal for the film.

The further injection of a thriller-driven narrative strand widens the potential audience of the film again, enabling Garland's story to move beyond the male-oriented technology-based pleasures of science fiction and to incorporate the enigma-driven pleasures of the thriller genre. As such, the film shifts from noir-style low-key lighting in its depiction of Caleb's surveillance of Nathan to more traditional science fiction presentations in which CGI-based action is placed centre stage. Genre hybridity, in this sense, enables the film to adopt quick tonal shifts and to prompt an alternating fear/ wonder-based response from *Ex Machina's* audience.

Experimental film movements

Surrealism's challenge to conventional narration

The development of surrealist film in Europe during the early twentieth century parallels that of European modernism – a stylistic and aesthetic revolution that cut across literature, art and architecture. Modernism was in part fuelled by the technological innovations of the period. In architecture, for example, the discovery of new building materials like concrete and steel radically altered building design. Modernists, too, focused on the subjective nature of human experience in ways that previous artistic movements hadn't considered. Artists like Edward Munch explored the effects of social change on the individual – the decreased role of religion and the corrosive effects of twentieth-century industrialisation – with Munch famously capturing the emptiness of modern living in his iconic *Scream* paintings.

In literature, too, writers like James Joyce and T. S Eliot sought to explore human psychology, using stream-of-consciousness prose styles and the unstructured rawness of free-verse to express their inner realities. It's no accident that modernism exploded at the same time that psychologists like Sigmund Freud were mapping human behaviour as the product of internal drives and instincts.

Film too was increasingly used by modernist artists. Indeed, the new technologies of cinema provided a set of new and expressive creative tools that artists could use. Certainly, film's ability to reimagine the real world coupled with its combined application of the disciplines of art, theatre, literature and painting attracted a number of creatives to use this new medium during the period. Perhaps one of the most significant groups to explore the possibilities of film was the European-based Dada collective that included artists like Marcel Duchamp, Salvador Dalí, René Magritte and Luis Buñuel – all of whom explored their interests in the subconscious via the new artistic possibilities that film opened up.

The origins of Dada were initially rooted in the burgeoning cafe culture of Europe during the pre-First World War period, a world where intellectuals, thinkers and artists discussed and debated a range of new political ideas. Dada surrealism, however, didn't truly adhere until the end of the First World War in 1917 when the hope and optimism of European intellectual thought was tempered by the deaths of over 20 million soldiers in the most destructive conflict ever witnessed.

For the Dada movement, the Europe-wide conflict exemplified the horrors of twentieth-century modernity. Trench warfare came to symbolise the mechanised destruction of human life, while the mental traumas induced by the war prompted Dada artists to look inwards to probe the origins of mankind's inhumanity in the modern era. In this sense, the inner worlds explored by the Dada surrealists provided both a refuge from the horrors of modern life while also pointing to the therapeutic capacity of introspection.

Film, of course, was readily used by the Dada surrealists, whose dream-soaked narrative style endures – to varying degrees – in filmmaking today. The most celebrated surrealist filmmaker of the period was Luis Buñuel, who's collaboration with Dada superstar, Salvador Dalí, produced the iconic short *Un Chien Andalou* in 1929, followed by the longer surrealist film *L'Age*

D'or in 1930. Both films carve out ethereal narratives that try to detail the power of the subconscious in disjointed, symbol-rich sequences. The film historian Michael Richardson, for example, tells us that, 'the central concerns of Buñuel's work, in fact, is with the establishment of authority: how it functions not simply to maintain itself through society, but also how it replicates itself within the individual and collective psyche' (Richardson, 2006, 35).

Buñuel's films not only articulate the power of desire in governing human behaviour, but also help us to understand the way that authority represses those desires. In a much celebrated scene in *L'Age D'or*, for example, two lovers are torn from their primal embrace by a mob of strangers and Church officials. Once separated, the female lover cross fades into a bubbling froth of sewerage. Here, Buñuel's less than subtle montage offers a clear critique of religion's role in suppressing sexual freedom.

Buñuel's filmmaking, as such, is hyper-subjective – less concerned with the interplay between characters and more interested in how the psychological processes that govern individuals are formed. The wider strategies used by surrealist filmmakers include:

- **Narratives abandon cause and effect progression:** real-world logic is readily abandoned in surrealist stories- timelines move forward using coincidence or via symbolic connections. Scenes transition using graphic matches or cuts that connect shots using patterns or textures rather than a sense of real-world continuity. We might further argue that surrealist narratives work through lateral connections or dream-based logic.
- **Central characters are passive:** where mainstream film stories progress as a result of character actions – heroes, for example embarking on quests in which their decision-making produces consequences and narrative progression – in con- trast, surrealist narratives often deliver passive characters who are positioned as witnesses to the actions of others.

- **Everyman characterisation:** surrealist films usually construct characters that lack personal details – names, identities or backstory. Characters, too, often assume archetypal roles such as mothers, fathers, lovers or priests. As such, surrealist film communicates using everyman characters who come to represent universal human experiences, or, conversely, who symbolise wider social forces.
- **Narrative sequences tend to be episodic:** where traditional three-act structures progress using an equilibrium/disequilibrium character journey, surrealist narratives offer disjointed episodic sequences in which the central character's world is consistently shown to be in a state of flux or change. Moments of disequilibrium, invariably, are succeeded by further moments of disequilibrium in a manner that suggests that the world at large is chaotic or all-consuming.
- **Meaning is constructed using visual symbolism:** surrealist narratives work using rich visual symbols that represent subconscious desires or repressive actions.
- **Time treatments are distorted:** surrealist narratives readily repeat sequences as well as stretching or speeding up time.

Table 12.7 Revise it: surrealism

Use the following questions to help you explore the meanings and impact of the surrealist films you are studying:

- Is the central protagonist active or passive in the film? What does this suggest about human experience in the modern world?
- What character archetypes are we given in the film? What do these characters suggest are the social forces that shape the human experience?
- What symbols are used within the narrative? What psychological or social forces do these symbols represent?
- How is time treated in films? What do elliptical sequences or stretched edits suggest about our experience of the world?
- What does the dream logic of surrealist narratives suggest about the way that the human mind works? What role do human instincts play in guiding our behaviours?

(*continued*)

Table 12.7 Cont.

Exemplar: *Un Chien Andalou* (OCR). Buñuel's *Un Chien Andalou* (see Figure 12.1) dream-suffused narrative conveys many of the themes of the modernist project as it stood in the early twentieth century. The lacerated eye of the opening sequence infers that the ensuing imagery of the film isn't a projection of an external reality but an internal portrait of the Freudian desires and repressions that make for the human subconscious. The film's female protagonist subsequently longs to revive her gender transgressing lover, her needs reciprocated with an animalistic and toxic masculine desire. Faceless forces, too, torment the film's protagonists, punishing the sleepers of the film in a show of social shame.

Buñuel's surrealist narrative progresses with a dreamlike logic that explores the workings of the human psyche. Swarming ants graphic match into the chaos of a circling crowd. We are reduced, Buñuel suggests, to the role of passive voyeurs: entranced by the misfortunes of others, yet simultaneously incapable of any sense of personal emotional fulfilment. And where Buñuel's film suggests that his everyman characters are passive, he asserts a much more potent role for the machinery that so invaded early twentieth-century life. Indeed, Buñuel forwards the modernist notion that twentieth-century life is somehow alienating – his use of bicycles, cars and guns in his films invariably playing a destructive role.

Figure 12.1 Un Chien Andalou (top): Buñuel's surrealist short explores the desires and repressive forces that lie within the human psyche. In the scene depicted above the film's dreaming protagonist is tied to two priests who prevent the dream hero from reaching his lover. *Vivre sa Vie* (bottom): Godard's unconventional composition presses the film's tragic protagonist into the lower half of the frame.

The French New Wave

The French film movement that came to be known as the
Nouvelle Vague or the New Wave was shaped by four distinct
influences:

- **Changing audience tastes:** by the late 1950s film
  attendance in France had declined steeply with major
  releases recording substantial losses. The industry responded
  with several measures to stimulate new talent. A combin-
  ation of industry subsidies and a new 'advance on receipts'
  funding system enabled a new generation of directorial talent
  to make their first features.
- **Technological advances:** the availability of lightweight
  cameras and the development of long lens technologies further liberated young French filmmakers. Filmmakers were
  no longer tied to static cameras – nor did they have to make
  films in expensive studio production facilities. Handheld
  cameras, instead, enabled a raw location-based aesthetic that
  looked more documentary than fiction-based.
- **Youth culture explosion:** a well-educated and politically
  savvy generation of young people also emerged in France
  during the late 1950s and early 1960s. The influence of
  Rock and Roll, Hollywood films and American Jazz, as
  well as the explosion in popularity of culturally savvy French
  intellectual writers like Jean-Paul Sartre and Albert Camus
  helped to nurture a countercultural youth movement who
  railed against the country's occupation of Algeria and French
  Indochina.
- **The influence of *Cahiers du Cinéma:*** the hugely influential film magazine *Cahiers du Cinéma* shone a critical spotlight
  on French film, simultaneously critiquing the 1950s French
  film industry that was overwhelmingly dominated by high-
  brow adaptations of literary classics, while also celebrating
  the output of maverick auteur filmmakers in Hollywood
  like Alfred Hitchcock, Orson Welles and Nicholas Ray.
  Indeed, it's no accident that many of the writers of *Cahiers*

– François Truffaut, Jean-Luc Godard and Claude Chabrol – transitioned from film journalism to filmmaking and were responsible for a great deal of the output that came to be labelled as French New Wave.

A personalised film movement

The youthful energy of the French New Wave provided a disparate range of films, hugely varied in terms of subject matter and style, but at the core of the movement lay a concern to revitalise French filmmaking and to invest films with personal storytelling. In many ways, that central concern is a reaction to French 'prestige' cinema of the 1940s and 1950s and the literary form of filmmaking that inserted established star power into epic and heavily romanticised film stories. The French New Wave movement, in contrast, is associated with the following narrative and aesthetic traits:

- **A documentary style aesthetic:** the use of real locations and handheld camera work constructed a documentary aesthetic with long-takes and observational camerawork used to dial up the realism of New Wave films.
- **Coincidence-driven narratives and existential themes:** much of the narrative excitement produced by the movement's films are created by episodic narrative structures where coincidence and chance meetings drive events. The use of coincidence also helps to suggest existential themes and the idea that individuals are subject to the forces of fate rather than acting as agents of free will. In *Vivre sa Vie*, for example, Nana's fate is determined by a chance meeting with her would-be pimp Raoul in a cafe – a meeting that leads, ultimately, to her tragic death.
- **Narrative irresolution:** French New Wave narratives lack the neat endings of traditional filmmaking. The use of unresolved endings helps to nurture a more active form of spectatorship, prompting audiences to determine for themselves how character dilemmas are resolved. New Wave

directors also resist the urge to punctuate their films with resolved endings in order to underline the objectivity of their films, with the lack of any resolution preventing New Wave films from constructing overriding judgements regarding the characters presented.

- **Youth culture celebration:** unlike French prestige films of the 1950s, the New Wave directors staged their stories in the gritty worlds of contemporary urban France – a world that young audiences of the period would be able to connect with. Directors also employed unknown actors to underpin the New Wave's audacious attempt to reboot the ailing French film industry. Films also work around anti-authoritarian plot points, using characters who freely commit crimes without compunction or who find themselves in confrontational situations with older authority figures.

- **Scene intensity:** New Wave directors revel in scene intensity, pushing audiences into a form of spectatorship that rejoices in the 'here and now' of a film moment. Where traditional film narratives use scenes as building blocks that deliver enigmas or that point audiences to the climactic thrill of a final act, New Wave films prompt us to revel in the intensity of scene exposition and to appreciate the zen beauty of the here and now. In *À Bout de Souffle*, for example, Godard pauses the overarching plot of the film for a staggering 24 minutes to give us an intimate portrait of Patricia's seduction by Michel. The jump-cut scene meanders, almost without motivation, in a way that underlines and celebrates the youthful innocence of both characters.

- **Metanarration and reflexive filmmaking:** the *Cahiers* inspired origins of the French New Wave and its highly intellectual assessment of film as art, unsurprisingly translates into the making of films that discuss and reference other films. In *À Bout de Souffle*, for example, Michel repeatedly mimics Humphrey Bogart in a way that pays homage to American film noir, while in *Vivre sa Vie* Nana's emotionless mask is allowed to temporarily slip as she watches Dreyer's *The Passion of Joan of Arc*. In both films, cinema is acknowledged as an important cultural filter that plays a significant role in shaping our identity.

- **Sound and editing experimentation:** yes, New Wave films used handheld cameras to produce a kind of documentary realism, but directors also apply a variety of stylistic treatments that elevate New Wave films beyond naturalism. Jump-cuts condense time in abrasive edits, soundscapes cut sharply to moments of prolonged silence, authentic newsreel footage and voiceovers are collaged to create a curious mix of fact and fiction – a mix that prompts audiences to draw narrative conclusions that convey a real-world political resonance.

- **Low-fi aesthetics:** the small budgets of New Wave films coupled with the limited access to equipment afforded to New Wave directors also resulted in the production of a raw lo-fi aesthetic. Dialogue was often dubbed onto films during post-production as a result of location shoots. The much-celebrated jump-cut editing style also associated with New Wave films was similarly deployed as a low-tech editing solution when Godard was asked to reduce the length of *À Bout de Souffle* so the film could be given an appropriate theatrical release.

Table 12.8 Revise it: French New Wave analysis

Use the following questions to help you explore and assess the experimental features of the French New Wave films you are studying:	
New Wave narratives	• How is the narrative of the film constructed? Does the film use an episodic structure? • Does the film's narrative feel fragmented? What is the effect of that narrative fragmentation? • What's more important in the film – the overarching story or individual scenes? What is celebrated about the human condition in key scenes? • Reflexive filmmaking: Why do French New Wave films reference other films? What is the director telling us about the value and position of cinema as a cultural force?

(*continued*)

Table 12.8 Cont.

The New Wave aesthetic	• What effect does jump-cutting have on audiences? • Which scenes exemplify composition-based experimentation? Why has the film been styled in this way? • Where is sound experimentation used? In what ways is sound used experimentally and for what reason? • Where in the film is a documentary aesthetic visible? How does this aesthetic affect the tone of the film? • In what ways do camera innovations of the 1960s help to construct the New Wave's documentary aesthetic?
Existentialism and youth culture	• What do New Wave films suggest about human existence? What do they tell us we ought to value in life? • What do the tragic narratives of the New Wave suggest about the human condition? • How do the locations chosen create connections to youth audiences? • What effect do actor choices have in shaping the New Wave aesthetic?

Exemplar: *Vivre Sa Vie* **(Eduqas).** In *Vivre Sa Vie*, Godard's compositional control feels deliberately amateur at times, pressing subjects into the corners of shots or deliberately framing Nana using long-take and low-eyeline compositions that emphasise the character's insignificance (see Figure 12.1). Nana is presented as a factual yet insignificant presence – presented in an observational documentary aesthetic in which camera movement is minimised to suggest an observational objectivity. The effect is peculiarly personal, helping us to connect with Nana's treatment by the authority figures who so nonchalantly pass through her life. Similarly, Godard's framing of dialogue and his use of rear headshots constructs a disorientating, unconventional and purposefully distanced portrayal of the film's central character: a fitting accompaniment perhaps to Nana's lifeless dialogue and compressed actor presence. Godard's intentions clearly were to construct a personal portrait while simultaneously distancing the alienated Nana from viewer alignment. Godard's approach seeks, as such, to observe tragedy in a way that doesn't over-sentimentalise the film's tragic subject.

Table 12.8 Cont.

A similar effect is constructed via *Vivre sa Vie's* fragmented score: snatches of lilting minor key phrases abruptly give way to silence – the musical accompaniment pointing out the emotional turmoil of Nana's life, yet also refusing to saturate the film with musical excess. *Vivre sa Vie's* narrative, too, is driven by abrupt coincidences – chance encounters in cafes and bars – with Nana's prostitution providing the perfect narrative frame for Godard to survey the underbelly of contemporary urban France in the 1960s. Importantly, the director uses those moments to intrude upon a series of characters in a way that produces psychological or philosophical insight. The episodic structure also produces contrasting vignettes: Nana's profound loneliness when she is rejected as a prostitute, for example, is immediately juxtaposed with an 8-minute-long treatise on the nature of love with the real-life French philosopher Brice Parain.

The film's crushing seriousness is punctuated too by occasional moments of humour: Luigi's balloon blowing impression and Nana's oddly youthful dance add moments of levity, while Godard's vignettes of Nana inject ample opportunity for his audience to revel in the youthful beauty of the then unknown Anna Karina.

Table 12.9 Challenge it: how experimental was the French New Wave?

Certainly, the French New Wave constructed a significant aesthetic contrast to the French prestige cinema of the 1940s, but can we really argue that it offers the same level of experimental storytelling of say surrealism or even of the Czech New Wave? In many senses, we might argue that Godard uses traditional storytelling that is augmented with several aesthetic or narrative flourishes. Consider the following questions to help you think about the extent to which French New Wave films were truly experimental:

• To what extent do films use linear plots that are driven by single-character action?
• To what extent do films recycle familiar themes – for example, the notion of unrequited love or familiar binary oppositions such as youth versus authority?
• To what extent do films deploy an overarching narrative structure?

(continued)

Table 12.9 Cont.

Exemplar: *À Bout de Souffle* **(OCR).** Godard's jump-cut, high-energy, hand-held approach in *À Bout de Souffle* offered audiences a new cinematic aesthetic. The use of ECU scene starters and circular camera tracking endlessly disorientates the audience, inserting spectators into a subjective filming style that hadn't been commercially used before, while long lens shoots in real locations also lend the film a documentary-like objectivity and a sense of raw realism.

Godard's style, perhaps, reflected the energy of a countercultural and youthful France in the 1960s, a France that was looking to free itself from its imperial past. The jump-cutting style, so celebrated within the film, perhaps also reflects something of the economic necessity of the production of the film in that Godard's abrupt editing is largely attributed to his need to radically reduce the runtime of the film so that it could be commercially distributed. The film's much celebrated documentary aesthetic too is symptomatic of the needs of the film's restricted budget – with location shoots and natural lighting used to minimise costs.

The film too recycles several common cinematic themes. It offers us a conventional set of binary concerns – action versus desire, honesty versus pretence, youth versus authority – while the overarching plot delivers a conventional story of unrequited love. True, the film offered audiences a youthful and defiant message, but even here, Michel's Humphrey Bogart inspired criminality recycled the narrative energy of American film noir and its love of anti-hero protagonists.

Table 12.10 Experimental film ten-minute revision

Essential knowledge: beyond three-act narratives

- Contemporary filmmakers subvert the three-act template using narrative-based subversions: flashbacks and flash forwards, narrative irresolution, circular narratives and frame-based storytelling.
- Filmmakers challenge the traditional three-act structure using character-based subversion: multi-character focalisations and unreliable narration.

Table 12.10 Cont.

- Filmmakers use postmodern stylistic devices to further subvert three-act storytelling, using both metanarration and intertextuality to prompt intellectual viewing responses.
- Avant Garde and surrealist filmmakers offer audiences alternative storytelling modes that use non-linear narratives that progress using coincidence rather than cause and effect action.

Genre subversion and postmodern stylings

- Filmmakers use genre-driven conventions as a template for filmmaking.
- Genre hybridity is used to widen audience engagement and to author quick tonal shifts.
- Intertextuality, bricolage and reflexive filmmaking are used to add stylistic and aesthetic complexity to films.

Experimental film movements

- Surrealism rejected cause and effect narration, instead constructing meaning through visual symbolism and narratives that progress using a dream-like logic.
- The French New Wave forged a highly personalised style of filmmaking that used a documentary aesthetic and a range of other stylistic innovations such as jump-cutting, collage and non-conventional framing techniques.

13 New Hollywood 1961–90

Table 13.1 Use it: why do you need to revise New Hollywood?

Eduqas
- **Component 1 Section A, Hollywood 1930–1990 (comparative study):** asks students to explore the potential impact that auteur filmmakers have on the construction of meaning in films. This section might also ask students to consider the extent to which individual auteurs or the collaborative efforts of filmmakers are responsible for the overall look and feel of a film.

OCR
- **Paper 1, Section A, film form in US cinema from the silent era to 1990:** the emphasis in exam questions in this section of the paper is placed on the use and selection of microelements to construct meaning.

Essential background

The foundations of a New Hollywood aesthetic

The 1960s produced a new and daring rejuvenation of the film industry in America. A variety of forces combined that presented a wave of new talent with the opportunity to make movies, hugely successful movies, that turned the Classical Hollywood aesthetic upside down. Young acting talent emerged from the television industry, alongside a small but hugely influential trickle of graduates from film courses in American universities. Those new actors injected new techniques, primarily the immersive method acting approach, while the director graduates of the newly formed film schools reworked and repurposed the Classical Hollywood film aesthetic using the filmic styles of European cinema.

The influence of this new wave of talent was greeted by the film industry with a lukewarm welcome at first, but the economic problems and declining audiences of the late 1950s and 1960s pushed the industry to reappraise its filmmaking approach. The Paramount Decrees of 1948, for example, dealt a series of economic blows to Hollywood during the period, forcing the major studios to give up their monopoly ownership of US cinema theatres, a move that allowed smaller film production companies to distribute their output more easily. The Paramount judgements also deprived the big studios of the huge profits they were able to generate from cinema-owned ticket sales.

Increased competition from independent producers also played a pivotal role in opening up Hollywood to new production ideas, and, moreover, prompted a switch from a production process that was controlled and managed by producers to a more creative production model in which films were placed under the artistic control of directors.

The Production Code breaks down

The expansion of independent filmmaking in America was slow, but by the late 1960s companies like American Independent Pictures (AIP) began to develop a significant market presence. AIP, under the creative direction of Roger Corman, made low-budget films for the burgeoning teen audience market – films that afforded a host of new wave directors and actors their first breaks in the industry, including Francis Ford Coppola, Jack Nicholson and Robert de Niro.

The increase in independent production also helped to erode the power of the once mighty Motion Picture Association of America (MPAA) – the organisation that was responsible for the regulation of films via its hugely restrictive Production

Code (informally referred to as the Hays code). Importantly, the only real sanction that the MPAA could enforce if their rules were broken was to prevent films from being shown in MPAA member theatres. Given that the Paramount Decree ordered the major studios to sell off those theatres, the code's most significant sanction was effectively blunted. As a result, independent producers increasingly flouted the MPAA's Production Code rules by including more sexually explicit and violent content to create youth appeal for their movies. Key changes prompted by the Production Code breakdown included the following:

- **Increased sexual content:** the Production Code prevented sexual references of all kinds as well as scenes of nudity, requiring Classical Hollywood films to use passionate embraces or symbolic references to suggest moments of intimacy. The gradual breakdown of the Production Code made for a sexier and more explicit form of filmmaking.
- **More violent content:** depictions of brutal killings, drug and alcohol abuse or criminal action that audiences might copy were similarly censored. Filmmaking, once freed of these restrictions, revelled in depictions of criminal violence, dialling up death scenes and placing morally dubious anti-heroes at the centre of film plots.
- **Anti-authority plot lines:** the MPAA Production Code also directed filmmakers to show respect to the American flag and to exercise caution when criticising American institutions. As such, MPAA policed films, by and large, exercised a patriotic and unquestioning tone. For several contextual reasons, filmmaking in the late 1960s adopted a more questioning presence, producing storylines that cast American authority in a less patriotic glow – the erosion of the Production Code further enabled those representations.

The post-war baby boom and youth-oriented cinema

America in the 1960s was also experiencing huge social change. The children of the baby boom explosion that occurred at the end of the Second World War were teenagers and young adults by the 1960s, and, where their parents before them had supported traditional values, the post-war baby boomers adopted a more countercultural outlook. In the 1960s, American youth celebrated anti-authoritarian rock stars, they attended civil rights demonstrations and held anti-Vietnam protests. The intergenerational tensions of the period were further reflected by the fragmented nature of film attendance, wherein older viewers continued to watch traditional Classical Hollywood fair, or replaced cinema going for the comfort of home television viewing. Younger audiences, in contrast, embraced the New Hollywood aesthetic that emerged from the deregulated and director-driven output of American filmmaking during the period.

New Hollywood in the 1970s

Arthur Penn's 1967 release of *Bonnie and Clyde* is often seen as a watershed moment in the history of contemporary cinema in that the film's overt sexualisation of its lead characters and its glamorisation of outlaw violence offered a direct challenge to the Production Code. More importantly, the film was a phenomenal success, and, as such, demonstrated to Hollywood that new themes and methods could be financially lucrative.

A rash of similar films followed, William Goldman, for example, penned the 1969 hit *Butch Cassidy and the Sundance kid* – recycling the bandit outlaw formula of *Bonnie and Clyde* to equally rave reviews. Mike Nichol's *The Graduate* introduced Dustin Hoffman in his morality bending tale of intergenerational seduction, while Dennis Hopper's drug-fuelled road movie *Easy Rider* further opened the door of cinema to the pleasures of immoral excess.

The countercultural films of the late 1960s also paved the way for a new generation of directors to emerge in the 1970s – an assertive circle of talent, known collectively as the New Hollywood. They were young filmmakers who had studied the director-driven New Wave films that emerged from France in the 1960s and who took inspiration from those filmmakers who operated within Hollywood on their own terms – directors like Arthur Penn and Stanley Kubrick. The New Hollywood directors – Martin Scorsese, Francis Ford Coppola, George Lucas, William Friedkin, Brian De Palma and Steven Spielberg – are household names now, but in the early to mid-1970s they fought to make films within an established production system that knew it needed to change but was simultaneously suspicious of new working methods.

The New Hollywood directors were lucky, too, in that they arrived at a time when the studio system turned to new talent as a means to connect with younger audiences and to rectify the plunging cinema attendance figures television ownership incurred. The New Hollywood filmmakers initially realised projects in the face of financial adversity, but once established, were able to dictate their own terms. Reputations, for example, were often established as a result of surprise blockbuster hits – with the phenomenal success of films like *The Godfather* (Coppola) and *Jaws* (Spielberg) generating enough studio clout to allow the New Wave of directorial talent to determine the direction of their own films thereafter. Key traits of the New Hollywood directors include the following:

- **European influences:** several directors of the New Wave were film school trained, and, as such, were influenced by European Cinema from France and Italy. The docu-style aesthetic of the French New Wave as well as Italian Neorealism were particularly influential and orientated directors towards stories that centred upon working-class American characters.
- **Stylistic experimentation:** the New Hollywood aesthetic didn't wholly abandon the cause and effect-driven storytelling mode of Classical Hollywood, but it did offer a much wider range of experimental stylistic flourishes. Freeze frames, telephoto shooting, increased use of extreme compositions (long-shots and extreme close-ups), sound and image mismatches as well as jump-cutting, improvised sequences and handheld shoots were more readily deployed.

- **Psychological insight:** films of the period also strove to reflect the psychological realities of their main characters – offering audiences a subjective storytelling style that sought to illustrate the inner worlds of characters. Harry Caul's unravelling mental landscape is depicted, for example, in Coppola's *The Conversation* via a smoke-filled dream sequence, while the inner voices of Scorsese's characters are often realised via mirror performed monologues – in Travis' seminal 'Are you looking at me?' moment in *Taxi Driver*, or Jake LaMotta's 'I could have been a contender' reflection in *Raging Bull.*

- **Pop culture links:** the New Hollywood directors, too, understood the importance of the explosion in pop culture that took place during the 1960s and 1970s. Directors piggybacked on blockbuster novels or connected films to celebrity musicians in a way that fashioned links to the burgeoning pop culture of the period. Scorsese's role, for example, in editing the film documentary of the iconic Woodstock festival of 1969 helped to carve out his Hollywood credentials, while Milos Forman established his cinematic pedigree by adapting Ken Kesey's bestselling countercultural 1962 novel *One Flew Over the Cuckoo's Nest.*

- **Authority mistrust:** directors too reflected the deep mistrust of established authority within their films. The Watergate scandal of the Nixon administration was a particular catalyst for the questioning mode of filmmaking that emerged in the early 1970s. President Nixon's resignation in 1974 followed revelations that he had ordered the Democrat party's headquarters to be bugged prior to the election of 1972. The deep-seated mistrust of authority that followed is a feature in several set texts, from Spielberg's shady government operatives in *E.T.* to Coppola's direct reference to the Watergate incident in his surveillance spy thriller *The Conversation.* Opposition to the Vietnam War also surfaced in several key films, explicitly so in Coppola's epic anti-war film *Apocalypse Now* and Michael Cimino's harrowing portrait of the Vietnam War in *The Deer Hunter.*

Table 13.2 Revise it: New Hollywood filmmaking traits

Filmmakers in the 1960s and 1970s were afforded more creative freedom as a result of the Paramount Decree, the erosion of the Production Code and changing audience tastes. Use the following questions to help you explore those contextual effects on set text films:	
Freedom from producer control	• How did filmmakers free themselves from the control of studio producers? Did they deliberately shoot films in remote locations or use non-studio-based financial support? • Did filmmakers manage to effect creative control as a result of the success of previous films they made? Which films? • Did filmmakers have to assert creative control in productions? Were there any director/studio conflicts produced as a result?
Production Code breakdown effects	• Does the film contain moments of explicit violence? For what purpose does the filmmaker use violence? • Is criminal behaviour referenced in the set text? Is criminal behaviour glamorised? • Does the film adopt a critical viewpoint of American authority? What is that viewpoint and where is that critique demonstrated most clearly? • Does the film use anti-heroes? What social forces does the anti-hero battle? • Does the film contain explicit sexual content? How does this content affect the portrayal of women in the film? • Does the breakdown of the MPAA Production Code help to construct a more realistic portrait in the film?
Youth audience effects	• Do central protagonists challenge conservative ideals? • In what ways do the central protagonists construct relatability for a youth audience? • Do films connect with pop culture of the 1960s? How and where?

Table 13.2 Cont.

European cinema influences and stylistic experimentation	• Does the film subvert the cause-and-effect storytelling of classical Hollywood? • Does the film use a non-linear narrative? • Does the film experiment with mise en scène, lighting, editing or sound? Where is this experimentation most obvious? • Do we see a similar aesthetic to that deployed by the French New Wave: docu-realism, working-class characters, handheld camera work, jump-cutting or subjective storytelling?
Psychological insight	• Does the film help audiences to understand the inner world of its central character? How? Are dream sequences, voice overs or monologues used in a way that gives audiences access to that inner world? • Do psychological portraits help to construct tragedy? • Does the film outline a character who is conflicted by the world they live in?
Authority mistrust	• Does the film critique government power or other sources of authority?

Exemplar: *Bonnie and Clyde* (Eduqas). Arthur Penn's slow motion resolution in *Bonnie and Clyde* presented audiences of the period with a shocking and controversially violent climax. The film's final scene in many ways also exemplifies the new found freedom that was beginning to be enjoyed by directors in the late 1960s. Freed from the hugely restrictive Production Code, *Bonnie and Clyde's* anti-hero-led plot was able to construct a glamorisation of violence that Hollywood films weren't able to do before the Paramount Decree stifled studio control (Figure 13.1). Warren Beatty's producer role in the film is also key to understanding the text's anti-authoritarian impulse and its eventual box office success. Beatty, for example, deliberately moved filming to Texas to help minimise undue interference from the film's Warner Bros. studio financiers, but when finally seen, studio executives were so appalled that *Bonnie and Clyde* was given a limited release in American cinemas. However, the film's fashion-conscious sex appeal – mostly realised through David Newman and Robert Benton's script – struck a

(continued)

Table 13.2 Cont.

chord with young British audiences, giving Beatty another window to convince Warner Bros. to agree an extended rerelease of the film in the United States.

Benton and Newman were themselves hugely influenced by the anti-hero glamour that underpinned so many films of French New Wave cinema. They understood the potential appeal that an anti-authoritarian film might have with a young countercultural American audience who were critical of the Vietnam War and the conservative attitudes that so dominated post-war America. In this sense, we might argue that the film foreshadows the collective auteurial zeitgeist of New Hollywood in the1970s. Freed from the control of Warner Bros. business-oriented producer-manager oversight, the actor/producer talents of Warren Beatty coupled with the subversive script of Benton and Newman and the then unrealised directorial talent of Arthur Penn enabled a more creative filmmaking model.

Links to exemplar film clips and exemplars for other OCR/Eduqas film texts can be found at www.essentialfilmrevision.com

Figure 13.1 Bonnie and Clyde (top): Penn's iconic gangster film
offered audiences levels of on-screen sexuality that hadn't
been seen before. *Apocalypse Now* (middle): Lt. Co.
Kilgore – *Apocalypse Now's* surfboarding squadron leader –
helps the film construct its anti-war critique. *Some Like it
Hot* (bottom): Cross-dressing in the film tested the rigid
gender-based norms of traditional America.

Table 13.3 Director focus: Francis Ford Coppola and the New Hollywood aesthetic

'I was into the New Wave and Fellini' Coppola tells us, 'and, like all the kids my age, we wanted to make those kind of films' (Biskind, 1999, 143). Coppola might have graduated from the newly established University of California film school with an idealistic outlook, but by 1970, Coppola and George Lucas' Zoetrope film production company was indebted to Warner Bros. to the tune of $300,000. Coppola had had enough of shooting film adaptations of popular novels, wanting instead to turn his attention to more serious film projects, but the scale of Coppola's debts forced him to accept an offer from Paramount to direct *The Godfather*.

Coppola continuously clashed with Paramount executives during the production of the film. He insisted upon the use of *The Godfather's* historical setting, and, moreover, that maverick method actor, Marlon Brando, play the lead role of Don Corleone. Shooting, too, quickly fell behind schedule – Coppola spent inordinate amounts of time working with actors during rehearsals, often shooting as little as one take a day. Coppola, too, agonised over casting decisions for extras in ways that Hollywood hadn't really observed before – his attention trained on constructing a kind of New Wave realism and a sense of authenticity that mainstream films usually bypassed.

The unexpected scale of *The Godfather's* eventual box office success – a staggering $150 million in sales in 1972 alone – gave Coppola the kudos and financial means to effect greater control of the production and direction of his later work in the 1970s – particularly that seen in *The Conversation* and *Apocalypse Now*.

Coppola auteur trademarks
In terms of Coppola's 1970s output we can detect several filmmaking traits that mark him out as an auteurial director – trademarks that were already present in the studio influenced adaptation of *The Godfather*. They include the following:

• **Life and death cycles:** the intellectual montages offered at the end of both *The Godfather* and *Apocalypse Now* infer Coppola's love of birth/death cycles. The murder of Kurtz and ascent of Willard as the new messiah of *Apocalypse Now* is hugely similar to Michael Corleone's dominion as the mafia figurehead in *The Godfather*.

Table 13.3 Cont.

- **Stories that reflect overt anti-authoritarian sentiments:** we already gain a sense of Coppola's anti-authoritarian impulses in *The Godfather* through the Corleone family's rejection and mistrust of law and order. Those concerns are magnified in the post-Watergate fuelled paranoia of *The Conversation* and in the countercultural apathy of Coppola's anti-Vietnam behemoth that is *Apocalypse Now*. Coppola's films, too, are concerned to show how authority can corrupt, whether it be Colonel Kurtz's descent in anarchy or his superior's willingness to use a covert operation in non-enemy territory to assassinate him.
- **Tragic anti-hero leads:** Coppola, too, readily uses compromised male leads in his stories – reluctant action figures who struggle with the demands of their masculine roles. Michael Corleone, for example, refuses, initially at least, to accept his criminal calling, while *Apocalypse Now's* hired assassin, Willard, similarly struggles to come to terms with the responsibilities thrust upon him by the narrative.
- **Method acting deployment:** Coppola is in many senses an actor's director and his penchant for method actors underlines his desire to inject maximum authenticity into his films. Method actors work hard to inhabit the role of the characters they play – indeed, their aim is to literally become those characters so that their reactions construct maximum believability. The hugely famous opening sequence of Willard's mental breakdown in *Apocalypse Now* is testament to that approach. Indeed, Martin Sheen was said to have inhabited the morally compromised world of Captain Willard so convincingly that he suffered a suspected nervous breakdown after filming was finally completed.
- **Tableau camera set ups:** Coppola's films are extraordinarily artsy in their composition. Objects and actors are blocked to construct symmetry or to emulate the golden triangle compositions used by master painters. As such, Coppola likes to keep camera movement to a minimum.
- **Ultra-realism:** Coppola's 1970s films regularly deployed epic casts while sets and costuming are honed to produce an ultra-realistic feel. Kurtz's camp in *Apocalypse Now*, for example, was deemed a health hazard by those working on it, with rotting meat and rats used to add tonal atmosphere. It was also rumoured that Coppola had shipped in real dead bodies to supply the set with as much grizzly impact as possible – only stopped when police turned up on set and took the bodies away.

(*continued*)

Table 13.3 Cont.

> • **Chiaroscuro lighting:** Coppola's films often explore the latent savagery of humankind, presenting us with characters who are forced into abject moral compromises – it comes as no surprise that Coppola readily uses a black canvas to affect those portraits, using nothing but the faintest of shafts of lights to suggest the hopeless and brutal nature of the human condition as Coppola sees it.

Rise of the blockbuster

The financial health of the big Hollywood studios was revitalised by the end of the 1970s, largely as a result of the success of blockbuster releases that brought in huge profits. Those blockbuster big hits – *Jaws*, *The Exorcist*, *The Towering Inferno* and *Rocky* – used television advertising to magnify ticket sales. The influence ironically, of the new directorial talent that helped to realise these blockbuster hits was already diminishing by the end of the decade as a result of the improved financial health of the big Hollywood studios.

Studios also moved from the use of a stepped distribution system that gave larger movie theatres priority access to new releases to a distribution model that encouraged as many cinemas as possible – both big and small – to show films on their opening nights. This move effectively introduced nationwide release dates and allowed the major studios to orchestrate more effective marketing campaigns. National releases also helped to generate simultaneous word-of-mouth appeal across the geographical expanse of the United States. This new general release distribution model increased ticket sales and oriented films towards more family-friendly storytelling.

Film critics further define 1977 as a pivotal year of change in which the $323 million box office success of the first *Star Wars* film signalled the start of that family-friendly form of filmmaking. Star Wars, too, alerted the big studios to storytelling formats that could exploit merchandising tie-ins as a means of increasing profits, and, more importantly, to the use of sequels to capitalise on the presold audiences and fan bases that began to adhere around big blockbuster successes. Other key traits of the New Hollywood style post-1977 include the following:

- **New Hollywood embraces science fiction and fantasy:** science fiction and fantasy epics were made to expand family-friendly cinema going. More importantly, the genre was able to take full advantage of new production technologies – computer-controlled stop motion animation and composite camera techniques, for example, enabled George Lucas to deploy realistic space-based fight sequences. Evermore sophisticated optical printing technology, too, helped Ridley Scott to wow audiences with his post-apocalyptic *Blade Runner* setting.
- **The cinema of spectacle:** science fiction, too, authored a form of cinema that constructed 'spectacle' based pleasures that were best experienced via big screen viewings. In the era of television and increasingly VHS home cinema, science fiction epics like *Star Wars* or the fantasy-based worlds of *Indiana Jones* lured audiences to ticket-buying big screen experiences.
- **The era of the big film score:** similarly, the integration of Dolby sound in cinema also encouraged a renaissance in sound-based elements. Long-term Spielberg collaborator, John Williams, perfectly understood the power of a fully immersive score in generating spectacle-based blockbuster cinema. Indeed, William's presence looms large in the blockbuster output of the 1980s and underpins much of the epic storytelling that took place during the period.
- **Less overt political messaging:** films of the early and mid-1970s were politically charged – Milos Forman's *One Flew Over the Cuckoo's Nest*, for example, laid bare the behavioural straitjacket of American society, while Coppola's nightmare portrait of the Vietnam War in *Apocalypse Now* provided a searing indictment of US foreign policy. The films of the late 1970s, conversely, provided a softer, more family-friendly critique. Spielberg's *E.T.*, for example, is largely concerned with family fracture despite its underlying anti-government messaging.

Table 13.4 Revise it: New Hollywood in the 1970s

Use the following questions to help you revise the changing nature of New Hollywood in the 1970s:	
Genre choices and family-friendly viewing	• Does the film operate within a family-friendly genre? • Did the film exploit merchandising opportunities? • In what ways does genre choice restrict the political messaging of blockbuster films in the 1980s?
Technology and spectacle	• In what ways does the film construct spectacle-based viewing? What sequences in the film were constructed to produce wow moments? • How was technological innovation used to author those wow moments? • How do the locations of the film help to construct an escapist feel? • How did the films provide an alternative experience to television viewing and video recording?
Film scores	• Is a fully symphonic film score applied to the film? Does the score exploit new audio projection technologies? Surround sound and so on? • Identify key moments where the score injects energy into the film? • What instrumentation does the score use? • How does the score help to underpin narrative excitement? • Does the score use leitmotif? Where and for who?

Exemplar: *E.T.* **(OCR).** Spielberg by 1982 had already cemented his reputation for blockbuster filmmaking, having scored huge box office hits with *Jaws* in 1975 and his science fiction epic *Close Encounters of the Third Kind* in 1977. Spielberg's *E.T.* blockbuster, however, steers a course that avoids both the political undertones of *Close Encounters* and the corrupt authority figures of *Jaws*. Perhaps by 1982, the Watergate scandal was a distant memory for filmmakers – perhaps, the reassertion of studio-based power also channelled films

New Hollywood 1961–90 265

Table 13.4 Cont.

to deliver more depoliticised narratives. Certainly, Spielberg's return to science fiction is markedly different from his previous films – its child-centred presentation of an alien encounter deliberately creating interest for a lucrative family-friendly audience.

E.T., moreover, echoes George Lucas' ground-breaking science fiction plus special effects formula that *Star Wars* laid out for the industry to follow in 1977. Industrial Light Magic's spaceship miniatures and the film's *E.T.* puppetry also utilised blue screen shooting and composite imaging to generate spectacle-based viewing pleasures (Figure 13.2). Such pleasures were deployed across cinematic output of the 1980s to secure ticket sales and were crucial to the marketing of films in an era that was increasingly dominated by television competition.

The film's otherworldly escapism is also driven by John William's immersive symphonic accompaniment. Williams' orchestration, for example, plays a crucial role in reinforcing the childhood innocence of the characters via its iconic unresolved flute refrain. That refrain repeatedly punctuates Spielberg's chiaroscuro lit action in a way that helps the film to induce family-friendly wonder rather than fear. Such was the importance of the score that Spielberg re-edited key moments to match the tempo of William's orchestration – Spielberg, too, was mindful of the terrifying effect that Williams had in bringing his lacklustre rubber shark to life in *Jaws*. Spielberg, moreover, implicitly understood the role of sound in the newly equipped Dolby Surround Sound auditoriums of the 1980s and the capacity for modern audio projection facilities to transmit symphonic subtleties that simply weren't possible in the mid-1970s.

Figure 13.2 *E.T.* (top): Spielberg's iconic family-friendly blockbuster
of 1982. *Do the Right Thing* (bottom): the use of wide-
angle canted shots with characters placed in the foreground
constructs a distorted representation of New York.

Table 13.5 Director focus: Spike Lee – new voices in Hollywood

The inclusion of Spike Lee's 1989 *Do the Right Thing* (Figure 13.2) on both OCR and Eduqas' specifications quite rightly draws attention to the restricted range of voices operating within Hollywood during the 1970s and 1980s. The anti-authoritarian filmmaking of New Hollywood in the early 1970s was restricted, almost exclusively, to white middle-class male directors, with Spike Lee's ground-breaking Hollywood intrusion not fully realised until the late 1980s. Lee, too, graduated from the UCLA film school, finding modest success with his low-budget *She's Gotta Have It* in 1986 – earning a respectable $7.1 million at the box office – enough for Lee to convince Universal that a sizable black audience existed for the studio to back a raft of Lee projects thereafter.

Lee's filmmaking style is energetic and experimental, packaging a complex diversity message in mainstream-friendly narratives. Use the following questions to help you define Lee's auteur style in *Do the Right Thing*:

- How does Lee use composition to underline themes of conflict?
- What effect does Lee's use of deep focus photography have?
- What kind of tone is constructed through the dialogue exchanges in the film?
- What kind of colour palette does Lee use in the film? How does this affect the representations constructed?
- In what ways does *Do the Right Thing* construct an ambiguous or complex representation of race relations in 1980s America?

Exemplar: *Do the Right Thing* (Eduqas and OCR). Despite *Do the Right Thing's* big studio financing, Lee retained a huge degree of control over the script, casting decisions and post-production treatment of the film. Lee's dialogue exchanges, as a result, bristle with aggression in the sweltering heat of the film's New York setting, while the multi-character plot shifts continuously in abrupt cameos of the inhabitants of Lee's downtown film set. Music systems clash, with petty arguments underpinning most character dialogue exchanges. Similarly, violent smash cuts and extreme close-ups are liberally deployed to charge scene intros with Lee's auteurial energy, while mismatched eyeline edits continuously agitate the idea of off-screen space – throwing the audience's sense of perspective into chaos.

(*continued*)

Table 13.5 Cont.

Lee's use of deep focus photography, too, when combined with a wide-angle lens further constructs the distorted world of his New York tableau, wherein his mismatched characters are deliberately placed in the foreground so that they loom large in the audience's vision (see Figure 13.2). Lee, too, readily uses tilt-ups during heated dialogue exchanges, situating the audience amid the inhabitants' swirling arguments and forcing the viewer to adopt a childlike viewpoint.
Yet despite *Do the Right Thing's* representation of a deeply segregated community, Lee's depiction buzzes with a celebratory energy: both set and costumes' using a primary colour palette, while the film's youthful performances and stylised realism coat the economic poverty of Lee's world with an upbeat veneer. Lee might also saturate the film's narrative in a racially driven culture war, but he also punctuates the film with moments of tenderness that leave open the possibility that the racially segregated world of New York might be able to find kinship. 'These people grew up on my food' Sal tells, 'and I'm proud of that'.

Table 13.6 New Hollywood 1961–90: ten-minute revision

Essential background
• The big studios were placed under pressure as a result of falling cinema attendance and the Paramount Decree.
• Studios responded to those pressures by producing films that targeted youth audiences.
• Films of the period were more critical of established authority, and, moreover, were more likely to include explicit content and experimental filmmaking.
• Changing audience tastes also eroded the hugely restrictive MPAA Production Code enabling films to include more explicit/violent content.

Essential knowledge: the New Hollywood aesthetic
• A new wave of film school educated directorial talent emerged in the 1970s. The New Hollywood directors were influenced by European film movements like Italian Neorealism and the French New Wave.
• A New Hollywood aesthetic emerged that used anti-hero leads. Films delivered tragic narratives and psychological portraits of characters.
• The New Hollywood aesthetic was stylistically experimental.

Table 13.6 Cont.

Essential knowledge: blockbuster films of the 1980s
• The blockbuster films of the late 1970s re-established studio power and resulted in a renewed focus on family-friendly output. • Blockbuster films used science fiction and fantasy-based storytelling to produce spectacle-oriented viewing pleasures. • Films used symphonic scores and computer-generated special effects to drive spectacle oriented-viewing pleasures. • Although the film industry was dominated by white male filmmakers, diverse practitioners like Spike Lee began to emerge.

14 Contemporary British cinema since 1995

Table 14.1 What do you need to revise contemporary British cinema for?

Eduqas
- **Component 1 Section C, British film since 1995:**
  students are asked to apply ideological perspectives to better
  understand the meanings and messages created by set text films.
  Students should also be able to evaluate the usefulness of these
  ideological perspectives as tools for understanding the set text
  films studied.

OCR
- **Paper 2 Section A, contemporary British and US film:**
  requires students to understand how film form, narrative and
  genre help to construct representations.

Essential background

A fragmented landscape

Undoubtedly, the scale and big-budget spends of Hollywood
have overshadowed British film production, making it harder
for UK filmmakers to find the financial backing or sufficient
audience interest to make domestic production truly sustainable.
Despite that, UK-based production does periodically achieve
huge commercial success despite its low-budget presence and art
house dominated distribution. For most UK producers, however,
commercial success is usually limited, or, equally problematically,
is used as a steppingstone to bigger Hollywood financed projects.

The UK film industry, as a result, offers us a fragmented and often eclectic cinematic history – a discontinuous history of ever-changing genre-driven output. In the 1990s, for example, a more commercially-oriented cinema is evident – an eclectic mix of laddish gangster flicks and optimistic reworkings of British social realism, where films like *The Full Monty* and *Billy Elliot* reflected the growing economic optimism of the New Labour era and the cultural cool of 1990s Brit Pop. The early 2000s, in comparison, are notable for their horror-oriented offerings: Danny Boyle's *28 Days Later* in 2001, and Neil Marshall's 2002 zombie flick, *Dog Soldiers*, providing notable stand out successes for British filmmakers.

Film form: British documentary realism

Arguably, a very British filmmaking traditional weaves its way amongst the various spurts of genre-based output of the last three decades: the ever-present tradition of British documentary realism, wherein long-standing filmmakers like Ken Loach and Mike Leigh have provided a constant supply of low-budget realist output alongside a raft of younger filmmakers who have used social realism, to greater and lesser extents, as springboards to other more experimental projects. Shane Meadows, Ben Wheatley, Andrea Arnold and Lynne Ramsay, for example, all made films that could be classified under the realist banner during the 1990s and 2000s – indeed, the genre still endures today via the work of Steve McQueen (*Hunger*) and Mark Jenkin (*Bait*).

British social realism, perhaps, has endured as a result of both the BBC and the BFI's role in funding UK production, whose diversity-oriented remits provide an easy fit for British documentary realism's regional settings and working-class characters. Other key traits of British documentary realism include the following:

- **Working-class settings:** British social realism provides us with narratives that document the lives of real people in marginalised communities. Andrea Arnold's *Fish Tank*, for example, is set in a council estate in a deprived area of East

London. The action of Loach's *Sweet Sixteen*, similarly, is located in the council tenements of Inverclyde. These sorts of narrative backdrops provide films with a raw and authentic purpose, enabling, too, an exploration of those UK regions that commercial cinema often neglects to represent.

- **Non-professional actors:** star power is rarely used in British realism. Directors, instead, cast unknown actors or even non-professionals to play key roles. Actors are often chosen because of their real-life experiences of the issues covered in story content, thus enhancing the authenticity of narratives.

- **Victim narratives:** often British realism places flawed or victim-based characters in plots that often resolve in tragic endings. Characters often fight injustice or economic poverty. Characters, too, are often depicted as outsiders to their communities. Narrative treatments of those leads often work through episodic structures, depicting a series of events in which central protagonists are overwhelmed by the worlds they live in.

- **Political/ideological subtext:** as a natural extension of victim-based narratives, realist films often deliver overt political messages. Ken Loach, for example, openly draws attention to the political purposes of his films and their underlying intent to draw attention to social injustice issues.

- **Documentary aesthetic:** a range of defined stylistic devices are also associated with the British social realist aesthetic. Handheld camerawork and long-takes are often used to produce an observational/docu-realist film style, while natural lighting and minimal sound scores further affect the sense that these films are representative of a working-class reality.

- **Alternative production practices:** realist filmmakers also employ a range of alternative production strategies to help concentrate realism effects. Mike Leigh, for example, uses improvised performances and minimal scripting to lend his films a sense of legitimacy. Loach and Arnold, too, film their stories in chronological order, often revealing crucial plot points to actors during takes to engineer authentic character responses.

British documentary realism, gender and race

Increasingly, the British realist tradition has focussed upon gender-based issues, using film narratives to explore the shifting expectations of both women and men in contemporary Britain. Films, for example, have sought to identify the destructive effects of toxic masculinity and female objectification, or to explore the search for alternative male identities in the wake of the shifting gender roles prompted by feminism. Social realism too has attempted to diagnose how gender and class intersect – to scope how poverty magnifies gender-based inequalities in the UK.

Shane Meadow's ground-breaking 2006 film *This is England*, for example, explores the loss of traditional masculine identity in 1980s Britain, offering two contrasting portraits of the responses men constructed in the wake of mass male unemployment during the period, wherein Woody's community-oriented masculinity is set against Combo's retreat into English nationalism and racist scapegoating. Meadow's film, ultimately, narrates the presence of a dark masculine energy that the film's male characters exorcise in a bid to reclaim lost patriarchal power. Combo's self-destructive impulses ultimately come to dominate in the film – a masculine explosion that ripples through Meadow's portrayal of 1980s Britain with deadly consequences.

Mike Leigh's *Secrets and Lies*, too, explores racial difference, offering us a shame-filmed narrative that probes racial sexual taboos while also narrating the diminishing power of white working-class communities. Ultimately, Leigh's film constructs a positive take on inter-racial relations in Britain in the late 1990s, offering us a narrative where characters connect rather than disconnect. *Secrets and Lies*, too, narrates the working-class shift towards more middle-class aspirations – a shift that Leigh questions via the hollow emptiness of Maurice's dysfunctional presence in the film.

Table 14.2 Revise it: ideological approaches and British realism

Use the following questions and prompts to help you construct ideological readings of relevant films:	
Use Marxian ideological approach to explore class-based representations	• How are lower class groups represented in the film? • What does the film suggest are the physical and/or psychological effects of poverty? • What effects do character circumstances have on the kinds of relationships they construct with others? • Does the film suggest that the lead character can escape the confines of their world? • In what ways are vulnerable characters exploited and by whom?
Use a gender-based ideological approach to explore male and female representations	• What kind of gender-based representations are constructed in the film? • What problematic roles are males and females expected to fulfil? Where in the film is this most poignant? • Does a character's gender lead to their exploitation or victimisation? • In what ways are women exploited in the film and by whom? • Are problematic attitudes and behaviours internalised by either male or female characters?
Use a postcolonial ideological lens to diagnose the representation of racial relations in contemporary Britain.	• Does the film focus on race-based issues? • How are white and non-white characters represented? • How do different racial groups interact? Are they segregated or connected? • Does the film focus on problematic interracial representations? What social forces are identified as problematic in those relations? • Does the filmmaker construct an optimistic or pessimistic view of racial harmony in contemporary Britain?

Table 14.2 Cont.

Exemplar: *Fish Tank* **(Eduqas).** *Fish Tank* clearly lends itself to Marxian ideological analysis – its social realist framed perspective clearly highlighting the effects of poverty in Britain during the 1990s. Arnold's single-character focalisation, moreover, is typical of the kinds of narrative tactics found within British social realist cinema, effecting a simplistic character alignment with the audience in order to explore class-based stereotypes (Figure 15.1). In *Fish Tank's* case, that exploration outlines the divide between the celebrity rich world of Mia's dancing ambitions and the harsh reality of her high-rise poverty.

Despite Arnold's high-key summer setting and the film's soul drenched musical interludes, *Fish Tank* makes for grim viewing as we are forced to watch Mia's childhood innocence forcefully taken from her. That uncomfortable portrait is further authored through the film's elliptical editing style, where shallow focus photography and lingering close-ups are used to confer Conor's grooming of the film's tragic female lead. Here, Conor's middle-class status also highlights the class-based divides of UK contemporary society, while also pointing towards white middle-class masculinity as the potential source of underclass exploitation.

Links to exemplar film clips and exemplars for other OCR/Eduqas film texts can be found at www.essentialfilmrevision.com

Extend it: ideological approaches

Visit Chapter 8 (Ideology) to read more about the ideological approaches that can be used to decode films and to think about the limits of those ideological approaches.

Figure 14.1 Fish Tank (top) and *Sweet Sixteen* (bottom): documentary
social realism has provided a steady output of films that
depict victim leads within tragic narrative structures.

The commercialisation of British realism

British realism, of course, is applied in different ways by different filmmakers. Mike Leigh and Ken Loach, for example, sculpt realist films using their own quirks and peculiarities. Leigh's use of black humour, for example, produces a lighter, bittersweet take on the genre when compared to Loach's harder narratives and political sloganeering. From the mid-1990s onwards, however, a distinctly different and more commercially viable form of realist filmmaking became visible – a form of British filmmaking that pushed realism beyond arthouse cinema distribution and into the mainstream.

Realist films in the 1980s and early 1990s often authored unequivocal critiques of the Conservative government of the period – Mike Leigh's 1993 film, *Naked*, for example, constructed a condemnatory portrait of youth unemployment, homelessness and middle-class apathy. In contrast, films from the mid-1990s onwards were buoyed by a more optimistic outlook – partly inspired by New Labour's landslide election victory in 1997 – also enabled by the presence of new Multiplex cinemas in the UK that gave commercially minded British filmmakers more opportunity to screen films that could compete with mainstream Hollywood fair.

The creation of the National Lottery in 1994 also helped a raft of new filmmakers find the finance for productions. *28 Days Later*, for example, was co-financed by Lottery cash to the tune of £3 million and helped Danny Boyle to resurrect his career after the filmmaker's first Hollywood foray *The Beach* was met with a lacklustre audience response. The burgeoning impact, too, of Film Four as a new financier and exhibitor cannot be understated. Film Four not only supplied filmmakers with new sources of funding, but also provided films with readymade television audiences via guaranteed Channel 4 screenings and later through its pay-to-view Film Four subscription service. The resulting commercial needs of Film Four prompted those films made under its banner to affect a more accessible or mainstream tone. Film Four's reliance on television advertising and pay-to-view subscriptions prompted it to finance projects that could command reasonably sized audiences, driving output towards more commercially friendly narratives. Established auteurs, however, like Loach and Leigh were also funded as a result of their ability to command pre-sold audiences for their films.

As a result, British realism tilted towards a more upbeat form of filmmaking: Mark Herman's Film Four co-funded *Brassed Off* in 1996, for example, was set in the industrial working-class heartland of Barnsley but effected an unusually cheery story structure – trading the tragic resolutions of documentary realism for a feel-good ending that celebrated rather than mourned the working-class community depicted in the film.

Significantly, British realism was also refashioned for youth audiences. Danny Boyle's Film Four adaptation of *Trainspotting* in 1996, for example, revelled in Irvine Welsh's working-class Scottish setting, yet also offered audiences moments of levity via its blackly comic take on underclass drug addiction (Figure 14.2). *Trainspotting's* working-class tenements, too, are constructed with stylised flourishes that lift the movie beyond a documentary-oriented aesthetic – expressive lighting, jump-cuts, freeze frames and it's cult soundtrack helping to nurture the film's alt-cool status for youth audiences in the era of Britpop. *Trainspotting*, undeniably, was branded British social realism – a slickly packaged version of the genre whose white-on-orange posters and relatable cast made Danny Boyle a household name.

Genre hybridisation and transnational cinema

We can also attribute the success of *Trainspotting* to its hybridised narrative and its packaging of documentary realism within an audience-friendly heist narrative framework. Boyle's multi-genre filmmaking formula continues to be used by contemporary filmmakers like Ben Wheatley who use social realism to affect a British feel to films while packaging the low-fi style of British realism within a more conventional – and entertainment-driven – narrative framework.

Wheatley's hugely successful 2012 film *Sightseers*, for example, reworks an audience-friendly crime-oriented plot via the unlikely characters of Tina and Chris whose caravanning holiday takes a darkly comic turn in a pencil museum. The film's story is packaged using a conventional three-act narrative which resolves in Tina's triumph over both her hyper masculine and controlling boyfriend and her overbearing mother. The film's quest-oriented structure is also conventional in that the central character's opening weakness is transformed using a predictable story formula. At times, however, the film's overarching plot feels secondary to its observational intentions, where Wheatley's exploration of the British landscape offers us episodic glimpses of a divided and class-ridden Britain – a Britain that feels hugely familiar to the kinds of social critiques offered by Ken Loach and Mike Leigh.

In contrast, films like Edgar Wright's *Shaun of the Dead* use story structures that are wholly designed to construct appeal for a global audience. Loosely labelled, transnational cinema, these sorts of films work within established narrative forms and deliver genre-driven storytelling to garner commercial success. Where Wheatley's *Sightseers* charts the peculiarly British idiosyncrasies of caravanning, Wright constructs a sanitised version of England that can be easily understood by cinema goers outside of the UK.

Characters, for example, work through easily decodable stereotypes: Shaun and Liz are the film's love torn heroes, Barbara and Philip are the quintessential essence of middle-class England, while David is the dastardly false hero who must be unmasked at the end of the story. Wright's zombie survival storyline, too, trades in a deluge of intertextual references that draw from an American film history. More problematically, the film's London setting is devoid of non-white leads. *Shaun of the Dead*, as such, minimises realism, instead deploying action-based storytelling to deliver a representation of Britain that constructs global appeal. Bond movies, too, exemplify this transnational approach to filmmaking: an approach that loosely hints at an iconic England – a globally recognisable version of Englishness that is packaged within an accessible three-act narrative format, while ending, predictably, in the triumph of a central hero.

Table 14.3 Revise it: commercialisation effects and British social realism

> The commercialisation of British realism in the mid-1990s impacted on the narrative structure and ideological effect of films. Use the following prompts to identify those effects:

Narrative considerations of commercial films
- Commercialised realist films use conventional narrative structures to create mainstream appeal.
- Narrative resolutions in films are more optimistic.
- Narratives present flawed characters, but characters overcome their weaknesses.
- Characters in commercial UK output are constructed using conventional genre-driven archetypes.
- Commercial films use star power to create appeal – stars inject their own auteur-driven characteristics into narratives.

The ideological impact of commercial output
- Commercial films often author escapist viewing pleasures – minimising the ideological messages and purposes of British social realism.
- Transnational films are constructed to generate global appeal rather than political impact.
- Representations of British culture in transnational films are often diluted.
- Elements of genres other than social realism are used to construct mainstream appeal. Genre hybridisation dilutes the authenticity of representations constructed of the UK.

Narrative analysis revision questions
- Does the film use a conventional three-act narrative structure?
- How does the narrative resolve? Does the narrative deliver tragedy or optimism?
- Does the narrative construct a political message?
- Does the film use genre-driven narrative devices? Why and with what effect?
- Does the film use star power? What effect does that have on the underlying messages of the film?

Ideology analysis revision questions
- Is the film constructed to produce escapist pleasures? What effect does this have on the ideological subtext of the film? Are political subtexts foregrounded or disguised?
- How does the distribution destination of the film (commercial television/art house cinema) affect the ideologies constructed?
- Does the use of non-realist genre conventions dilute the ideological effects of the film?

Table 14.3 Cont.

Exemplar: *We Need to Talk About Kevin* **(Eduqas and OCR).**
Ultimately, we might argue, the UK film industry and its most
prominent filmmakers have had to adopt a more commercial style
for their output to be viable in the globalised film industry. Lynne
Ramsay's adaptation of Lionel Shriver's bestselling novel *We Need
to Talk About Kevin* (WNTTAK) demonstrates the extent to which
the British film industry has sacrificed UK-oriented realist-based
representations in favour of a more transnational and commercially
friendly form of output. Funded by the BBC, WNTTAK
looks and feels very different to Ramsay's 1999 Scottish realist
masterpiece *Ratcatcher* – a lyrically detached observation of
working-class youth in 1970s Glasgow. In contrast, Ramsay's
2011 project sacrifices the natural authenticity of *Ratcatcher* for a
more conventionally structured narrative, alongside an expressive
aesthetic that again is hugely different from the detached realism of
Ramsay's first film.

WNTTAK, in many senses, is driven by horror-oriented narrative
conventions: Kevin is the archetypal demonic child, while the
film's nightmarish revelations are realised through slow-motion
compositions and a horror-driven jump-cut editing style. The
film, too, revels in moments of visceral body horror, delivering a
highly predictable narrative denouement in its revelation of Kevin's
macabre high school killing spree. In terms of mise en scene, the
film too constructs vividly coloured settings to symbolically infer
the nightmarish nature of Eva's existence, deploying a palette that
is dominated by crimson reds to foreground the film's eventual
horror. And where *Ratcatcher* delivered a relatively unknown cast to
dial up the film's authenticity, WNTTAK delivers Tilda Swinton-
oriented star power to help seal the narrative's commercial success.
WNTTAK, ultimately, is a film that uses a British actor and UK-
based finance to tell a wholly American story. It is a film, more
interestingly, whose feminist impulses – as evidenced by Eva's stigma
as a failed mother – are obscured by a narrative that foregrounds
enigma and horror-based shock.

British science fiction

Given the inclusion of *Ex Machina,* and *Under the Skin* and *Moon*
as set text choices in specifications, it is worth considering in
some detail the use and application of the science fiction genre in

contemporary British film. Certainly, a long tradition of science fiction filmmaking exists in the UK, driven in part by the reputation of the literary British SF cannon which includes high profile writers like H.G Wells, J.G. Ballard and George Orwell. That literary pedigree has attracted a number of big-name directors to the UK to make adaptations of key novels: Stanley Kubrick's reworking, for example, of Anthony Burgess' *Clockwork Orange* (see Figure 14.2) and Alfonso Cuarón's adaptation of PD James' *Children of Men* are considered as classics in the genre of science fiction.

British science fiction, too, is synonymous with an aesthetic style and form of storytelling that feels very different to mainstream Hollywood science fiction, with, primarily, the lower budgets of UK-funded films necessitating a small-scale application of the genre. Key traits include the following:

- **Realism is affected instead of CGI rich spectacle:** as a result of limited budgets, British science fiction often constructs dystopian visions using settings that look and feel realistic. Instead of transporting audiences to off-world locations or using ornate tech-based settings, British science fiction conventionally deals in narratives that are hugely relatable to audiences. As a result, the aliens in British science fiction films tend to live amongst us rather than in distant galaxies or far-away worlds. The low-fi emptiness of Danny Boyle's *28 Days Later* stands out as a prime example of a low-budget British realist SF aesthetic, likewise, Jonathan Glazer's realism in *Under the Skin* affects a no-frills approach.
- **Slower paced narration and horror-based verisimilitude:** without the energy of CGI-driven spectacle, British SF tends to progress at a much slower or introspective tempo than Hollywood equivalents. Alex Garland's *Ex Machina*, for example, provides an interesting example of the slow-moving intensity of British science fiction, while its enigma-driven narrative structure and creepy intrusion of technology into a world that feels hugely familiar produces horror-oriented storytelling. A similar dynamic is authored by *Under the Skin,*

wherein Scarlett Johansson's meat processing hideout feels more horror-house than high-tech alien lair.

- **Limited finance restricts casts:** restricted budgets also tend to produce films that feature smaller casts. As a result, British SF tends to lean towards a more subjective storytelling style wherein filmmakers focus on the psychological effects of the dystopian fears outlined in plots. *Moon's* limited cast stands as a clear example, wherein Duncan Jones' lone character narrative is trained squarely on the singular experiences of Sam, enabling the film to fully explore the isolation and vulnerability of the clone at the hands of his Earthbound employers.

- **Political dystopian subtexts:** British science fiction also effects narratives that use dystopian settings to readily critique authority. Mainstream Hollywood SF output tends to deliver humans versus alien survival narratives that are underpinned with romance-based subplots. UK SF, conversely, tends to deliver more austere or fatalistic messaging, with greater emphasis placed on outlining wider social themes or political issues.

Figure 14.2 Trainspotting (top): Boyle's 1996 film constructs a more commercially savvy form of British social realism. *Clockwork Orange* (middle) and *Moon* (bottom): a rich tradition of British science fiction filmmaking exists, a tradition that often offers critical social commentary.

Table 14.4 Revise it: the British science fiction tradition

Use the following questions to help you diagnose the ideological subtexts and narrative effects of the UK-based science fiction set text you have studied:	
Realism effects	• Where is the film set? Does this setting construct or use a realistic aesthetic? • Does the setting defy the CGI rich conventions of Hollywood-based science fiction?
Subjective narrative concerns	• Does the film use a limited cast? How does this change the dynamic of the film? What themes or ideas does this limited cast enable the film to pursue? • Does the limited cast enable a more psychological or subjective filming style? What is revealed about the character's inner world as a result?
Themes of isolation	• Are themes of isolation or vulnerability emphasised?
Ideological subtexts	• What social forces or trends does the film highlight as problematic? • How do these forces affect the world of the central character? • Who or what triumphs at the end of the film? In what ways does the ending of the film construct an ideological effect?

Exemplar: *Moon* (Eduqas). *Moon's* slick commercial advert at the start of the film suggests the presence of a false utopia via the ad's high-key lighting, optimistic voiceover and feel-good natural imagery. The subsequent contrast with the film's black desaturated moonscape and Clint Mansell's eerie soundtrack – replete with non-melodic fragments of piano – constructs a deliberately unnerving binary opposition. That opposition forwards a dystopian warning of corporate control and global warming, an overt political message that Duncan Jones' dials up via his clinically white Moon base setting in which Sam can be permanently monitored by his Moon mining exploiters.

Sam, too, presents as an unconventional SF hero – his dishevelled and frayed persona symbolised through his costuming (see Figure 14.2), while the film's subversion of mainstream science fiction is further enabled through the narrative's single-character focus and its fragmented story structure in which a discontinuous series of hallucinatory episodes are related to align audiences with

(continued)

Table 14.4 Cont.

> Sam's collapsing mental state. Editing, mise en scene and narrative
> subversion, in this sense, combine to construct a Marxian vision
> of a dystopian future wherein corporate power sanctions human
> slavery for the purposes of capital gain. We might argue that the
> political subtext of *Moon* falls neatly within the tradition of British
> science fiction film output – a rich tradition of low-budget/limited
> cast storytelling that delivers much sharper social critiques than
> equivalent Hollywood SF fair.

Table 14.5 Contemporary British cinema: ten-minute revision

Essential background

- As a result of fragmented film financing, a disparate range of film styles and forms have flourished in British filmmaking over the past 30 years.
- British social realism has offered one thread of continuity within that fragmented landscape.

British documentary realism

- The long-standing presence of filmmakers like Ken Loach and Mike Leigh have had a huge influence on British cinema.
- British realism uses a documentary aesthetic to highlight social issues.
- British realism tends to use tragic narrative structures, victim characters and real settings to inject a sense of authenticity into films.
- Documentary realism also uses a variety of experimental production techniques – improvisation, linear filming and non-professional actor input – to further construct authenticity
- Documentary realism in the 1990s sought to explore gender and race-based issues in addition to the class-based concerns of social realism in the 1980s.

Commercialised realism, hybridisation, transnational cinema and British SF

- Social realism shifted to a more commercial form of filmmaking in the 1990s.
- Commercial realist projects used more optimistic storylines to construct mainstream audience appeal.
- Commercial realism also used narrative features from a range of other genres to widen audience appeal.
- British science fiction films draw upon a rich literary tradition of UK-based SF writing. British SF films tend to construct harder social commentaries than those offered in Hollywood financed SF.

15 Documentary film

Table 15.1 What do you need to revise documentary film for?

Eduqas
• **Component 2 Section B:** students are asked to consider the role played by digital technologies in relation to the key films studied and also to explore documentary set texts using the approaches taken by the following documentary filmmakers: Peter Watkins, Nick Broomfield, Kim Longinotto and Michael Moore.
OCR
• **Paper 2, Section B Documentary Film:** requires students to understand the use of narrative and film form as well as the conventions of the documentary genre in constructing meaning. Students should also be able to understand the influence of John Grierson and D. A. Pennebaker on chosen set texts.

Essential background

Film has always been used to document real life. Indeed, the Lumière Brothers' revolutionary showreel of the very first projected films in 1895 was composed of a series of real-life vignettes: workers leaving a factory, a train arriving at a station and a demolition crew laying waste to an old house. Early films like these had no choice but to record the real world given that the infrastructure of fictional filmmaking hadn't yet been realised, yet the public's appetite for watching real life didn't diminish once that infrastructure was put in place. Early documentary filmmakers in the 1920s like Robert Flaherty, for example, found commercial success with documentary output like *Nanook of the North* – an intimate portrait of the remote Eskimo Itivimuit tribe who lived inside the arctic circle – a hugely difficult area in which to film given the size and weight of production equipment at the time.

In Making *Nanook of the North*, Flaherty spent over a year befriending the Eskimo tribe, lugging his camera everywhere they went, and, in so doing, amassed vast reams of footage that were later edited into Flaherty's first hit in 1922. Flaherty realised early on, however, that using the camera as a purely observational tool – as a means of just recording reality – didn't produce a great deal of viewer interest. Documentary films, if they were to engage audiences – Flaherty realised – had to package that observed reality inside of stories that spectators could connect with – using narration, editing and characterisation to tease out a higher truth. In *Nanook*, for example, Flaherty didn't just observe, he reconstructed or recreated events, directing his Eskimo cast towards moments of rehearsed action to help him weave a more lyrical or poetic portrait of their community.

In Flaherty's documentary, for example, the film's onscreen family weren't really related – but were selected by Flaherty for their looks and potential screen appeal, nor did they hunt with traditional harpoons as portrayed in the film, using, in reality, the kinds of modern weaponry that the filmmaker's audience would have been familiar with. As such, *Nanook of the North*, as beautiful as it was, is often accused of constructing an overly romanticised version of inuit life. Flaherty's work, more interestingly, provided later documentary filmmakers with a blueprint for documentary storytelling: a blueprint that combined both creativity and observation.

Table 15.2 Discuss it: should creativity play a role in documentary filmmaking?

Flaherty's work raises several critical questions that documentary filmmakers have tried to grapple with ever since *Nanook of the North's* release in 1922. Discuss the following to help you understand the thorny relationship that exists between creativity and observation in documentary filmmaking:

- Was it dishonest of Flaherty to recreate scenes in his film?
- Would audiences be interested in documentary films that are purely observational?
- Why do audiences enjoy documentaries? What pleasures or gratifications do they construct, and, more importantly, is it possible to produce those pleasures without refashioning reality?
- Flaherty defended his creative refashioning of material in his films because they helped him tell stories that narrated higher truths. Is the use of fabricated content in documentaries defensible?

John Grierson

Grierson's influence on the documentary form cannot be underestimated – his eclectic storytelling approach has provided a creative template that many filmmakers have emulated ever since. Although Grierson personally directed only two films – *Drifters* in 1929 and *Granton Trawler* in 1934 – he nevertheless oversaw a number of key documentaries in the 1930s as a producer-manager for both the Empire Marketing Board and the General Post Office. Notable films made under his tenure include *Coal Face* (1935), *Housing Problems* (1935), *Night Mail* (1936) and *Spare Time* (1939).

Grierson's documentary style was influenced by the work of Flaherty as well as the expressive editing style of Soviet Montage. Grierson, much like Flaherty, also believed that documentary films ought to play a role in informing and educating the masses – mixing entertainment and artistry with observational camera work to immerse audiences into worlds that might ordinarily be hidden from view. Key features of Grierson's approach include the following:

- **Montage-based storytelling:** Grierson advocated a narrative style that mixed sequences of observational footage alongside a range of to-camera interviews: an approach that underpins documentary filmmaking even today. Observational montages often affected lyrical or poetic depictions of subject matter – portraying workers with expressive backlighting or using close-ups of found imagery in which shapes, textures or patterns were celebrated. Grierson's montage formula, in this sense, provides visual interest while also connecting audiences to the human subjects of his films via the use of talking head interviews.

- **Voice of God narration and narrated exposition:** a key feature of Grierson's approach was to overlay voice overs on top of footage that outlined the argument or expositions presented by the film. Narration, too, anchored the rich mishmash of imagery presented in montages, using middle-class male narrators to inject films with an air of authority that ordinary viewers wouldn't question.

- **Creative sound treatments:** films also fully exploited the introduction of sound – collaging ambient soundscapes with musical interludes, often matching sound tempos with editing cuts to create carefully controlled rhythmic edits.

- **A concern for ordinary subjects:** Grierson's films squarely focused on the living conditions of ordinary people – whether they be the working conditions of miners in *Coal Face* or the difficulties of living in slum housing in the East End of London in *Housing Problems*. As a result, Grierson was one of the first directors to deploy the documentary format as a political tool. Certainly, he opened up the genre as a filmmaking form that gave voice to working-class subjects.

Direct cinema and D. A. Pennebaker

Donn Pennebaker's observational approach provides an interesting contrast to that of Grierson. In the late 1950s and early 1960s, the invention of lightweight cameras afforded documentary filmmakers a newfound mobility, allowing them to record subjects with an immersive intensity that Grierson could never achieve. Pennebaker, alongside other members of the direct cinema movement, rejected the use of voice overs and controlled story structures. Instead, taking their newly mobile cameras into the worlds of subjects in a way that tried to affect an invisible presence.

Pennebaker, too, resists the urge to shape visual content via reconstructions, formal interviews or staging, instead pursuing a raw documentary aesthetic that immerses audiences in the lived experiences of his subjects. In *Don't Look Back* (1966), for example, Pennebaker follows a young Bob Dylan during his first tour of Europe – the film capturing an authentic slice of Dylan's backstage persona, a portrait that at times is less than flattering. In *Monterey Pop*, Pennebaker's seminal documentary of the iconic 1967 music festival, a showreel of 1960s countercultural pop royalty is showcased, yet Pennebaker's film feels more interested in the crowd – deploying long-takes of the festival's audience to document the spirit and energy of 1960s youth culture without the intrusive presence of a narrator or an overbearing narrative structure.

Key features of Pennebaker's approach include the following:

- **Observational camerawork:** Pennebaker uses the camera in a quiet and unobtrusive way, often producing shots from vantage points that don't impact on the subjects being filmed. Shots too are less concerned by compositional concerns and more interested in effecting a voyeuristic presence.
- **An immersive editing style:** editing too lacks the montage-based organisation of Grierson, with films often progressing through linear storytelling to reflect the lived experiences of the film's setting. Long-takes and single perspective edits dominate, and where cuts do appear in footage they usually proceed via jump-cutting or scene transitions.
- **Minimal sound-based application:** soundscapes mostly reflect diegetic sound only, with minimal application of any sound-based elements that aren't present in observational footage.

Table 15.3 Comparing set text documentary films with Grierson and Pennebaker (OCR)

Use the following questions to help you explore connections that exist between the OCR set text documentary you are studying and the filmmaking styles of Grierson and Pennebaker:	
Grierson	• Does the film outline a clear exposition or argument for the audience to follow? • Does the documentary use a 'voice of god' to narrate the film's exposition? Does the voiceover construct authority via select language use or diction? • Does the documentary use a mixture of to-camera interviews and observational footage? How does this technique construct variety? Who is interviewed and why have those subjects been included? • Does your chosen set text use composition or lighting to construct an expressive representation? • Does the film use a specific camera style or post-production treatments that are expressive? What are the emotional effects of those expressive moments? • Does observational footage construct a lyrical tone? Are textures, shapes or patterns foregrounded? Are subjects romanticised or celebrated? • Does the documentary explore the lives of ordinary people? What is suggested about those lives? • Are creative sound treatments applied to films to help build the documentary's exposition or to help channel audiences towards a specific emotional response? • In what ways does the film's narrative structure/voiceover reveal the bias or underlying motives of the filmmaker?

Table 15.3 Cont.

Pennebaker	• Does the documentary use an observational film style? What is revealed through those observations? • Does the filmmaker play a less intrusive role in the film's exposition? • Does the documentary's use of observational sequences stimulate a more active form of spectatorship? • Does the observational style allow for a more natural representation of the film's subject matter? • Does the filming style immerse the audience in the raw experience of the film? What is that raw experience? What effects does that immersion have? What do the audience learn as a result of watching the film?

Exemplar, *Man on Wire* (OCR). *Man on Wire* clearly uses the mixed narration model pioneered by Grierson in the 1930s, combining to-camera interviews with observational footage to create a documentary that blends information and entertainment. Interestingly, Marsh also recreates footage via dramatisations during the pre-title sequence to narrate historical events – the justification of these fictionalised moments, presumably, is that it was impossible for the filmmaker to locate or create authentic footage.

The extent to which this initial recreation uses expressive ingredients, however, is pointed and suggests that Marsh wanted to channel the film towards a set of entertainment rather than information-based gratifications. The use, for example, of a grainy high-contrast black and white post-production treatment infers the sequence's historical nature, but also helps deliver an ominous rendition of the Twin Towers stunt that it depicts. The deployment, too, of extreme close-ups and shallow depth of field in the car journey element of the recreation also foregrounds a sense of impending danger, channelling the film's audience towards fear-based gratifications, while also working to construct a heroic representation of the film's subjects. In interviews, too, low-key lighting and black backdrops are used to further magnify the danger of the impending stunt, while the use of an escalating editing tempo in the recreated footage/interview cross-cuts further suggests the imminent danger of the stunt.

Links to exemplar film clips and exemplars for other OCR/Eduqas film texts can be found at www.essentialfilmrevision.com

Kim Longinotto

Longinotto's approach is very reminiscent of the direct cinema style of D. A. Pennebaker in that she uses, predominantly, observational camerawork and a low-key filmmaking presence to document her subjects. Longinotto, too, avoids voice overs and to-camera interviews, instead deploying a fly-on-the-wall filming style alongside slow-tempo edits. As such, the stories of her films attempt to accurately mirror the reality of the worlds she immerses herself within. Longinotto, however, isn't afraid to tackle difficult subjects: *Sisters in Law* (2005), for example, follows the often distressing cases of female abuse that are brought to trial in a family court in Cameroon, wherein Longinotto's immersive approach details a trail of harrowing witness accounts. Longinotto's skill, as such, lies in her ability to sustain her stories in the most trying of situations – situations that a lot of filmmakers would probably find too difficult to endure. 'I want, Longinotto tells us, 'to make films which create a situation where the audience gets close to another individual, often from a completely different background, and feel a shock of understanding. I want the whole experience to be a strong and emotional one' (Cranston, 2019).

Key features of Longinotto's approach include the following:

- **An observational film style:** in contrast to the performative expositions of Michael Moore and Nick Broomfield, Longinotto uses a much quieter style that builds engagement through observational camerawork. She affects a reduced presence in films, with camera movement reduced to the bare minimum needed to follow the subjects of her stories.
- **Functional editing:** occasionally, Longinotto's films might necessitate an establishing shot or the use of an explanatory intertitle so that her audience might orientate themselves within a wider narrative – with the exception of those brief stylistic necessities, Longinotto affects a minimal editing presence.
- **Authentic storytelling:** importantly, Longinotto reminds us that the camera can be trusted to represent the world in an

objective way – nothing in Longinotto's films is fabricated or reconstructed.

- **Feminist subtexts:** Longinotto's filmmaking is driven by a feminist-driven concern to document gender-based injustice around the world.

Table 15.4 Comparing set text documentary films with Longinotto (Eduqas)

Use the following questions to help you explore connections that exist between the documentary set text you are studying and the filmmaking style of Longinotto:	
Observational filmmaking	• Does your set text use an observational film style that's similar to Longinotto's work? What is revealed through the observations recorded? • Does the filmmaker of your set text effect a non-intrusive presence in the film's exposition? • Does the film construct a natural or unmediated representation of the film's subject matter? • Does the filmmaker immerse the audience in the raw experience of the film? What is that raw experience? What effects does that immersion have? What do the audience learn as a result of watching the film's observations? • Does the film use character-focused storytelling? What do we learn about characters? What universal truths are exposed as a result of those observations?
Functional editing	• Does the film affect a slow editing tempo? How does the tempo help to build the exposition of the film? • Does the film apply a no-frills approach to storytelling? • Does the filmmaker resist the use of recreative storytelling?

(*continued*)

Table 15.4 Cont.

Feminist subtexts	• Does the film specifically explore the experiences of women? • Are the problematic experiences of women presented in a challenging way? What challenges do women endure? • How does the film align us with a female viewpoint?

Exemplar: *Sisters in Law* (Eduqas/OCR). Longinotto's slow-burn narrative approach is abundantly evident in *Sisters in Law*. The film constructs a pointed and highly emotive exploration of the entrenched gender-based inequalities that exist in Cameroonian society, yet Longinotto's low-key approach – her minimal use of varied shot distance and the metric tempo of her editing – constructs that exposition without the visual or aural presence of the filmmaker herself. Instead, a carefully presented collection of character cameos is delivered, with Longinotto's direct cinema approach giving space to her subjects to reveal their often-tragic circumstances with a raw first-hand clarity. The lack of any narrative voiceover further immerses her audience in the lived experiences of the film's subjects, and, more interestingly, means that her audience are left to form their own conclusions regarding the harrowing judgements handed down by the Cameroon court that Longinotto records.

To suggest, however, that Longinotto doesn't use any expressive techniques to magnify the representations of her female subjects would be misleading. Intertitles are used to foreground the broken relationships of her conflicted characters, while emotive reaction shots are given extended screen time in the final edit of the film, firmly anchoring the trauma of *Sisters in Law*'s female victims as a primary focus. Longinotto, too, uses narrative juxtaposition: a judge, for example, is seen playing with her grandchild after delivering a damning verdict in a child sex abuse case – the contrasting moments revealing the capacity for female tenderness to nurture growth despite the all-pervading presence of masculine exploitation in the film.

Peter Watkins

Peter Watkins' ground-breaking *Culloden* (1964) and *War Games* (1966) use performance-based reconstructions to give presence to events that couldn't be directly filmed. *Culloden* (see Figure 15.2), for example, reimagines the 1746 battle of the same name, using an immersive handheld filming style alongside mocked-up interviews to imaginatively recreate the experiences of those who took part in the battle. Watkins' film also fuses history with an incongruous war reportage news style, enabling the film to produce a charged political subtext and an open critique of British imperialism and the UK class system as it stood in the mid-1960s. Watkins' use of a fake news crew to record the battle also drew parallels to the media's presentation of the Vietnam War during the 1960s, producing a timely critique of the use of observational footage for the purposes of entertainment.

Watkins repeated his recreative approach in his openly political *War Games* documentary of 1966 – an emotive portrait of an imaginary nuclear war in 1960s Britain (see Figure 15.2). Again, Watkins used mocked-up actor performances to generate an emotionally charged film that was so controversial that the BBC refused to show the documentary for some 20 years after it was made. Again, the film produced a stinging critique of the authoritarian undertones that Watkins felt were a hallmark of British society.

Key elements of Watkins' documentary approach include the following:

- **Overt political intentions:** *War Game's* anti-nuclear message and the anti-imperialist subtext of *Culloden* deliberately author a politically charged form of documentary filmmaking.
- **Faux actuality:** Watkins stretches the idea that documentary film must connect with observed reality to breaking point. His use of fake news crews and actor-based performances point to a more imaginative form of the genre. Watkins also opened up documentary filmmaking to a range of creative techniques that filmmakers might use to tackle subjects where direct observation is difficult to realise.

- **Active spectatorship:** Watkins deliberately constructs moments that seek to shock or that elicit an extreme emotional response from his audience. The execution scene in *War Game* serves as an example of the lengths that Watkins was prepared to go to in his bid to stop audiences from producing a passive engagement with his material.
- **Mixed documentary style:** much like Grierson, Watkins fuses voiceover narration with to-camera interviews and observation-based montage to construct a blend of information and entertainment in his films – albeit with a much sharper political focus.
- **Subjective camerawork:** Watkins' handheld camera style also produces an immersive approach – using the camera to construct an eyewitness-oriented viewpoint.

Table 15.5 Comparing set text documentary films with Watkins (Eduqas)

Use the following questions to help you explore potential connections that exist between the documentary set text you are studying and the filmmaking style of Watkins:	
Faux actuality	• Does the film contain reconstructed moments? • Why are reconstructions used? Are reconstructions used because the filmmaker can't create or access footage? Are they reconstructed to add dramatic impact? • Does the film use professional or amateur actors in reconstructions? With what effect? • How does the filmmaker persuade audiences that reconstructions are tied to real experiences?
Active spectatorship and political subtexts	• Does the film outline an overtly political exposition? What political arguments or viewpoints are articulated? Where in the documentary are those viewpoints given the most presence? How?

Table 15.5 Cont.

	• Does the film critique authority figures? How and where? • Does the filmmaker deliberately include moments that are uncomfortable for the audience to watch? What is the aim of those moments?
Mixed narration	• Does the documentary use a mixture of to-camera interviews and observational footage? • Are to-camera interviews used to give audiences direct access to the subjects of the film? • Is observational footage stylised? How is footage edited? Are images juxtaposed in montages? Are metric edits or intellectual montage techniques used?

Exemplar: *The Arbor* **(Eduqas).** *The Arbor's* use of actors who lip-sync the interviews of the documentary's real-life subjects provides audiences with the kind of recreative documentary film work that was pioneered by Peter Watkins in the 1960s, an approach he used as a result of his inability to access footage of *Culloden's* historic battle scene. *The Arbor*, too, presented Clio Barnard with a similar difficulty in that documentary footage of Andrea Dunbar's early life simply didn't exist, while the emotive revelations of child abuse in the film necessitated an approach that would protect the identity of key participants.

Barnard's actor-based recreations are equally as provocative as Watkins' politically charged commentary in *The War Game*. Barnard, for example, offers a Watkins-esque critique of the media's exploitation of conflict and poverty, highlighting the use of Dunbar's Northern realism to supply escapist entertainment for a middle-class audience. Barnard's performance-based approach in *The Arbor* also deploys similar levels of expressive styling as Watkins' work, and where *Culloden and The War Game* used a roving handheld camera style to dial up the emotive impact of his work, Barnard applies a flat low-key lighting style in interviews, alongside a desaturated post-production treatment. The combined effect of both approaches drains *The Arbor* of any emotional levity, while the use of assertive fourth wall breaks by the film's actors during their monologues (see Figure 15.1) further constructs an accusatory undertone – an undertone, perhaps, that authentic to-camera interviews mightn't have achieved so effectively.

Figure 15.1 *The Arbor* (top): Barnard's use of actors enables *The Arbor* to affect an assertive and accusatory exposition. *Amy* (bottom): Kapadia's documentary portrait of Amy Winehouse collages found footage to create an intimate portrait of the singer.

Figure 15.2 The War Game (top) and *Culloden* (bottom): Peter Watkins'
use of recreation and performance allowed his documentaries to broach historical or imagined subject matter.

Nick Broomfield

Broomfield's presence within his films marks a subtle, but hugely important shift in the development of the documentary genre. Where observational filmmakers like Longinotto and Pennebaker hide their presence from view, Broomfield deliberately steps in front of the camera to openly acknowledge his influence and creative steer in making the films he produces.

Broomfield, as such, plays a starring role in his films, with his visibility used to outline to audiences that they are watching an authored text – that interviews, for example, are the result of Broomfield's line of questioning or that contributors have been deliberately chosen to provide a select viewpoint.

Broomfield's trademark headphones and boom carrying presence further signify his intention to lay bare the production processes used to author his work, while the use of unusually reflective commentaries purposefully rejects 'voice of god' exposition in favour of a more confessional approach. Broomfield, in this way, openly acknowledges his filmmaking motives while also using his own emotional responses during filming to signpost audience engagement.

Key features of Broomfield's approach include the following:

- **A performative documentary approach:** performative documentaries are those where the filmmaker's presence is brought into focus within a film. Often, material is shaped around their involvement with a subject, with voiceovers used to expose their thoughts regarding the things they are filming. Performative documentary makers tell us what they feel or think about the subjects they are filming.
- **Celebrity-oriented subjects:** Broomfield uses celebrity-oriented subjects as content for his documentaries – using their stories to reveal uncomfortable truths about the world we live in. In *Aileen Wuornos: The Selling of a Serial Killer*, for example, Broomfield focuses on the media's role in vilifying one of America's most notorious female serial killers and the undue influence that the American media played in Wuornos' death sentence judgement.

- **Political subtexts:** Broomfield, too, evidences much of the politically charged energy of Watkins. Broomfield's profile of the South African nationalist, Eugene Terre'Blanche, for example, in *The Leader, His Driver and the Driver's Wife* (1991) delivers a critical assessment of far-right politicians and their ability to influence others via their charismatic appeal.

Michael Moore

Moore, too, uses a performative approach, but replaces Broomfield's soft-spoken reflective demeanour for an uncompromising film-making style that is underpinned by Moore's hard-left political viewpoint. In *Bowling for Columbine*, for example, Moore attacks American gun culture, comically satirising those American institutions that promote gun ownership despite the rising death toll produced by mass-shootings in the United States. *Fahrenheit 11/9*, too, constructs a polemical commentary of Donald Trump's 2016 election victory, with Moore's trademark voiceover providing the film with a double helping of black humour and cynical analysis.

Key features of Moore's documentary-based approach include the following:

- **Participatory content:** Moore often positions himself as the focus of his documentaries. In *Bowling for Columbine*, for example, he films himself applying for a bank account that gives away free guns to demonstrate the problematic nature of America's lax gun laws. That presenter-based focus moves beyond Broomfield's interview-oriented methodology, and, instead, positions Moore at the centre of his films in a presenter-oriented role.
- **Cannibalising of found footage:** Moore in *Fahrenheit 11/9* evidences an approach that constructs exposition using found footage, using archived news reports and other professional media as well as mobile phone footage and social media feeds. Moore's lack of self-filmed material points to the deluge of visual material that is produced in the digital era – an era where events are readily documented

by smartphone devices. Moore's cannibalising methodology suggests, perhaps, that a documentary filmmaker's job isn't to contribute to that deluge of observational footage but to make sense of it.

- **Rhetorical excess in expositions:** generally speaking, most documentary voice overs routinely use emotive phrasing or guide audiences towards predefined conclusions, but Moore's accompanying commentaries, without doubt, are magnified to the point that any sense of an objective assessment is very difficult to locate.

Table 15.6 Comparing set text documentary films to Broomfield and Moore (Eduqas)

Use the following questions to help you explore potential connections that exist between the documentary set text you are studying and the filmmaking styles of Broomfield and Moore:	
Participatory content and performance-based presence	• Does the filmmaker affect a visible presence in your set text documentary? Where and in what form? • How does the filmmaker's presence help to reveal the film's underlining exposition to the audience? • Does the filmmaker offer reflective commentary? Do accompanying commentaries reveal the filmmaker's rationale or motives? • What presenter-based moments do you think are the most important in the film? Why are they important? • How do filmmakers treat their subjects in interviews? Do they use an emotive or objective interview style? Do they use a hard line of questioning that helps them to establish a political statement?
Overt political bias	• Does the filmmaker construct an overtly political exposition? How do sound and imagery applications help to frame those political messages?

Table 15.6 Cont.

Use of found footage	• Does the filmmaker rely upon found footage to help build the film's exposition? • Is smartphone video or social media material used? For what purposes?

The impact of digital technology in documentary film

Questions in Eduqas' exams might ask students to consider the effects of digital technology in documentary films. In response to these questions, students might consider both the production and distribution-based advantages/disadvantages of digital technology use, as well as the degree to which digital innovations have been integrated into documentary films. Certainly, the availability of digital practices offers filmmakers a range of advantages that include the following:

- **Cheaper production:** celluloid-based production requires filmmakers to purchase and develop film stock. This adds considerable expense to production costs.
- **Ease of production:** digital cameras are, comparably, easier to operate than filmstock equivalents, and, generally speaking, are smaller and more portable, enabling filmmakers to access locations and subjects that bigger cameras might struggle to operate within. The comparative ease of use of digital technologies also has the potential to democratise film production – to enable, in other words, a wider variety of filmmakers to engage in documentary filmmaking.
- **Easier editing:** digital film can also be edited using relatively accessible software packages. Again, this accessibility has the potential to open up the documentary filmmaking genre to a wider range of voices and subjects.
- **Easier access to found material:** digital media also presents filmmakers with a wider range of found footage to tell stories. Social media feeds, amateur footage and digitised

news, for example, can be used to provide visual variety in edits or to add essential backstory.

- **Wider distribution potential:** advances in digital technology have also expanded the distribution platforms that filmmakers can use to release material. Semi-professional films, for example, can gain significant audiences via YouTube, while the popularity of streamed television networks has provided documentary filmmakers with a new and highly viable distribution platform that can generate instant global audiences. Indeed, the genre's popularity on platforms like Netflix and National Geographic has prompted a resurgence of long format documentary making, with film financiers demonstrating a renewed enthusiasm to back productions knowing that costs can be more easily recouped through streaming sales.

Despite the advantages presented by digital technology, most documentary filmmakers continue to covet the celluloid format, arguing that physical film stock provides a richer and more organic look than digital recording. Digital distribution, too, has produced an overcrowded market, making it much harder for filmmakers to create products that can stand out in the ever-burgeoning world of semi-professional documentary filmmaking. The drive to create unique marketable content, perhaps, has pushed documentary filmmaking to explore ever more polemical subjects or to use star power to command audience interest. Asif Kapadia's documentary profiles of Amy Winehouse, Ayrton Senna and Diego Maradona, for example, generated a degree of pre-sold interest from the pre-existing fan bases of the personalities his films profiled. Certainly, Kapadia's star-based 'kiss and tell' storytelling offers a radical departure from the everyday realism of early documentary filmmakers like Grierson.

Table 15.7 Revise it: assess the impact of digital technologies on your chosen set text film

Use the following questions to help you explore the potential impact that digital technology has had on your chosen set text film:	
Archive/social media footage use	• Does the film rely on the use of found footage? • How is found footage recontextualised? Do voice overs or other over dubbed sounds enable us to view the footage in a different light? Are post-production effects applied to archive footage for expressive purposes? • How does found footage help to broaden the film's viewpoint? • Does found footage create relatability for the audience? Is social media content or home video used to provide access to the private world of a film's subject? • What cost/production-based advantages does the use of found material present?
Increased competition effects	• Does the filmmaker use a specific strategy or approach to differentiate their work from the huge pool of observational films that digital technology has enabled? • What is it that your set text documentary filmmakers do that is idiosyncratic or that differentiates them from increased competition? • Has increased competition resulted in documentary filmmaking moving away from its roots as a means to tell the stories of everyday subjects? Have documentary filmmakers stopped telling the stories of ordinary people? • Has increased competition resulted in a more polemical or extreme approach being taken by the filmmaker?

(continued)

Table 15.7 Cont.

Exemplar: *Amy* (Eduqas). Asif Kapadia's 2015 *Amy* documentary signals its intent to provide a highly personal profile of Amy Winehouse from the outset. The film's title suggests, for example, a first name intimacy with the singer, an intimacy that is further enabled through the filmmaker's careful collaging of home video and smartphone footage. The overall effect feels not to dissimilar to Michael Moore's *Fahrenheit 11/9* in its repurposing of found footage to form the bulk of the visual material used in the film, and, moreover, testifies to the digital age's presence and capacity to document our lives in a way that has never been achieved before.

Kapadia's editing of that found material, however, builds a conventional star-oriented portrait of a pop icon who was driven to an equally familiar self-destructive end, weaving personal anecdotes over archive footage to maintain narrative purpose. Footage, too, is used to anchor the overdubbed observations of Winehouse's acquaintances, providing audiences with candid moments that seemingly reinforce the singer's underlying vulnerability. Kapadia, too, treats his catalogue of Winehouse's private video to some emotive post-production effects: slowing down key moments to suggest an eerie and fatalistic tone, magnifying other shots to focus attention on the singer's emotive expressions (see Figure 15.1), while other moments are looped and replayed to emphasise their importance. The overall effect of that treatment is powerful – more so when the footage is synched to emotive moments in Winehouse's back catalogue of songs.

Table 15.8 Documentary film: ten-minute revision

Essential background
• Documentary film is grounded in a presentation of the real world.
• Documentary filmmakers use expressive ingredients to add interest to their real-world representations

Key practitioners
• John Grierson (OCR) and his production teams helped to refine the mixed documentary style. Grierson's films used observation-based montages and to-camera interviews to construct their expositions. Voice of God narration was also used to construct exposition authority.

Table 15.8 Cont.

- Grierson's teams focused on telling stories that were concerned with the lives of ordinary people – often using lyrical/romanticised treatments to tell those stories.
- Donn Pennebaker (OCR) exemplifies a less intrusive approach to filming, rarely using voice overs or interviews. Pennebaker's approach constructs an immersive/voyeuristic experience for the audience.
- Peter Watkins (Eduqas) uses actor-based recreations. His work is overtly political in tone and directs audiences towards a more active form of spectatorship.
- Kim Longinotto (Eduqas), much like Pennebaker, uses an observational filming style to narrate stories that explore feminist themes.
- Nick Broomfield (Eduqas) evidences a performative approach to filmmaking, foregrounding his own presence within films to channel audience reactions.
- Michael Moore (Eduqas) again takes a central role in his films but uses an abrasive and sometimes humorous presentation style. His films produce overt political subtexts.

The impact of digital innovation

- Digital innovation has the potential to revolutionise documentary filmmaking – giving practitioners access to a range of found footage to help them tell stories.

16 Contemporary American cinema since 2005

Table 16.1 What do you need to revise American film since 2005 for?

Eduqas
- **Component 1 Section B American film since 2005:** students are asked to apply ideological perspectives (structuralism, feminism or post-Marxian theories, for example) to understand the meanings and messages created by set text films. Exam questions might also ask students to consider the impact of spectatorship on the meaning-making capacity of films.

OCR
- **Paper 2: Section A Contemporary British and US cinema:** requires students to consider the use of narrative and genre in key films and their importance in constructing representations of societies and cultures. Students are also asked to consider the impact of viewing conditions on spectatorship.
- **Paper 2: Section C ideology:** requires students to analyse a US independent film text using relevant ideological perspectives to diagnose the meanings and effects of set texts. Students also need to consider the impact of social, political and historical contexts on the meanings produced by films.

Spectacle-based cinematic appeals

Contemporary cinemas are under increasing threat from digital streaming services. Flat-screen televisions and elaborate home projection systems now enable audiences to recreate big screen viewing experiences in the comfort of their own home, while digital streaming services like Netflix and Hulu have given contemporary audiences unlimited access to extended libraries of film back catalogues for relatively cheap subscription costs.

Major production studios have sought to counter increased competition from home viewing services by focussing their output on content that is best experienced on big screens. As such, the mainstream film market is rich in output that induces spectacle-based narrative pleasures, using science fiction or fantasy-oriented settings to immerse audiences in image-rich experiences. That spectacle-driven output means that it's not unusual for big blockbuster releases to include over 2,000 individual visual effects, necessitating elaborate post-production processes that can involve thousands of personnel to realise. Those effects construct photo-real cinematic universes via computer-generated imagery, digital painting and the use of complex miniatures and virtual sets. The effects-driven cinema of contemporary Hollywood isn't just restricted to science fiction or fantasy-based output either, indeed, most films deploy an invisible range of post-production digital touch-ups that darken shadows or recolour individual frames to ensure palette consistency across a product.

Contemporary blockbusters are also organised around elaborate and extensive marketing strategies, driven by budgets that often exceed production spends with big-name directors engaged to produce event driven releases. Films, too, are increasingly driven by franchise-oriented storytelling, using sequels, serialised output and spin-offs to engage inherited audiences and to exploit fan-based interest as a means of generating ready-made profits. Major Hollywood studios also look to film projects that can be recycled into commercial opportunities for ancillary subsidiaries. Disneyland, for example, uses the Star Wars film franchise to theme resort park attractions, while Universal's Orlando theme park has built its own Jurassic World resort.

Filmmakers, too, use a variety of projection-based innovations to enhance the experience of watching films in cinema auditoriums, and much like the initial introduction of 3D projection in the late 1940s and early 1950s, contemporary 3D releases have tried to re-establish cinema's dominance in the wake of rising competition from television-based consumption. 3D production can either be achieved during filming, or, conversely, is applied as a post-production process (as used on *Guardians of the Galaxy* and *Star Wars: The Force Awakens*). 3D releases have also helped to boost associated Blu-Ray DVD sales – offering 3D viewing experiences that streaming services don't yet provide. The reintroduction of 3D cinema was initially greeted with a great deal of audience interest as a result of its novelty value, with James Cameron's 3D release of *Avatar* in 2009 heralding the start of this projection revolution. Recent interest, however, has waned with audience complaints drawing attention to the limited impact of 3D applications and to the darkened colour palettes that 3D production tends to produce.

Several contemporary filmmakers have also voiced criticism of the 3D trend, most notably Christopher Nolan who eschews the format in favour of the mega-screen capacities of IMAX filming. IMAX's 65 mm film format not only allows for distribution using the super-sized projection capacities of IMAX auditoriums, but also enables cinematographers to capture unparalleled set detail in longshot sequences. Nolan, for example, used IMAX film for both his award-winning war epic *Dunkirk* and for some sections of *The Dark Knight Rises*. Neither is Nolan alone in his use of the 65 mm format, with J.J. Abrams' reboot of the Star Wars franchise using 65 mm stock to film some of the introductory scenes of *The Force Awakens* – using the colour/detail-oriented brilliance of 65 mm filming to maximum effect during Rey's Millennium Falcon escape.

Table 16.2 Revise it: what effect does auditorium viewing have on spectators?

OCR exam questions might ask you to consider the effect that viewing conditions have on the audience. Is, for example, the ideological effect increased if a film is experienced in the cinema, or is home viewing more likely to engage audience alignment? Discuss the following questions to explore the effects of spectatorship further:

- Which of your set text films would be enhanced if viewed in a big screen environment?
- Does home viewing enhance or diminish the ideological impact of a film?
- Does watching a film in an auditorium affect an audience's response?

Some key arguments to consider:

- **The enhanced experience of cinema-based spectatorship might concentrate impact**: superior sound projection combined with the inescapable presence of a large cinema screen might make it less likely for audiences to question the narratives or representations constructed. We might further argue that 3D projection or viewing the film in an IMAX auditorium would further concentrate this effect.
- **Viewing a film in an auditorium is more likely to align the response of the spectator with that of the audience in the auditorium:** it might also be argued that our emotional response to a film could be guided or unduly influenced by the collective response of an auditorium audience if we view the film in a big screen environment.
- **Private home viewing might dilute the ideological effect of a film as a result of the less invasive presence of television screens:** audiences can also discuss imagery in an open manner with family members.
- **Private home viewing enables repeat viewing:** conversely, streamed viewing or DVD-based consumption allows the spectator to pause or rewatch key moments. Repeat viewing might enhance or indeed reduce any ideological effects of a film.

Exemplar: *Dark Knight* (OCR). The low-key night-time suffused ambience constructed by Nolan's *Dark Knight* builds a portrait of a violent and crime-ridden America in which casual violence and gun crime are the norm. Problematically, that portrait positions white masculinity as a dominant and morally virtuous presence, while the film's absence of non-white protagonists and the equally problematic

(continued)

Table 16.2 Cont.

use of Baine's vaguely foreign accent links foreignness with criminality (see Figure 16.1).

Nolan's use of IMAX's supersized distribution format might also help to exacerbate the problematic nature of those representations. We might argue that spectatorship of *The Dark Knight* in the film's intended IMAX format might magnify the emotional impact of the film, or, at the very least, amplify the subtextual fears presented. Viewing the film in theatres, as opposed to home viewing, will certainly foreground the energy of the film's action sequences and could make it much harder for individual audience members to resist an alignment with Batman in mass audience viewing conditions.

Links to exemplar film clips and exemplars for other OCR/Eduqas film texts can be found at www.essentialfilmrevision.com

Figure 16.1 The Dark Knight (top): Bane's non-American antagonist presence constructs a problematic representation of race. *Guardians of the Galaxy* (bottom): Star-Lord constructs an ironic and potentially ambiguous masculine lead.

Figure 16.2 No Country for Old Men (top): Chigurh's toxic masculinity is forwarded as the film's antagonist. *Winter's Bone* (bottom): the film's ending suggests the inescapable and circular nature of underclass poverty in America.

Family and home: a reappraisal of gender in contemporary American film

Perhaps one salient feature of contemporary Hollywood output centres around its reappraisal of gender. Where once lone-wolf male heroes took centre stage in American mainstream output, contemporary films offer more flexible adaptations of traditional gender-based stereotypes. From *No Country for Old Men's* reappraisal of cowboy-based masculinity to *Carol's* emotive exploration of female sexuality, most of the film's selected for study offer audiences characters who defy and stretch traditional gender roles. Key contextual influences that have prompted this appraisal of gender in contemporary film include the following:

- **Second wave feminism:** the women's liberation movements of the 1960s and 1970s questioned the idea that a woman's primary ideal role was connected to child rearing and running the family home. Second wave feminists sought equality in education, the home and also in employment. Second wave feminism, too, questioned the routine object-ification of the female body – critiquing the presentation of sexualised females in both the media and film. We might argue that Katniss' lone-wolf hero status in the *Hunger Games* constructs a second wave-oriented depiction of femininity in that she occupies the same kind of role that was once the preserve of male actors in the action/SF genre.
- **Third wave feminism:** perhaps of greater influence in the films specified for study by both exam boards is 1990s third wave feminism. Where second wave feminists sought equality of the sexes, third wave feminists embraced trad-itional female values in addition to the second wave's more radical ideals: women, third wave feminists argue, can choose themselves whether they want to be mothers, or, indeed, whether they want to nurture career-driven aspirations. In many ways, a number of female representations in set text films confirm these third wave ideals: in *Jurassic World*, for example, lead female protagonist, Claire, learns that her

career-driven ambitions can also work alongside a more maternally oriented outlook. In *La La Land*, too, Mia's Hollywood dreams nestle against more traditionally aligned goals of romance and family.

- **Fourth wave feminism:** buoyed by social media, the feminist movement of the early 2000s pursued a more radical agenda. The #metoo movement, for example – as prompted by the Harvey Weinstein scandal – used social media to draw attention to the persistent and often invisible acts of everyday sexism in society. Fourth wave feminists also question the kinds of female objectification that are sanctioned by third wave feminism, and, more importantly, draw attention to difficulties women face in terms of career development. In many senses, Rey's tough no-nonsense and desexualised femininity in *The Force Awakens* offers audiences a more radical femininity that aligns with fourth wave contextual concerns. It is interesting to note, however, that only two female directors feature in the set text choices of both exam boards offering Film Studies – Ava Duvernay (*Selma*) and Debra Granick (*Winter's Bone*). We might argue, as a result, that many of the films presented for study continue to reflect a masculine view of womanhood.

- **Gender fluidity:** undoubtedly, LGBTQ groups are slowly gaining mainstream acceptance in American film, with a range of non-heteronormative storylines beginning to appear in mainstream film output as well as that of independent film. Again, that fluidity is largely absent from the texts selected for A Level study with only *Carol* featuring any non-heteronormative lead characters.

- **Redefined masculinity:** as a reaction to the ongoing redefinition of femininity in film, masculine ideals too have been realigned. Lots of set text films offer us more versatile male characters who openly reject the macho hero values offered by traditional media products and films. *Boyhood*, for example, points to Olivia's refusal to accept outdated versions of toxic masculinity in the form of Bill and Jim, while *No Country for Old Men* explores the changing social attitudes regarding masculinity through a range of broken and dysfunctional male leads – none of whom provide a resounding affirmation of traditional male heroism.

- **Masculine backlash:** while some film's explore alternatives to the hard-emotionless masculinity seen in traditional American cinema, other films react to the shifting social expectations of our contemporary world with a reactionary reaffirmation of traditional masculinity. Christopher Nolan's male dominated films, for example, provide audiences with the dark brooding loneliness of Batman and the hyper-masculine action-based energy of *Inception*. *The Dark Knight* resoundingly reaffirms traditional masculine power through Batman's single-handed rescue of Gotham City, while *Inception's* action-filled narrative marginalises the only substantive female lead, Ariadne, to a largely supportive role.

- **Contemporary American films also construct ironic masculine identities:** contemporary films also generate characters who demonstrate traditional values but undercut outdated presentations with the use of accompanying humour. Both *Guardians of the Galaxy* and *Jurassic World*, for example, exploit Chris Pratt's ironic alpha-male star presence – an ambiguous representation that simultaneously supports and critiques Pratt's attempts to assume the heroic lead of both films (see Figure 16.1).

Outsiders and conflict: a reappraisal of race

Race-based representations have also been brought into much sharper focus in contemporary American cinema. Where filmmakers like Spike Lee were once marginalised as maverick voices in the 1980s, contemporary American mainstream film has started to offer an increasingly broader range of race-related film representations. Ava Duverney's 2014 *Selma* biopic of Martin Luther King, for example, sits alongside a host of racially aware movies made in the early 2010s – including Steve McQueen's *12 Years a Slave*, Theodore Melfi's *Hidden Figures* and Tate Taylor's *The Help*. Such films explore America's problematic treatment of non-white communities. Jordan Peel's much celebrated *Get Out*, too, injected racial issues into the horror genre while Disney's mainstream hit of 2018, *Black Panther*, broke box office records with its Afrofuturistic treatment of the superhero genre.

Contextual factors that have helped to throw a spotlight on film diversity in the last ten years include the following:

- **Post 9/11 considerations:** perhaps the singularly most potent news imagery of the twenty-first century is that of the Twin Towers attack in 2001. President Bush's subsequent decision to invade Iraq in 2003 features in several films in the decade that followed. Cinematic treatments of the war are often critical of the effects of the invasion and of the patriotic rhetoric of the period.

- **Hurricane Katrina:** Hurricane Katrina was a catastrophic category 4 storm that devastated New Orleans in 2005, killing over 1,000 inhabitants of the largely black community who lived there. President Bush's delayed military response to the disaster was widely criticised and brought accusations that America was riven with institutional racism. Katrina, even today, acts as a potent symbol of the economic disparities that exist between the largely white affluence of America and the corresponding poverty of the black American populous. Indeed, Behn Zeitlin's 2012 film *Beasts of the Southern Wild* uses a Louisiana setting that is rendered destitute as a result of a hurricane strike – its residents abandoned by local authorities in the aftermath of the disaster in much the same way that New Orleans was left to fend for itself in the wake of Hurricane Katrina.

- **Changing political landscape of America:** the historic election of Barack Obama in 2008 to the White House brought to the fore the presence and power of Black America. We might similarly argue that Trump's 2016 election victory and the widespread accusations that he has encouraged an anti-libertarian backlash has similarly produced a critical and more racially aware cinematic response.

- **The rise of the Black Lives Matter movement:** the shooting of the unarmed black youth, Trayvon Martin, by George Zimmerman in 2012 was a pivotal moment in American social history, providing one of the catalysts for the expansion of the Black Lives Matter movement (BLM). BLM's protest-based responses to racial injustice – both political and economic – undoubtedly brought race-based issues to the fore in contemporary American politics.

While black representations in American film have undoubtedly increased, the complete lack of nominations for non-white filmmakers in the leading categories of the 2015 Oscars exemplifies the extent of the problems that black filmmakers face today. The omission of films like *Selma* from award nominations led to accusations that Hollywood was, and remains, institutionally racist. Certainly, the absence of black representation in many films chosen for study by both exam boards provides a great deal of evidence to reinforce the idea that black American representations are absent or at least marginalised in both mainstream and independent cinema.

Table 16.3 Revise it: gender and race in contemporary American film

Use the following questions to help you assess the gender and race-based presentations constructed by your set text films:	
Gender-based representations	• What kinds of representations of femininity are constructed by the text? Are women empowered in the film – where and in what way? Are females constructed using a second, third or fourth wave feminist lens? • What kinds of representations of masculinity are constructed by the text? Are males disempowered in the film – where and in what way? • Are traditional representations of masculinity/femininity reasserted in the film? Are audiences aligned to agree or disagree with those representations? • Is gender fluidity presented in the text? How are audiences aligned with those representations?

(*continued*)

Table 16.3 Cont.

Race-based representations	• What effects have historical and political contexts had on the race-based representations that are constructed in your set text film? • Are non-white characters empowered within the film? • How are audiences aligned with non-white characters in the film? What moments produce the biggest emotional effects for audiences?

Exemplar: *No Country for Old Men* **(Eduqas).** The Coen Brothers' western/crime drama hybrid offers audiences a range of complex male representations that mirror the wider repositioning of masculine identity in contemporary America. Sheriff Bell's older masculinity, for example, contrasts with the certainty and power of Chigurh's antagonist presence in the film (see Figure 16.2). The film's antagonist and protagonist, in this sense, embody the range of male-oriented identities that are presented to men in the real world: Chigurh embodies a darker hyper-masculine energy that destroys all that it comes into contact with, while, conversely, Bell's epilogue – his revelation of his dreams to his wife – offers an uncertain vision that connects male identity both to the more nurturing purposes of child care and also to the self-sacrificing vision of his own father. It is the latter vision, ultimately, that haunts the viewer, with Bell's revelation trumping Chigurh's desperate and humiliating escape after his car accident.

Independent American film

The 'independent' label, as applied to American film, is highly contentious. Indeed, some commentators and critics have suggested that the existence of financially independent film production is relatively rare and that most independent producers form strategic pacts with the Hollywood majors to ensure the theatrical distribution of their films and to help mitigate the huge costs incurred when making and marketing film.

As a result, Hollywood majors often engage in a co-dependent production financing model that farms out film production to independent satellite producers while also granting major Hollywood conglomerates like Disney or Universal exclusive access to distribute films. This production model provides the major studios with a steady stream of high-quality, low-to-mid budget output that they can subsequently monetise via their ancillary distribution networks – streaming services, cable television and so on.

The co-dependent production model, moreover, gives high profile auteurs the ability to market themselves as alternative filmmakers – their 'independent' labelling helping to underline to audiences the idea that the films they make are different to more commercially mainstream output. The Coen Brothers, for example, work under the Mike Zoss Productions label, yet their films are given a global high-profile distribution presence via their links with Paramount. Independent labelling, as applied here, helps to determine a set of predefined expectations for spectators, helping to infer that films contain a critical viewpoint or that they are styled using a non-mainstream aesthetic.

The co-dependent production model might be a necessity given the extraordinary sums of money needed by filmmakers to give their output a commercial presence in today's film landscape, but the emergence, however, of the Sundance organisation in the mid-1980s produced something of a mini revolution for independent film – enabling truly independent filmmakers to find audiences and to finance productions without the help of major Hollywood studios. The Sundance Festival by the late 1980s established its reputation for finding new talent, while also affording filmmakers a window to showcase projects. Indeed, several of the films identified for study gained public prominence and valuable distribution deals as a result of winning the Sundance Grand Jury Prize: *Winter's Bone* in 2010, *Beasts of the Southern Wild* in 2013 and *Whiplash* in 2014. The Sundance Institute also provides filmmakers with finance to make projects, again helping a number of outsider films to be made, including *Beasts of the Southern Wild* and *Whiplash*.

Independent film has also expanded as a result of digital technology. In terms of production, digital film and editing processes have enabled outsider voices to make and assemble films more cheaply, while streaming services like HBO, Netflix and Channel 4 have widened the distribution outlets that independent producers can use beyond those of the major Hollywood conglomerates. New streaming services, too, have provided finance to independent filmmakers in a bid to provide a staple stream of innovative content that can satisfy the needs of discerning subscription paying customers.

Transcoding as narrative subversion

Despite the effects of Sundance and the emergence of new distribution outlets, major Hollywood companies continue to affect huge control of the independent film production market. As a result, film academics like Geoff King argue that the 'independent' label as applied to contemporary American cinema doesn't allude to the use of independent finance to make films, but, instead, describes a specific aesthetic style or a type of narrative content that is distinctly different from mainstream cinema. King tells us, that 'Independent films are far more likely than Hollywood productions to confront us with prickly central characters and less likely to offer fantastical reconciliatory dynamics in which such characteristics are washed magically away' (King, 2009, 259).

Other key features of independent American cinema include the following:

- **A subjective narrative style:** in contrast to spectacle-based mainstream cinema, independent films construct detailed explorations of marginalised characters who live in equally marginalised worlds. Independent cinema, as such, focuses on class or race-based portrayals – often using victim-based characters to assert sympathetic portraits.
- **Outsider character alignment:** independent films align spectators with marginalised protagonists – positioning viewers to understand better the circumstances or experiences of those characters.
- **Use documentary realism:** independent films are often based within settings that audiences are familiar with, while

also using camera and editing styles that emphasise cinematic realism.

As such, the labelling of films as 'independent' produces a guarantee to audiences that a film will contain content that is ideologically challenging or that will provide critical commentary regarding key social or economic inequalities in contemporary America. Those challenges are often framed via what cultural theorist Stuart Hall called stereotype trans-coding – where character-based representations are given critical depth or are associated with values/experiences that force audiences to rethink their assumptions.

Table 16.4 Revisit it: character and ideology

Go to Chapter 8 (Ideology) to remind yourself of the various ways that character stereotypes can produce ideological effects.

Trans-coding in independent films

Two of the most common transcoding strategies used in both independent and mainstream film include the following:

- **Character countertypes:** counter typical representations occur when a character inverts or reverses stereotypical expectations. In *The Dark Knight*, for example, Anne Hathaway's Catwoman offers audiences an active female representation whose actions in saving Batman at the end of the film defy conventional Proppian Princess character-based expectations. In *Selma*, a countertype is deployed through Duvernay's foregrounding of Martin Luther King's pacifism – with Luther King's quiet defiance inverting the more conventional association of black masculinity with violence and crime. In *No Country for Old Men*, too, countertypes are used to outline an alternative to action-based hyper masculinity, with Sheriff Bell's cowardice inverting the heroic lawman stereotype that we so often find in both the western and crime genres.

- **Deconstructed stereotypes:** these occur when stereotypical characters are used but are subsequently placed within narratives that explore in detail the causes and significance of the negative behaviours associated with the stereotype. Linklater's *Boyhood*, for example, invokes the teenage slacker stereotype, but contextualises that character within a detailed exploration of the boy's family history to reveal a sense of the character's fragility rather than his villainy. Similarly, Terrence Malick's dream-soaked psychodrama *The Tree of Life* invokes a problematic teen male, Jack, who's troubling behaviour is explained as the result of his father's abusive actions. In *Winter's Bone*, too, Ree is outlined using the conventional underclass trailer trash stereotype, but is positioned within a narrative that deconstructs the effects of her inescapable underclass status.

Table 16.5 Revise it: trans-coding effects in contemporary American film

• Do your film set texts deploy counter typical representations? What stereotypical attributes are reversed by countertypes? What assumptions are challenged? • Which films explore stereotypes via deconstructions? Which moments in the text could you use to provide the examiner with relevant analysis? • In what ways does trans-coding create positive representations of outsider groups? • Does the use of trans-coding shift perceptions of marginalised, demonised or powerless social groups?
Exemplar: *Winter's Bone* (Eduqas). The impoverished winter setting, handheld filming style and slow-paced narration of *Winter's Bone* effects a European documentary realist aesthetic that is readily found in contemporary American Independent productions. Realised as a result of funding from the Sundance Institute, the narrative intentions of *Winter's Bone* deconstructs the effects of underclass poverty in Midwest America. The story's single-character tale unpacks the economic and social marginalisation of Ree's family and their abandonment at the hands of American authority. That authority is symbolised through

Table 16.5 Cont.

Sheriff Baskin's pursuit of Ree's criminal father, and, moreover, his desire to affect a family-wide punishment for the father's crimes despite his absence. The narrative's subtext, like so many contemporary independent films, deconstructs the myth of the American Dream, while also pointing to the huge disparities in wealth that exist in the United States. Ree, importantly, is motivated enough to want to escape her enclosed world, indeed, she offers to enlist in the army so she might find a better life, but is rejected in a way that underscores the vindictive treatment of outsiders in American society. The film's ending, moreover, constructs a resoundingly depressing resolution in which Ree's sister's banjo playing is used to suggest the inescapable and circular nature of American underclass poverty (see Figure 16.2).

Table 16.6 American cinema since 2005: ten-minute revision

A cinema of spectacle
• Mainstream cinema faces increased competition from home viewing technologies and has sought to reignite theatre-based viewing using 3D projection and other technological innovations.
A reappraisal of outsider representations
• Both mainstream and independent contemporary films construct representations that are more socially diverse.
Independent cinema
• The use of the independent label is hugely problematic. Independent filmmakers are highly reliant on the major studios to distribute and market films. • Independent American cinema is likely to use a subjective narrative style and a documentary realist aesthetic. • Independent cinema is more likely to produce challenging representations of class, race or gender.

Bibliography

anon. (n.d.): "Broomfield, Nick (1948–)". *BFI Screenonline: Broomfield, Nick (1948–) Biography*. Retrieved on 30.11.2020 from www.screenonline.org.uk/people/id/501784/index.html.

Biskind, Peter (1999): *Easy riders, raging bulls*. London: Bloomsbury.

Bordwell, David; Staiger, Janet; Thompson, Kristin (2015): *The classical Hollywood cinema film style & mode of production to 1960*. London: Routledge, Taylor & Francis.

Brown, Blain (2002): *Cinematography theory and practice; imagemaking for cinematographers, directors & videographers*. Amsterdam: Focal Press.

Caughie, John (1995): *Theories of authorship: a reader*. London: Routledge.

Chatman, Seymour Benjamin (ed.) (2006): *Coming to terms: the rhetoric of narrative in fiction and film*. New York: Cornell University Press.

Cook, Pam; Bernink, Mieke (2005): *The cinema book*. London: BFI.

Coppola, Eleanor (1995): *Notes:* London: Faber and Faber.

Cranston, Ros (2019): "Where to begin with Kim Longinotto" *British Film Institute*. Retrieved on 30.11.2020 from www2.bfi.org.uk/news-opinion/news-bfi/features/where-begin-kim-longinotto.

Deleuze, Gilles (2005): *Cinema*. London: Continuum.

GLAAD (2019). *Where we are on TV*. [online] Gay and Lesbian Alliance Against Defamation. Available at: http://glaad.org/files/WWAT/WWAT_GLAAD_2018-2019.pdf [Accessed 12 April 2019].

Grant, Barry Keith (2011): *Film genre: from iconography to ideology*. London: Wallflower.

Grant, Keith B. (ed.) (1996): *The dread of difference: gender and the horror film*. Austin: University of Texas Press.

Grieveson, Lee; Krämer, Peter (2004): *The silent cinema reader*. London: Routledge.

Hall, S. (1999): Encoding/Decoding. In: S. During, ed., *The Cultural Studies Reader*, 2nd ed. New York: Routledge.

Hall, S.; Evans, J.; Nixon, S. (2013): *Representation*. 2nd ed. London: Sage.

King, Geoff (2009): *American independent cinema*. London: I.B. Tauris.

Krämer, Peter (2005): *The new Hollywood: from Bonnie and Clyde tot Star Wars*. London: Wallflower.

Lévi-Strauss, C. (2004): *The savage mind*. Oxford: Oxford University Press.

Millerson, Gerald (1998): *The technique of lighting for television and film*. Boston: Focal Press.

Monaco, James (2009): *How to read a film: movies, media, and beyond: art, technology, language, history, theory*. Oxford: Oxford University Press.

Mulvey, Laura (1989): *Visual and other pleasures: collected writings*. Hampshire: Palgrave Macmillan.

Neale, S. (2001): *Genre and Hollywood*. London: Routledge.

Nelmes, Jill (2012): *Introduction to film studies*. Oxon: Routledge.

Orpen, Valerie (2009): *Film editing: the art of the expressive*. London: Wallflower.

Procter, James (2004): Stuart Hall. London: Routledge.

Propp, V. (2009): *Morphology of the folktale*. Austin, TX: University of Texas Press.

Richardson, Michael. *Surrealism and Cinema*. Oxford, Berg Publishers, 2006.

Shaviro, Steven (2000): *The cinematic body*. Minneapolis: University of Minnesota Press.

Stam, Robert (2000): *Film theory: an introduction*. Oxford: Blackwell.

Thompson, Kristin; Bordwell, David (1994): *Film history: an introduction*. New York: McGraw-Hill.

Todorov, T. (1977): *The poetics of prose*. Oxford: Basil Blackwell.

Tucker, Patrick (2015): *Secrets of screen acting*. New York: Routledge.

Tzioumakis, Yannis (2017): *American independent cinema: an introduction*. Edinburgh: Edinburgh University Press.

UCLA (2018): *Hollywood diversity report*. [online] UCLA. Available at: https://socialsciences.ucla.edu/wp-content/uploads/2018/02/UCLA-Hollywood-Diversity-Report-2018-2-27-18.pdf [Accessed 15 April. 2019].

Valk, Mark De; Arnold, Sarah (2013): *The film handbook*. London: Routledge, Taylor & Francis Group.

Wharton, David; Grant, Jeremy (2005): *Teaching auteur study*. London: BFI.

Index